LADY CONSTANCE LYTTON

LADY CONSTANCE LYTTON

Aristocrat, Suffragette, Martyr

Lyndsey Jenkins

Biteback Publishing

First published in Great Britain in 2015 by
Biteback Publishing Ltd
Westminster Tower
3 Albert Embankment
London SE1 7SP
Copyright © Lyndsey Jenkins 2015

Material from Olive Schreiner's letters © Olive Schreiner Letters Project

Unless otherwise credited, all images © Knebworth House Archive: www.knebworthhouse.com

Every reasonable effort has been made to trace copyright holders of material reproduced in this book, but if any have been inadvertently overlooked the publishers would be glad to hear from them.

ISBN 978-1-84954-795-6

10 9 8 7 6 5 4 3 2 1

A CIP catalogue record for this book is available from the British Library.

Set in Adobe Caslon Pro

Printed and bound in Great Britain by

CONTENTS

ACKNOWLEDGEMENTS

My first and most sincere thanks are to the Cobbold family for their interest in and support for this project. Henry Cobbold gave freely of his time and answered many questions which helped put pieces of the puzzle together; David Cobbold likewise shared his memories and knowledge. The archivist at Knebworth, Clare Fleck, is an incredibly kind and unrivalled source of wisdom on all things Lytton, and her help went far and above the call of duty. Both the family and their archivist allowed me to pore over original letters, diaries and photographs without constraint and I am incredibly grateful for this generosity.

Other members of the extended family were also very helpful. Thank you to Michael Brander for permission to quote from the Balfour papers at the National Archives of Scotland and Lady Alison Kember for photographs of Betty Balfour. Professor Jane Ridley shared with me her immense knowledge of the Lutyens family. Thank you to Adam Pallant for permission to quote from the works of Emily Lutyens and for a photograph of her, as well as the loan of Mary Lutyens's books – and thanks to Candia Lutyens for alerting me to the existence of Mary's work on Edward and Elizabeth Villiers.

The extremely warm and welcoming Samantha and Talitha Pollock-Hill gave me a lovely afternoon at Constance's former residence, Homewood. Laura Ponsonby and Kate Russell kindly allowed me to quote from two letters of John Ponsonby.

I wish to thank the staff at various other libraries for their assistance and permission to quote from their sources: these include Beverley Cook and Richard Dabb at the Museum of London and Bridget Gillies at the University of East Anglia archives, as well as staff at the British Library, the National Archives, the National Archives of Scotland and the Sheffield Archives, as well as the Gloucestershire archives on behalf of the Blathwayt family.

Thank you to my agent, Humfrey Hunter, for unfailing enthusiasm and to Olivia Beattie and all the team at Biteback for their sterling efforts to make it the best possible book.

This book came out of my MA at the University of East Anglia and I wish to thank the tutors, Professor Kathryn Hughes and Dr Helen Smith, who improved my work immeasurably. Thanks also to the students who made me think and laugh in equal measure, particularly Alexis Wolf, who is an inspiration in every way.

Thank you to my former colleagues who didn't mind too much (or at least didn't say anything) when I starting muttering about votes for women instead of contributing anything sensible, especially Dan Forman and Kirsty Buchanan.

Thank you to Steve Gregson (www.youshouldbeshot.co.uk) for all the excellent headshots and to all the friends – Jennifer Sunderland, Aleksandra Kulas, Jane Houghton, Patricia Gondim, Francesa Lopez and Holly Thompson – who helped choose the best one. That was the hardest bit.

Thank you to my best friend and first reader, Natalie Black, who gave up her holiday to read the final draft on her phone. She was by the pool in Thailand, though, so you don't need to feel too sorry for her.

Final thanks and love always to my immediate and incredible family: Kathryn, Mike, Isabella and Amber Smith, and Becky Jenkins; but especially to Pauline Jenkins and Jeegar Kakkad, who did everything that I was supposed to be doing. I am sure they think I am mad, but I hope they think it was worth it.

My lovely daughter Cerys used to climb up to where I was working and say, 'You are doing a great job, Mum!' and 'I want to do important work too.' This just meant she wanted to type her name on my computer, but I hope when she grows up, she really does do important work. This book is for you, my darling.

In memory of David Jenkins (1956–2011).

LADY CONSTANCE LYTTON
FAMILY TREE

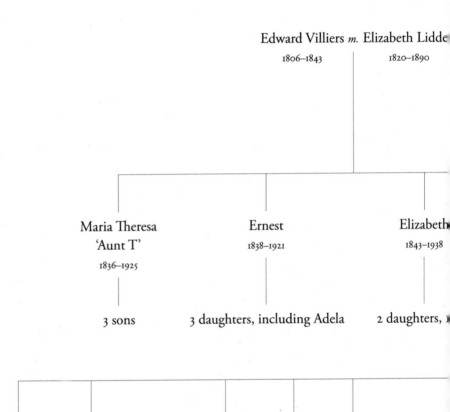

Edward Villiers *m.* Elizabeth Lidde
1806–1843   1820–1890

Maria Theresa
'Aunt T'
1836–1925

Ernest
1838–1921

Elizabeth
1843–1938

3 sons

3 daughters, including Adela

2 daughters,

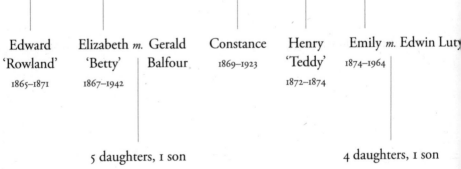

Edward
'Rowland'
1865–1871

Elizabeth *m.* Gerald
'Betty'   Balfour
1867–1942

Constance
1869–1923

Henry
'Teddy'
1872–1874

Emily *m.* Edwin Luty
1874–1964

5 daughters, 1 son

4 daughters, 1 son

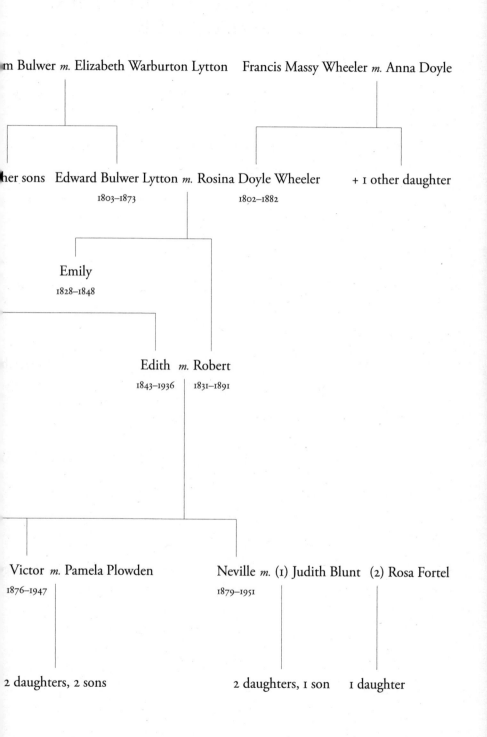

...m Bulwer *m.* Elizabeth Warburton Lytton   Francis Massy Wheeler *m.* Anna Doyle

...her sons   Edward Bulwer Lytton *m.* Rosina Doyle Wheeler   + 1 other daughter
1803–1873   1802–1882

Emily
1828–1848

Edith   *m.* Robert
1843–1936   1831–1891

Victor *m.* Pamela Plowden   Neville *m.* (1) Judith Blunt   (2) Rosa Fortel
1876–1947   1879–1951

2 daughters, 2 sons   2 daughters, 1 son   1 daughter

'How glorious those Suffragette days were!
To lose the personal in a great impersonal is to live.'
– Christabel Pankhurst

'She was a light to our generation, lighting something which
will never go out.'
– Anonymous suffragette

'Whether or not victory is for your day, at least each one of you make
sure that the one course impossible to you is
surrender of your share in the struggle.'
– Lady Constance Lytton[1]

The cast of characters involved in the suffragette movement is a large and diverse one. Thousands of women took part, irrespective of age and class, from different walks of life, from all parts of the country and even from beyond. It is also a cast full of women who grew in stature as they put the cause of women's rights to vote above their own struggles, their comforts and day-to-day living. However, these pioneering, feisty women rarely lived alone: many family members were supportive and also became engaged in the cause in complex and interrelated ways, while others shunned and ejected their wayward relatives.

One of the central characters in danger of being forgotten in the reductive narrative about the movement was Lady Constance Lytton. Luckily, this biography by Lyndsey Jenkins brings her back out of the shadows. Lady Con, as she was often called, was symbolically important as an example of a woman from the upper classes (albeit an impoverished one) who joined the struggle, lending her name in order to legitimise it. She was, however, even more important as someone who managed to challenge the privileges of her status. She exposed the double standards of a government that released her from prison with little harm once she was identified as Lady Constance whilst meting out harsh, vicious and dangerous treatment when she disguised herself as Jane Warton, a poor unknown nobody. This episode, her own idea, was picked up by the media and the general public and is evidence of a growing rejection of class-based injustice – even before the First World War, the cataclysmic event to which the tremors that shook the class system are generally attributed.

It was a sensational deed and, as Lyndsey Jenkins puts it, 'In a campaign marked by daring feats of bravery, great moments of theatre and spectacular leaps of imagination, this act of Constance Lytton/Jane Warton still stands out. The suffragettes immediately turned her act into the stuff of legend.'

However, there is much more to Lady Constance than this well-publicised incident, her associated work on prison reform and her book *Prisons and Prisoners*, which was the first personal testimony of a suffragette to be published in a book. This biography makes an important contribution to our understanding of a whole life, rather than of the single moment of notoriety.

The biography shows the person over time with all her frailties, her shyness, the inconsistencies in her attitude to class differences, and her personal disappointments. At the same time, it reveals her intrinsic kindness and compassion, her bravery and her selflessness. Particularly interestingly, it also sheds light on the personal and household contexts: how one woman's engagement in the movement ricochets around her close and extended family, who respond in different ways ranging from support or endorsement of the cause to distancing and dismay; from expressing fear of the dangers she was submitting herself to in an increasingly militant cause to worrying about the family's name and reputation. Beyond the family, Lady Constance used her networks and status to lobby Conservative and Liberal MPs, gaining greater access than could be achieved by most. For example, her sister Betty married into the Balfour family, Arthur Balfour, the then Leader of the Conservative Party, being her brother-in-law. Her brother Victor Lytton, meanwhile, sat in the

House of Lords and was friends with Winston Churchill. Despite these contacts, her lobbying arguably did not achieve much impact.

As the book progresses, we see how Lady Constance gained massively from the movement, which gave her a sense of purpose and direction, a chance to live a fuller, more exciting life, and introduced her to women who became lifelong friends. However, she also became a casualty of the movement. Her health, never the strongest, was battered by her experiences, particularly of force feeding. She is shown to be incapacitated at different points in her life with depression, heart murmurs, bronchitis, breathlessness, partial paralysis and a stroke. Even more sadly, she was increasingly on the fringes of events, partly due to extreme ill health, and was taken in by a charlatan parading as a psychotherapist at the end of her life.

This is an objective, unsentimental, unbiased account of Lady Constance's life, revealing a woman whose life was punctuated with, in the author's words, 'acts of kindness typical of Constance, more so than the grander gestures designed to attract attention and maximise impact. Such acts came from the heart, without an eye on political strategy.'

Lyndsey Jenkins's book also provides a broad-brush portrayal of a woman within the context of an influential family, making sense of the historical changes at play over more than half a century. At its core, it provides an overview of the suffrage struggle and as such provides a stark reminder of how long and painful that struggle was and how many set-backs there would be before women finally got the vote on the same terms as men in 1928.

In Jenkins's words, 'As the centennial anniversary of women winning the vote approaches, and we reflect on the suffragettes' achievement and their legacy, it's time that this exceptional woman and her extraordinary story became better known. Though these events took place a hundred years ago, they still have resonance and parallels today. Think, for example, of the misogynistic vitriol and hate directed at many women who dare to have a voice and express an opinion in public. The suffragettes would find that all too familiar. We've not come as far as we'd like to think.'

PROLOGUE

24 February 1909, London

Lady Constance Lytton picks at her food. Around her, the rest of the suffragettes are eating hungrily: this will be their last meal before they are arrested. These veterans are cheerful enough not to worry too much about their upcoming ordeal. They've done this many times before.

This is Constance's first protest. She is almost forty years old and has spent the afternoon lying in the dark with a headache. She has come in disguise, with her hair arranged differently than usual. She is worried the police will consider her an 'awkward customer' because her well-known family might kick up a fuss – as well they might.

Elsa Gye has been assigned to keep an eye on Constance. New recruits are often very nervous, and as Constance pushes her dinner around her plate, Elsa can see how troubled she is. Elsa is only in her twenties but is already a seasoned campaigner. Constance feels terribly guilty that this nice young woman will have to accompany her to prison. Constance is wearing a white muff and feather boa. She is told, gently and kindly, to leave them behind or they will be torn to shreds.

The women assemble at Caxton Hall, putting on their 'Votes for Women' sashes as if they were battledress. Always disorganised, Constance has forgotten her ticket to get in and has to rush back to get it. The sense of anticipation hardens into determination and dread. There are speeches but Constance can hardly hear them. Instead she nervously asks Elsa what she needs to do.

'You needn't bother about what you'll do,' Elsa says matter-of-factly. 'It will all be done to you. There is only one thing you must remember. It is our business to go forward. Whatever is said to you and whatever is done to you, you must on no account be turned back.'

In theory, the goal of tonight's protest is to march to the House of Commons and present a petition to the Prime Minister. But all the women know their mission is hopeless as they will inevitably be stopped and arrested. Constance is secretly glad about this. She is almost more afraid of success. What on earth would she say to the Prime Minister if she actually met him face to face?

The women have barely set foot in the street before the police close in. Constance has little sense of direction and clings desperately to Elsa. Nothing in Constance's genteel upbringing has prepared her for the jostling and jeering of a hostile mob. She can hardly breathe. The suffragettes break away from their neat lines and begin running through the side streets of Westminster. Constance is pushed and pulled in all directions and falls to the floor several times. She is picked up, manhandled and thrown to the floor by a policeman. Elsa is out of sight. Constance is desperate and tells another woman, 'I can't go on. I simply can't go on.'

'You will be all right presently,' is her answer. It's enough reassurance to pick herself up and try again. The dark evening is lit up again and again by the flash of press photographers.

Eventually Constance makes it as far as the gates at the entrance to the Palace of Westminster. A policeman takes her by the arm and steers her away. Exhausted and confused, she follows him obediently. It's not till they arrive at a police station that Constance realises she has been arrested. She is oddly relieved. At least she is out of the scrum and cannot be hurt any more.

In the police station, Constance is reunited with her comrades, who are covered in scrapes and bruises and blood. The leader of that night's work, Emmeline Pethick-Lawrence, is greeted as a heroine. For the first time, Constance tastes something of the rewards of being a suffragette: the friendship, the solidarity and the delight in each other's achievements. She has never felt useful in her life until now. She is part of something at last.

Her only regret is for her mother, and the shame Lady Lytton will feel in the morning as she unfolds the newspaper and sees the family's illustrious name being dragged through the mud. The day before the protest, Constance had written to her mother in an attempt to explain the inexplicable: why a gentle and delicate lady of leisure should throw her lot in with the militant suffragettes.

'Prisons, as you know, have been my hobby,' is the best she can do. Constance's hobby is about to become a full-time occupation.[1]

18 January 1910, Liverpool Gaol

Jane Warton hears hurried footsteps outside her cell. The doctor is coming.

The door opens and he appears, trailed by a series of wardresses. Jane has decided not to resist and lies down obediently on the wooden bed. But the staff are taking no chances. One wardress grips her head and another pins her feet down.

'There's a choice. A wooden gag or a steel one. The steel one hurts.'

The doctor explains in detail just how much it hurts. Jane ignores him. Defiance, an absolute refusal to comply in any way, is part of her resistance strategy. Eventually, and it is hard to imagine he doesn't take some pleasure in this choice, he selects the steel gag. He begins screwing her mouth open. It pries her jaws apart, much wider than a mouth would normally stretch, into a gaping silent scream.

Then the doctor pushes a four-foot long tube into her mouth and down into her stomach. He pours the 'food' – a white slop of milk, egg and brandy – down a funnel. Jane's stomach automatically revolts and she is sick. Her body convulses, head straining forward, knees going automatically to her chest. But the wardresses hold her down tighter so she can't struggle. The food is simultaneously going down and coming up. It seems never-ending. Eventually Jane forgets who she is. She forgets why she is there. She forgets everything but the pain and the sensation of simultaneously being choked and suffocated.

After the doctor has finished, he slaps her in the face.

Jane lies gasping on her cell floor. The wardresses try to comfort her, but she cannot move. She is covered with sick. It is in her clothes, through her hair and even across the cell on her bed. The wardresses say it is too late in the day to get her washed and changed. She will have to stay like that all night. Despite the squalor, Jane feels only relief that the torment is over: she can breathe again without the suffocating tube.

Jane listens through the wall as her neighbour, Elsie, is force-fed in turn. It's almost worse than being tortured herself. When all is quiet next door, Jane bangs on the wall and screams 'No surrender!' into the silence. 'No surrender,' Elsie echoes back through the brick wall.

The next day, Jane decides to make a last desperate protest at her treatment before she becomes too weak to act. She takes her shoes off and uses them to smash the gas jet that heats her cell. Glass shatters all around her. The wardresses sent to clean up are frightened of this dangerous, raving woman. They take her shoes away before she can do any more damage.

Then the doctor returns.[2]

Later, Jane will try to find the words to talk about what happened. But she can't. 'The horror of it was more than I can describe.'[3]

❧

This is the story of how Lady Constance Lytton became Jane Warton.

Over the course of 1909, Constance turned herself from a respectable spinster into a die-hard suffragette. It meant rejecting her upbringing, abandoning her class and defying her mother. She did it all without hesitation and with barely a backward glance at her former life.

Her life until then had given no hint of the rebellion to come. She was often ill and always cripplingly shy. She was devoted to her mother, her siblings and their families. Her spare time was spent in clumsy but well-intentioned efforts to help the working women who lived around the family estate. She had little interest in politics and even less in voting.

Today, it is all too easy to see the suffragette victory as inevitable, a natural and logical development in a society becoming ever more liberal and progressive. But when Constance Lytton joined the suffragettes in 1909, there was nothing inevitable about it. Since Emmeline Pankhurst had set up the Women's Social and Political Union (WSPU) in 1903, the decades-old struggle for the vote had gained new force and momentum. But after six years of exhausting campaigning, the sense of optimism and vigour was draining away. There was no end in sight. The women were tired of signing petitions, marching on parades and even going to prison when none of it seemed to have any effect. The Liberal government, led by Herbert Asquith, had no interest in 'votes for women', and were grimly set on ignoring these women, however loud and aggressive they became.

To break the deadlock, the suffragettes needed more effective weapons. Almost by chance, they hit upon a deadly solution: the hunger strike. The battle between the government and the suffragettes now entered a new and perilous phase, in which the women risked their lives every time they were arrested. Why on earth would Lady Constance Lytton join them?

⁂

We think we know the suffragettes. We have mental images of them, smartly dressed Edwardian ladies chaining themselves to railings and setting fire to postboxes. We've absorbed them into our culture and our history. In a measure of how iconic the suffragettes have become, Danny Boyle brought them to life in the 2012 Olympic opening ceremony – and there they were, alongside Shakespeare, the Industrial Revolution and the NHS, defining modern Britain.

The trouble with this stereotype is that it obscures the real women who were involved: women who gave up their time, their energy and in some cases their lives for the idea that they were worth something and they should be counted. For daring to stand up for themselves, they were heckled and ridiculed. For daring to keep trying, in the face of government indifference, public condemnation and even police brutality, they were imprisoned. Even today, they are sometimes dismissed and belittled as well-off single women who had nothing else to do. There are even those – historians as well as contemporaries – who claim that their focus on women and gender was a distraction which took the focus off the 'real' problems facing the nation: class, inequality and poverty. But it's not easy to change the world unless you first are allowed into it, and the suffragettes broke down the barriers that had kept women out for centuries. In doing so, they did not just win the vote: they also changed how women were seen by men, and how women saw themselves. The suffragettes helped women become a force to be reckoned with, politically, socially and culturally.

When it comes to the suffragette movement, biography has a great deal to add to traditional history. It allows us to understand the complexity and the rich diversity of the suffragette movement that is hidden by the image of the Edwardian lady gone wild. Every suffragette was different and was drawn into the movement for different and very personal reasons. Some were steeped in the labour movement and became disillusioned with a socialism that didn't recognise the specific problems women faced. Some saw it as a natural progression after women had taken their first tentative steps into higher education, medicine and other professions. Some believed it was the only way to address the grinding poverty of women in the slums and inner cities. Some wanted recognition that women were equal to men. Others believed that women were different from men and that this very difference meant their voices should be heard and their views acknowledged. Some even wanted suffrage simply because they couldn't vote and their butler could.

It's by remembering and re-telling their stories that we do these women justice. They made acts of extraordinary acts of bravery and heroism part of their everyday routine. But Constance Lytton's story is exceptional, even by suffragette standards. No less a person than Emmeline Pankhurst claims that 'Constance Lytton did one of the most heroic deeds to be recorded in the history of the movement'.[4] She was loved and admired by the suffragettes, almost as much as the Pankhursts themselves. After she died in 1923 one of her suffragette sisters said, 'If someone could write the story of that spiritual pilgrimage, showing the atmosphere of the home where it started, and the contemporary current of thought among women that led Con out of that shelter into Jane Warton's cell, a great deal that cannot be understood now would be made clear.' No one has yet done so.

This is partly because Lady Constance Lytton is so different from the others. Her story is not a 'typical' story of a suffragette, and not only because there was no such thing as a 'typical' suffragette. It is also partly because Constance remained utterly loyal to Christabel and Emmeline Pankhurst, even as many of their followers deserted them. Though history is supposedly written by the victors, many historical accounts of the Pankhursts have been critical of their leadership, and their followers have suffered by extension. More recently, historians have been keen to shift the focus away from the Pankhursts, and they are right to do so. The vote wasn't won by just two women, however determined they may have been. The emphasis has been on restoring working-class women to the picture, but important as that is, it has left even less room for the anomalous stories of the upper-class suffragettes. However, as the centennial anniversary of women winning the vote approaches, and we reflect on the suffragettes' achievement and their legacy, it's time that this exceptional woman and her extraordinary story became better known. Though these events took place a hundred years ago, they still have resonance and parallels today. Think, for example, of the misogynistic vitriol and hate directed at many women who dare to have a voice and express an opinion in public. The suffragettes would find that all too familiar. We've not come as far as we'd like to think.

This is a conventional biography, in that it begins at the beginning and continues on to the end, but Constance is not a conventional subject. She packed all the action and incident of her public life (though not her inner, emotional life) into a few short years. It seemed only right to reflect that when writing her biography. That makes this book a more uneven shape than a traditional biography, as it canters through the first forty years of her life and then slows right down to explore those turbulent months in detail – but, after all, whose life is as neat and linear as a traditional biography would have us believe?

Biographers are always faced with the conundrum of what to call their subjects. It's a uniquely unbalanced relationship. We think we know them. We spend our waking hours poring over their letters and poking into their secrets. But of course we hardly know them at all. Biographers of women have an added consideration. Male subjects are almost always called by their surname, whereas women are usually called by their first name: an unconscious reflex, perhaps, demonstrating that men are approached with respect and women with familiarity. In this case, as many Lyttons will appear, it would be confusing as well as jarring to use the surname. The same is true of the Pankhursts, and in the end, I have chosen to use the first names of most of the people who appear in these pages.

The *Oxford Dictionary of National Biography* calls her Lady Constance Bulwer-Lytton, but no one else, at the time or subsequently, uses the prefix Bulwer. No one called her Constance either. She was Conny or Con to her siblings and Lady Con among the suffragettes. That seemed too familiar for me though it would be tedious to continuously refer to 'Lady' Constance. I have compromised in using Constance.

Unlike many biographers, I have not struggled with a lack of material. But it is important to note that the material I have had has been carefully edited. Constance told her own version of her story in her autobiography, *Prisons and Prisoners*. Her early life is dispatched in just a few pages and her 'real' life does not begin until she becomes a suffragette. She appears as an accidental heroine, hopelessly naive but enlightened and saved by the Pankhursts. *Prisons and Prisoners* is astonishingly religious in tone. It is a spiritual quest as much as an autobiography and reads almost as though it has been written to be declaimed from a pulpit. There is a powerful moment during one of Constance's stays in prison when Emmeline Pethick-Lawrence recites one of Olive Schreiner's stories and it gives the women new strength. *Prisons and Prisoners* is likewise written to give the suffragettes new strength at a moment, in 1914, when increasingly audacious and violent attacks on private property had alienated public opinion. It expresses the fierce longings of a woman forced to leave the battle but desperate to rejoin it.

Constance's family, led by her sister Betty Balfour, told another story when they printed her letters. They wanted to present a picture which fitted with the family image of 'Con' as dutiful daughter and sacrificial lamb: Francis of Assisi in female form. In these letters, we also see clearly the struggles of a family who loved Constance and did as much as they could to support her but couldn't understand her. The letters aren't entirely sanitised, and Betty sometimes makes surprisingly modern editorial choices for a book published in the 1920s: for example, in the published letters, Constance speaks frankly about her dislike of her famous grandfather; her depression; and even her impulse to kill herself. However, Betty also left out a great deal. There is no mention, for example, of the unhappy love affair that coloured a decade of Constance's life. This family story of duty and sacrifice was reinforced in later Lytton writing, including in her sister Emily's collection of letters and her brother Neville's memoir. But this was by no means the whole picture. This biography therefore draws heavily on letters which were left out of the published collection and have not appeared in print before.

The suffragettes, too, had their own version of Constance's life. This was a society deeply riven by class, and when Constance reached across the divide they responded with genuine love and admiration. But many of them were also slightly dazzled by her privilege, and this comes across in the way they talk about her, their aristocratic martyr. Constance does appear in histories of the suffrage movement, but just briefly. The focus is usually on two key moments in her life: her decision to join the suffragettes and her decision to become 'Jane Warton'. This book explores what it was in her personality, her circumstances and her history that influenced those decisions, and argues there was much more to Constance Lytton than Jane Warton.

The two stories of Constance Lytton's life are so contradictory that they almost seem to belong to two different people. But they are both correct, and both important to Constance's own identity and sense of self. She was both utterly loyal to her family and totally committed to the suffragettes, and to emphasise one over the other is to do her a disservice. I have done my best to tell both stories at once and, wherever possible, I have let her speak for herself.

CHAPTER ONE

DIPLOMAT'S DAUGHTER

'They thought for themselves, they thought differently from others; they often thought even more differently from each other. There is no pattern about the Lytton family, except a consistent strain of unconventionality, almost non-conformity, even inconsistency. All the Lyttons were originals: they did not go in for carbon copies.' [1]

By far and away the best-known of Constance's ancestors is her paternal grandfather, the novelist and politician Edward Bulwer-Lytton. The youngest of three sons, he lost his father when he was just four years old. He was the only son to stay at home with his mother Elizabeth through childhood and they were very close. But when Edward married Rosina Doyle Wheeler in 1827 against his mother's wishes, he was cut off. He had already published a few volumes of poetry: now, out of necessity, he turned to writing in earnest. His 1828 novel *Pelham* was a great success, and marked the first step in a literary career which put him second only to his great friend Charles Dickens in the literary popularity stakes. He was a versatile and prolific writer of historical fiction and mysteries, and he had a strong interest in horror and the occult. His later work *Vril: The Power of the Coming Race* was an early science fiction classic and, incidentally, lends its name to Bovril. He coined any number of phrases which have passed into the vernacular: 'the pen is mightier than the sword', 'the great unwashed', 'the pursuit of the almighty dollar' and, most famously, 'it was a dark and stormy night.'

Edward was also a notable statesman. He won St Ives as an independent radical in 1831 and Lincoln the following year, holding the seat until 1841. When he returned in the early 1850s, it was to represent the Tory Party, alongside another great friend, Benjamin Disraeli. His estrangement from Elizabeth did not last long and, after she died, she left him her family estate at Knebworth in Hertfordshire. To honour her, he added her family name, Lytton, to his father's name of Bulwer.[2]

But despite the fame and fortune of her grandfather, Constance's female forebears were just as remarkable. Rosina's mother, Anna Wheeler, was one of the first women in England to actively campaign for women's rights. Born in Tipperary in the 1780s, she married Francis Massy Wheeler aged just fifteen, only to discover that he was an abusive alcoholic. Twelve years of such a marriage was as much as she could stand and she fled to the protection of an uncle in Guernsey with her two young daughters, Henrietta and Rosina. Four other children died. Already familiar with the radical ideas of Mary Wollstonecraft, now she taught herself French and became an avid reader of French political thinkers. She moved to France, where she fell in with a group of utopians and socialists who called her 'the Goddess of Reason'. Her children were left in Guernsey with an affable great-uncle until they were old enough to go to school in Kensington and pay her periodic visits in Caen.[3]

When her husband finally died, Anna settled in London and became part of a set of social reformers which included Robert Owen and Jeremy Bentham. This group, the Owenites, were very concerned with issues of gender and wanted to see the establishment of co-operative communities where class and sex would be irrelevant. The publication of James Mill's 'Essay on Government' was vitally important in Anna's intellectual development. Radical insofar as it called representative government 'the grand discovery of modern times', Mill's tract nevertheless wrote off the idea of women voting, since their interests could more than adequately be represented by their husbands and fathers. Anna would not stand for this. In 1825, her close friend William Thompson published *An Appeal of One Half of the Human Race, Women, Against the Pretensions of the Other, Men*, which critiqued the way society expected women to live without education, employment or property rights. It challenged the institution of marriage for keeping women as helpless dependents and compared the position of women to that of slaves. The logical conclusion, Thompson argued, was to grant women political rights as well as to abolish marriage in favour of communal family life and free love.[4] Anna, a staunch socialist as well as a committed feminist, had become far more radical than her inspiration, Mary Wollstonecraft.[5]

Though Anna did not write *An Appeal* herself, Thompson attributed many of the ideas in the book to her and considered it a work of joint scholarship. Anna began to campaign for her feminist ideals in public, speaking at what is now Conway Hall and publishing her own work under the pseudonym Vlasta. She was even a vocal advocate of contraception. It is no wonder that the stately Elizabeth Lytton balked at the idea of Anna's daughter Rosina joining her aristocratic family.

In fact, Elizabeth was soon proved right. Rosina and Edward had two children, Emily and Edward (known as Robert, to distinguish him from his father), but had serious disagreements over the best way to raise them. But this was not the main point of contention. Victorian society understood that male infidelity was only to be expected, and Bulwer-Lytton took full advantage of this. Wives should look the other way and not say a word. But Rosina had inherited her mother's independence and would not tolerate such hypocrisy. In 1833, on a European trip when Edward was researching and writing *The Last Days of Pompeii*, she began a flirtation of her own. Edward was outraged, and became violent. On at least one occasion he threatened her with a knife. The last straw, according to Rosina, was when she arrived unexpectedly in London one night to look after Edward, who was supposedly ill, only to find him with two cups of tea and a young lady beating a hasty retreat.[6] They separated soon after. Edward would only grant her a divorce if she acknowledged her own infidelity but kept his a secret. Rosina would not consent to this; so they were stuck with each other.

Their relationship descended quickly into bitterness, hostility and very public recriminations. Despite the fact that his unfaithfulness had led to the collapse of their marriage, in the eyes of the law Edward was blameless. That meant, in theory at least, that he kept the children. But in practice he was not much interested in them. For the next few months, they lived with Rosina and a family friend, Miss Mary Greene, in Ireland, which Robert would remember as among the happiest months of his life. This was the last time Rosina and her children lived together. Edward realised the power of making the children a weapon in his battle against Rosina, and refused to let her see them. Afterwards, they lived with Mary Greene in Cheltenham while Rosina divided her time between London and Europe. Edward, meanwhile, went on to have at least three long-term mistresses, and seven children. One, Eleanor D'Ewes Thomson, was his housekeeper. Another had the intriguing name of Marion Wollstonecraft Godwin Lowndes; he used to dress her up as a valet in order to take her around Europe. Miss Lowndes also took in Miss Thomson's children when she died.[7] Like his friend Dickens, Bulwer-Lytton kept all these mistresses as secret as he could.

In 1848, Rosina heard that twenty-year-old Emily was suffering from typhoid, and muscled her way into the boarding house where her daughter lay dying. In a scene worthy of Edward's most lurid fiction, there was a shouting match over Emily's deathbed in which Rosina accused her ex-husband of neglect and murder. Rosina would not go quietly, and turned to literature, not just for financial support, but for revenge. Writing about her own position illustrated broader points about the precarious position of women in the Victorian age. In 1839, she published a merciless portrait of Edward in her novel *Cheveley, or The Man of Honour*. A series of novels was to follow: increasingly bitter satires of her husband, his family and their friends. She thought it unfair that while his books were bringing him fame and fortune, she was kept on an allowance of just £400 a year (though to put this in context, it represents something more like £20,000 today).[8] Time did not diminish her righteous fury. In 1851, when Queen Victoria attended a performance of his play *Not So Bad As We Seem*, Rosina wrote to Prince Albert threatening to pelt her with eggs (and began to advertise an alternative play, *Even Worse Than We Seem*). When Edward stood for election in Hertfordshire in 1858 Rosina appeared at the hustings to shame him. There is another legend about this scene which has Edward fainting at the sight of his ex-wife, dressed in Liberal yellow, climbing up on the platform and listing his crimes against her to a cheering crowd. 'Fiend, villain, monster, cowardly wretch, outcast,' she – allegedly – said. 'I am told you have been sent to the colonies. If they knew as much about you as I do they would have sent you there long ago.'[9] (He was being made Secretary for the Colonies.) Bulwer-Lytton won the election but felt humiliated. He hit back by claiming that Rosina was insane, and had her committed to an asylum.

Rosina's story is a stark reminder of the absolute power of men and utter powerlessness of women in the mid-nineteenth century. Children, money, even freedom: all could be taken away on the say-so of a man. All he needed was two signatures from the medical profession – which Edward, with his money, power and influence, found easy to obtain. In the asylum, Rosina went on hunger strike in an effort to prove that she was of sound mind. She only gave in and ate again when it was pointed out to her that this would be used as evidence of her insanity.[10] Fortunately for Rosina, her female friends were outraged at the way she was treated. She may have been angry and resentful – and with good cause – but she was not mad. They campaigned for her release and she was let out after three weeks. Bulwer-Lytton's case was not helped by the fact that he had been advised by a John Conolly, an asylum reformer who subsequently got in trouble when it was discovered that asylums were actually paying him for referrals. Rosina's experience may have helped inspire *The Woman in White*: Wilkie Collins moved in similar circles to Bulwer-Lytton and it is impossible that he would not have been aware of this cause célèbre.[11] Rosina read this book and wrote to Collins:

> The great failure of your book is the villain; Count Fosco is a very poor one, and when next you want a character of that sort I trust you will not disdain to come to me. The man is alive and constantly under my gaze. In fact he is my own husband.[12]

Their son Robert was hopelessly caught in the middle of this acrimony. With the death of his sister, he had lost his closest companion and was almost totally friendless. Edward had visited him just twice a year through his childhood. Despite this neglect, Robert idolised and adored this absent father, and submitted to his wishes even as an adult. After being sent to Harrow, he spent lonely holidays at school, with a tutor, or with his father's friend John Forster. Best remembered as Dickens's friend and biographer, Forster took the young Robert under his wing and nurtured his interest in poetry and literature. Robert was grateful for the attention and the two remained close as Robert grew up. After the scandalous asylum episode, Robert took Rosina out of the country to the Pyrenees in order to try to restore some semblance of peace. Instead, he found himself right in the centre of the quarrel, both parents expecting his allegiance. After three months in Europe, Rosina and Robert fell out in Paris. Robert gave up and went home. He never saw his mother again.

Meanwhile, what was Robert to make of his own life? Encouraged by John Forster, Robert hoped to be a poet. Edward, though, wouldn't have it. 'I don't think whatever your merit, the world would allow two of the same name to have both a permanent reputation in literature,' he wrote.[13] Instead, Robert was sent into the diplomatic service. Aged just eighteen, he went to work for his uncle William, Edward's older brother Baron Dalling, who was then ambassador to the United States. He later followed his uncle to Florence and then began a steady rise up the ranks in his own right. But he continued to write poetry and in Florence, his talent was discovered and nurtured through friendship with Robert Browning and Elizabeth Barrett Browning. His first volume of poetry was published under the pseudonym Owen Meredith in 1855 and was quietly well received. His most successful and lasting work was *Lucille*, a novel in verse, published 1860. But his writing increasingly had to take a back seat to his public service.

Robert entered into European diplomatic society enthusiastically. He was eccentric, dressing 'in the fashion of his father's day with bell-bottomed trousers and square-cut toes to his shoes and a good deal of jewellery',[14] but he was charming and attractive, blessed with a natural ease and grace that helped him both personally and professionally. With so few family members to rely on, he was eager to make good friends.[15] In Europe, he discovered women. There was at least one serious relationship in Florence and another during his next post at The Hague, which eventually resulted in an engagement. Edward at first refused to countenance the marriage and by the time he came around, the young woman herself had changed her mind. Robert's next post was in Vienna, where he spent four years and became close friends with the ambassador's wife, Lady Georgina Bloomfield. Lady Bloomfield saw Robert needed a wife, so when Robert went home on leave in 1864, she sent him to visit her sister, Elizabeth Villiers, a widow then living with her last unmarried daughter, Edith.

Lady Bloomfield thought Edith Villiers would be a perfect diplomatic wife and she was correct. Edith came from a long line of aristocrats: one of her ancestresses had been a mistress of King William III.[16] Edith's father, Edward, had been the brother of Lord Clarendon, the Foreign Secretary. When Edward died in 1843, Lord Clarendon invited his widow, Elizabeth, and her four children to live on his estate in Hertfordshire. Elizabeth, already suffering serious financial difficulties, gratefully accepted.

When Robert met Edith, two of her sisters had recently married. Teresa, married to Charles Earle, would become a major part of Constance's life, known fondly as 'Aunt T'. Edith's twin sister, yet another Elizabeth, had married the diplomat Henry Loch. The family story goes that both twins were in love with Henry and he accidentally proposed to the wrong woman but was either too proud to admit his mistake or too gentlemanly to go back on his word.[17] Regardless, he married Elizabeth, and Edith pined.

Edith was incredibly beautiful. Around this time she was painted by G. F. Watts in a Pre-Raphaelite portrait which became famous and much admired. Perhaps because she was better known for her looks, she has been treated harshly by Robert's biographers: 'She loved him too uncritically to be of any intellectual stimulus to him … she had no originality of mind, no intellectual sparkle,' says one (her own granddaughter). Because she did not come from the same sort of literary family, these writers have considered her relatively stupid. Of course, Edith had no formal education apart from the music, drawing and dancing, which, together with winters in Europe, were essential for girls of her class. She is allowed to be 'sweet tempered, gentle, gracious and tactful'[18] but these traits are undervalued, and her contribution to Robert's career has been seriously underestimated. Not by Constance, though, who truly appreciated and admired her mother. She could see how much Robert had benefited from Edith's influence. Around 1892, reflecting on her family history, she wrote to her cousin Adela that it was a

> sheer miracle that father came forth from such generations of undesirables ... the whole family history, as one looks back on it, gives me an awed sense of the fearful power of wrong-doing and of the yet more wondrous power of right doing ... if there ever was a crude moral tale, it was grandfather's life.

For Constance, 'the great turning point in generations of misery' was when 'mother married into our family ... an upright, conscientious, dutiful, law-abiding, sane and normal woman! Whatever her shortcomings, her outlook on life was high-minded and unselfish in aim.'[19]

Edith was everything that Robert was looking for, and they soon became engaged. Predictably enough, Edward was also opposed to this marriage. This time, it was because Lord Clarendon was one of his political opponents – and a local one to boot, as Clarendon's estate was in the same county as Knebworth. Eventually, he was persuaded to allow the wedding to go ahead, though with bad grace. He would not allow the newlyweds to use Knebworth for their honeymoon.

Edith and Robert then set out for their new lives together in European capitals. She was fortunate in that his postings were relatively undemanding and close to home; her sister Elizabeth had to move to South Africa with Lord Loch. Their marriage was professionally very successful, and seems to have worked personally too, though Robert's reputation as a flirt was well established and entirely justified. They began in Athens, then moved to Lisbon, Madrid and then Vienna. Here, Robert invited disapproval by taking George Henry Lewes, then on 'honeymoon' with his new partner MaryAnn Evans – George Eliot – into the official box. The two couples would become friends and Edith rather surprisingly became a correspondent of George's – she particularly enjoyed *Daniel Deronda*.[20] Robert would always surround himself with writers, especially poets. His closest friendship was with the poet Wilfred Scawen Blunt, formed in Lisbon when Edith was away in England. Edith disapproved of Blunt and his rackety lifestyle, but he would be a lasting part of their lives (almost with disastrous consequences for one of their daughters).[21]

Robert and Edith's first child, Rowland, was born in August 1865, followed by Elizabeth – known as Bina as a child and Betty as an adult – in June 1867. Their third child, Constance Georgina, was born on 12 February 1869 in Vienna.[22] Her second name was a tribute to the great-aunt who had brought her parents together. In the summer of 1871, all the children had whooping cough. Rowland never recovered and died. Eight months later, a second son, Henry, known as 'Teddy', was born.

In the autumn of 1872, Robert spent his leave with his father at Torquay; a reunion which also became a farewell as Edward died early in the New Year. He was at the height of his fame, having outlived his friend Dickens and taken his place as the nation's most popular author. He left countless essays, reams of poetry and several plays, as well his wildly successful novels. But as literary fashions changed, Bulwer-Lytton was left behind, and he is no longer as widely read as some of his Victorian contemporaries. He was buried in Westminster Abbey, which suggests how successful he had been at hiding his colourful private life. Along with Knebworth, Robert inherited financial responsibility for Edward's mistresses and children. In 1875, he was in regular correspondence with Marion Lowndes and her daughter Lucy as they asked for more support; in return he asked for Marion's help in preparing his memoir of Edward.[23]

In a terrible echo of Rowland's death, towards the end of 1872 the children all suffered flu, and this time Teddy died. Just afterwards, on Christmas Day, another daughter, Emily, was born. Robert now seriously considered resigning from the diplomatic service and moving home to Knebworth. He had served his country competently for nearly a quarter of a century but with no great distinction. Finally freed from his father's long shadow and enormous ego, he could at last devote himself to poetry and see if his talent was as great as his desire. But while he was still considering his future, he received a telegram from Benjamin Disraeli which would change his life. It was an invitation to be the Viceroy of India. 'I believe if you will accept this high post, you will have an opportunity, not only of serving your country, but of obtaining an enduring fame,' said the Prime Minister.[24]

Robert did not want to accept. Aside from his renewed commitment to poetry, his health wasn't very good. He battled with depression, and piles made his life a misery. He had already turned down the offer to be the Governor of Madras precisely for this reason. Then there were the children. Having lost two sons already, Edith and Robert were understandably protective of their girls, and worried about the many possible diseases and illnesses. Typhoid, cholera and malaria were major killers, as were smallpox, tetanus and dysentery.[25] Edith was also pregnant again.

But the call to serve at such a high level eventually proved irresistible. To give an idea of just what a significant promotion this was, Robert had been earning £4,400 in his last role at Lisbon, and his salary in India would be £25,000.[26] But far more important than the money was the prestige. This was the high point of British rule in India and the glamour and glory associated with the viceroyalty was extremely attractive to Robert. Edith refused to be separated from the children so leaving them at home was not an option, but they consulted various doctors who put their minds at ease about the possible risks to the girls. Once Robert had made up his mind to go, Edith supported him utterly. This was her duty and it was not her place to question his decision, whatever her private feelings might have been.

One of Robert's first and most important tasks as viceroy would be to proclaim Queen Victoria the Empress of India. The British public was baffled by Victoria's preoccupation with India, as she had been living in a permanent state of mourning for years, with seemingly no interest in being Queen of her own country, let alone Empress of another. Acquiring this new title was the start of a process which tempted Victoria back into public life and reconnected her with her people. Aside from organising this ceremony, Robert's main task – as Disraeli and his Foreign Secretary, Lord Salisbury, made clear – was to bring Afghanistan to heel. Russia was increasingly making trouble in the region, which was a direct threat to India because of the long border they shared. Robert's assignment was to get relations with Afghanistan on an 'intimate and friendly' footing, and ideally to establish a British mission in Afghanistan, which would give the British a more secure footing in the area.[27] At the same time, Robert would have to contend with the day-to-day running of this vast subcontinent and effectively address long-standing Indian grievances, without causing undue resentment among the British. Robert had to contend with myriad complicated issues in India, including a growing middle class which was increasingly, and rightly, discontented about its lack of representation in government; a British civil service becoming ever more insular and disconnected from the people it was supposed to be governing; and periodic catastrophes of famine and disease. Change in India was at once extremely rapid and extremely slow. Where it occurred, the impact of new transportation and communication was swift and dramatic, but away from the centres of activity, life in the villages continued much as it had done for centuries.[28]

It seems obvious in hindsight, but apparently not at the time, that Robert was hopelessly unprepared for, and totally unsuited to, this immense task. He was charismatic and charming, but had little regard for hierarchy and protocol, features which dominated Anglo-Indian society. Moreover, most of his experience in Europe was irrelevant. He had no direct experience of government and certainly nothing even approaching the scale of Indian rule. Furthermore, having spent so much of his career abroad, he did not have good connections with the British Cabinet to rely on in difficult situations. Instead, Robert confidently assumed that his own instincts, together with Disraeli's support, would carry him through. He did, however, have something very important going for him: Queen Victoria (unusually) genuinely liked and respected him. This was important, because the Queen took a strong personal interest in India. She wrote in her journal that Robert was 'a man full of feeling'.[29] He was the only person who was allowed to address her in the first person in his letters, a breach of protocol that became a mark of their mutual respect and affection.

Robert now had to go on a crash course in the government of India. It is almost impossible to overstate just how complicated this was. Since the Indian Mutiny in 1857, the Crown had taken over direct rule from the East India Company. Relations between governed and government now appeared stable, but underneath the surface there was still considerable tension. Successive viceroys tried to manage this with a hands-off approach to ruling which was more respectful of Indian customs and traditions, however incomprehensible they were to the British. But it was a mammoth task simply to understand how the administration of this vast continent worked. The new viceroy would have to contend with an advisory council, a legislative council and an executive council, several governors, and nine provinces divided into innumerable districts. Robert was fortunate to find an excellent guide through this maze of bureaucracy in Fitzjames Stephen, brother of Leslie. Fitzjames, who had spent years in the Indian civil service, gave Robert a crash course in Indian government and became Minister of Finance. Robert's other great ally in India was Richard Strachey, another senior government administrator, who named his son, Lytton Strachey, after Robert.[30]

The Lyttons left London on 1 March 1876, spending more than three weeks on a boat before reaching India. Robert and Edith then separated so that he could start his official duties in the capital while she settled the children in to their new home. This was Government House in Simla, the summer capital of Indian government, where Constance and her siblings would spend six months of the year.

Simla was an odd place, imagined and built to remind people of a country that they had not seen for years. Each summer, the government packed up and moved 1,200 miles into the hills to avoid the greatest extremes of the climate. There were something like 400 houses, built along a strip a mile long, along with everything that you would expect to find in an English town – a church, library, bank, town hall, a club for the gentlemen – as well as a hall for 'rinking', or roller skating.[31] The houses were 'little islands of Englishness' and 'the gardens were planted with ferns and roses and familiar vegetables'.[32] There was also a valley which was used for cricket, archery, fetes – and as a racecourse. All Anglo-Indian society spent their leave at Simla, so there was a permanent holiday spirit, which the Lyttons entered into enthusiastically. Edith caused something of a stir by the apparently radical innovation of seating dinner party guests in small groups rather than along one long table.[33]

Though her first impressions of India were not favourable – 'everything we touched was baking hot, and the bread at luncheon quite hard, and napkins stiff'[34] – Edith liked her new home. Robert hated the way it leaked and resented having to spend any money on it. Having been used to moderate and temperate European cities, the Lyttons now had to adapt to a climate that went rapidly from one extreme to the next: freezing in April and boiling in May; utterly dry in June and rains heavy enough to wash away houses in September. It made Robert ill and for four months he was forced to give up champagne and smoking.[35]

Edith diligently threw herself into the extensive duties required by Robert's social position. Not all of these were tedious, and the Lyttons found pleasure where they could: one of Robert's biographers describes them as the 'first Viceregal couple to bring some glamour to Simla'.[36] Robert encouraged theatre and the arts, while Edith, a talented piano player, tried to nurture a musical scene and had a tennis court built. Aside from entertaining the British, Edith had a strong interest in education, especially for Indian girls, and made a steady stream of official visits to schools, hospitals and army barracks, to meet the wives and children of British soldiers. She was so busy with her official duties that for the first time, she did not nurse her new baby. This was, to their great relief and joy, a boy, born on 9 August 1876. The Queen had asked to be godmother, and the baby was named after her: Victor Alexander George Robert. A final child, Neville Stephen, would be born in February 1879, between the first and second suppers of a ball.[37] When Victor himself served in India in the early 1920s and saw what was expected of the Vicereine, he wondered how on earth Edith had managed to do it all, especially with two babies.[38]

Robert did not make a good first impression on the expatriate elite. His first significant intervention was a legal case in which a

British man, named Fuller, struck his coachman, who collapsed and later died. It was brought to trial but Fuller was fined only thirty rupees. This became a focus for Indian grievances, and Robert rightly intervened, rebuking the judge. He was supported in this by the Queen and both British and Indian press, but Anglo-Indian society felt he had let them down. In their view, he was not on their side, and so they mistrusted him from the outset.[39]

Robert began preparations for the ceremony to proclaim Queen Victoria as Empress. This was to be expensive and extravagant, which began to look grotesque when a series of natural disasters struck. A cyclone in Bombay was followed by an outbreak of famine in Bombay and Madras. The ceremony was held on New Year's Day 1877 and Robert, for once, stuck rigidly to formality and protocol. There were princes and chiefs, ambassadors and envoys, soldiers and bureaucrats, as well as thousands upon thousands of ordinary people.[40] The assembled multitudes were surprised to see Edith and her girls present, though at least Robert was able to refrain from smoking during the ceremony. Constance was seven, old enough to be impressed and young enough to be bored.

Meanwhile, the famine grew worse. Famines were frequent and hardly unexpected, but the government had no structures in place to distribute relief. Nothing in Robert's previous career had prepared him to face such a crisis and his response did not match the magnitude of the disaster. The last major famine had struck parts of Bihar and Bengal. It had been dealt with successfully by importing rice, setting up an effective distribution system and establishing work programmes, which helped avoid major casualties. But there had also been a great deal of waste, and this led Robert to focus on efficiency rather than human suffering. He introduced tests to determine who was eligible for help, and the systems in place forced people to walk long distances for relief. In Madras, the Governor introduced a much more generous and liberal system of help. Robert tried to put a stop to it, worried about the likely costs, and sent instructions to reduce the rations and cut down the relief operation.

This famine was one of the worst disasters of the century in India, resulting in five million deaths. As a result, the government created an Indian Famine Commission which drew up a Famine Code, setting out how the government would respond in future. Plans were drawn up for new railways and better irrigation in areas prone to famine, district officers were told how to share out food and organise relief, and provisions were made to reduce taxes and offer loans to help farmers recover. This was a vast improvement on the formerly shambolic and piecemeal approach to famine relief. However, it allowed the British to feel complacent and did not prevent further severe famines over the next few years.[41]

Robert's handling of the delicate situation in Afghanistan did more lasting damage to his own reputation. There was a division of opinion back home about the best policy towards Afghanistan, and by implication, Russia, which was aggressively expanding through Asia every year. Afghanistan was a fragmented and tribal land, and if Russia wanted to invade India, the easiest way to do so was along the huge north-western border between India and Afghanistan. One school of thought held that Britain, through India, needed to have a strong influence over Afghanistan in order to hold Russia back and dissuade any chance of invasion. Another view was that Afghanistan was so divided as to be almost ungovernable, and if it came to a fight with the Russians, that would be easier on the frontier of India than in the mountains of Afghanistan. Disraeli and Salisbury were advocates of the former policy and sent Lytton to India with clear instructions to bring Afghanistan closer to India and thus Britain. They had put their faith in one of the chiefs, Sher Ali. Robert spent months negotiating with him, making very little progress and becoming increasingly frustrated. The issue became more pressing when Russia went to war with Turkey in 1877. The

British Cabinet decided to stay neutral but Robert thought this was the wrong decision, believing it would look like weakness to the Russians. After the Turkish war was concluded in July 1878, the Russians sent a mission to Afghanistan. Sher Ali had been resisting a British mission and Robert was outraged. The Cabinet urged him to tread carefully. But instead he sent his own mission to Afghanistan, and when that was turned back, he sent an invasion force. This began the second Anglo-Afghan war.[42]

Disraeli and Salisbury were extremely angry. Newly embroiled in war in South Africa, the last thing Disraeli needed was another unpopular war on the other side of the world. Worse, Robert seemed to be deliberately disobeying orders – though actually those orders had never arrived, victims of the late-Victorian inter-continental postal system. Although the invasion force was initially successful – and Sher Ali was killed in the fighting, meaning the British could install a friendlier successor – in September 1879, the British residency in Kabul was attacked, with many casualties. Robert had to pour money and troops into Afghanistan to bring the situation under control. Stability was finally restored after the Battle of Kandahar in September 1880, but only at great cost and for little obvious benefit except restoring the status quo.

The press, both in India and Britain, turned against Robert, and not just his policy but his personality.[43] He was attacked again and again in Parliament, but the government was more worried about preserving relations with Russia than protecting their viceroy, so did very little more to defend him. He felt let down and his depression returned with a vengeance.

Robert's reputation as a flirt grew during his time in India and his name was consistently linked with two of the most attractive women in Simla, Mrs Batten and Mrs Plowden. There was even a whisper that his godson, Lytton Strachey, may have actually been his son. In truth, Robert's womanising does not seem to have crossed the line from flirtation into anything more serious. His love life was by no means as colourful as his good friend Wilfred Scawen Blunt's, and Mrs Batten and Mrs Plowden were actually having affairs with his two aides-de-camp. (Though Robert implored her not to, Blunt also slept with Mrs Batten.)[44] To Robert, Blunt represented the life that he might have chosen: romantic, bohemian and free. That didn't mean he followed Blunt's example, but neither did he feel at home in the stifling atmosphere of Anglo-Indian society. Robert was courtly and affectionate, an unconventional romantic poet. He liked smoking, and pretty women; he did not attend church. It was his misfortune to find himself in a stuffy, uptight society which saw his chivalrous nature as simply louche. Luckily, he had Edith, who was conscientious where he was rebellious, always ready to smooth over slights and engage in the small talk that Robert loathed. A more serious flaw was Robert's tendency to spend money wildly. One theatrical production alone in Calcutta cost him £2,000. By 1880 he was beginning to realise the consequences of this, and warned Edith that they would be going home as 'titled paupers'.[45]

The girls were too young to be concerned by the troubles of their parents. They lived apart for weeks, even months, at a time. This bothered Edith, though there was not much she could do about it. Her duties as a wife came before her duties as a mother. The girls felt the separation intensely. Betty wrote to Edith early in their stay, before they had got used to their new situation: 'Poor Con often says to me, "Oh, Bina, I wish I could see dear Mother's face again. I do try to comfort her, although I feel just as unhappy myself."'[46]

All Edith wished for the girls was 'good health, charm and the power of adapting to their husbands'. She wanted them to be pretty but not too beautiful, as she told her mother: 'I hate a girl to have enough to be stared at.'[47] The girls' weight was a frequent cause for concern: Constance was always thought too thin, and Betty and Emily too fat.

The girls' education was not a priority. 'Charm, and a power of adapting themselves to their husbands, we consider far more essential than great study which might only ruin their healths,' Edith told her mother. The girls had a governess but their studies were not especially rigorous, as Edith remarked. 'A gentleman reads English history with them, and teaches them arithmetic, which amuses them. They are also drilled, and the arm exercises are the best things for making them hold up.' There was an art teacher, as the older girls loved painting, and Constance was thought to have some talent. 'I think illuminating on very small things will be her style,' Edith wrote in her diary.[48] A few years into their stay, part of the veranda was closed off into a huge private doll's house, which they all enjoyed.

Like Robert, the girls were interested in the theatre. First they watched the adults in amateur theatricals. 'They looked so pretty in white cachemire [sic] dresses over pink – and had stools in front of us for the Play. Con's eyes looked as if they would drop out of her head with excitement.' Later, they were able to get up their own productions. For Constance's ninth birthday, there was a production of Cinderella in which Constance played the prince, 'though she is more an actress in originality and really killed me with laughter', Edith wrote.[49]

Otherwise, their main occupation was riding, and the girls shared two horses, Tommy and Bill. Seven-year-old Conny did not mind Tommy rearing, and said, 'If Tommy likes to go up a tree I shall not mind.' On important occasions they also rode elephants. For the first part of their time in India, Constance had her own parrot, named Polly, and was disconsolate when he died: especially when the replacement parrot quickly followed suit. 'I had to scold her,' their nurse disapprovingly told Edith, 'because when once she begins crying it is difficult to stop her.'[50] Eventually, she was given her own dog, who did survive and even came back to live with them in Knebworth. Constance would keep dogs all her life.

For all that Constance would later claim that she had been a virtual invalid, she seems to have had no trouble keeping up with her sisters. 'One day I found the girls all together in their petticoats, with their hair streaming, doing gymnastics on their beds,' wrote Edith ruefully to her mother. 'Con had been so often head downwards that her nose was bleeding.' She was a good eater and seemed to cope with the stifling heat. On another occasion, 'after a long scrambling walk', Constance begged to be allowed to run up the hill afterwards.[51] These were not quite the perfectly brought-up children to be found in a Victorian picture-book.

Neither was this an entirely idyllic childhood, however much freedom and fun there may have been. Emily recalled a 'sense of being a prisoner, caught in a long tunnel of childhood which would never end'. She and Constance despised each other as children and there was a constant tension between them which occasionally exploded into rows. Constance was deeply sarcastic about Emily's excessive piety, and took a vow not to speak to her. Emily experienced an ongoing sense of injustice and felt it deeply. 'No child was believed or treated with respect,' she wrote later. 'One had just to endure the wrongs in silence and grow bitter with brooding over them.'[52]

Betty had her father's eyes and expression; otherwise she was a Villiers in temperament. 'She is quiet, but chatty and cheerful and answers gently if contradicted,' said Edith. Emily was forthright and independent, unafraid of speaking her mind. 'I wonder', she pondered to her nanny, 'if I should be prettier if I was better, but naughtiness will come and I can't help it.' Constance was a quieter and more thoughtful child, 'generally so much more silent than Bina', wrote Edith to Mrs Forster.[53]

Conny is tall and very thin and stoops a good deal; the heat tires her so that she is perhaps more silent and sad than she was, but she has the same lovely eyes and active movements, and her character always gentle and easy, and she never gets into a scrape with anyone.[54]

Robert believed that Constance bore a 'haunting resemblance' to Rosina, but Edith saw her differently: 'Such a mixture of Villiers and Lyttons, and will be like my father I think.'[55] At eleven, Constance's figure was just as Edith's had been as a child. Edith wrote to her mother that she had really beautiful eyes, and hoped that, 'the lower part of her face' would improve in time.[56] Victor, by comparison, was 'rather like an owl and a monkey, with long skinny arms, but with eyes that redeem all the other features'. Neville was thought to look like Constance, with the same dark hair and chin. Edith's fears about the climate proved to be groundless, as 'the children are all very rosy and perfectly strong, and much better than they could be in England'.[57]

In March 1880, Disraeli dissolved Parliament and called an election. The Conservatives were hopeful of victory, but the Liberals, led by William Gladstone, went on the attack. People had been suffering with poor harvests and high prices. Gladstone offered peace and prosperity compared with Disraeli's unpopular and expensive wars. As a result, Robert came in for renewed abuse over the Afghanistan war. Robert was not accustomed to being dragged into party politics and found this extremely difficult to cope with, especially as Edith's family at home remained prominent Liberal supporters. But halfway around the world he was unable to defend himself.

Gladstone won the election and Robert resigned his post. Viceroys usually served a five-year term, but Robert believed that there was no way that the two could have worked together effectively. His reputation took a further battering when Gladstone's first Cabinet discovered a major miscalculation in the costs of the war. Fitzjames Strachey had underestimated these by millions of pounds. The mistake was Strachey's rather than Robert's, but Robert was still ultimately responsible and this catastrophic error was yet another stick to beat him with.

Robert was gratified and consoled to find that both Disraeli and the Queen remained loyal. The Queen had made him an Earl as thanks for his service in India and Disraeli wrote to ask for Robert's continuing support when he entered the House of Lords. The people of Knebworth were also very supportive and lined the streets to welcome the family home, on 9 August 1880. It was Victor's fourth birthday.

CHAPTER TWO

A MISFIT AMONG ECCENTRICS

*'Conny had exceptional talent; she had also an infinite capacity for
taking pains; she hated society and yet she loved humanity; she had such
nobility of character that if she had lived in the gutter she would have
purified its mud and yet remained unstained herself.'*[1]

Edith was delighted to leave India. She felt she had hardly
seen Robert for four years, and loyally counted the cost to his
health, reputation and sense of self. Robert himself was consumed
with regret. He never came to terms with his failures in India and
he never recovered from the damage to his personal reputation: his
period as viceroy is still judged critically today.[2] In part, this is because his contemporaries blamed him, to an extraordinary degree, for
the famine and the war. Both were regarded as personal rather than
political failures. In the popular parody, Robert was seen as almost
single-handedly starting the conflict and killing millions of people.
The reality, of course, is far more complicated. Later, his daughter
Betty Balfour and his great niece Mary Lutyens wrote more nuanced
histories which show Robert's time in India in a more balanced light
but, writing as relations, these were understandably seen as partisan
accounts. In any case, the damage had already been done.

Constance and her family spent the next few years of her life
living, as quietly as it is possible to do in a great house, at Knebworth. It had been in the Lytton family for 400 years, and was

originally a Tudor manor house, built round a courtyard. Elizabeth Bulwer-Lytton had pulled three sides down, leaving only the west wing, and started an extensive programme of renovations, complete with griffins and gargoyles. This was continued by Edward Bulwer-Lytton, who remodelled and redecorated Knebworth to suit his gothic imagination.

It is best known today as a venue for rock concerts. Freddie Mercury played his last gig with Queen at Knebworth, while Robbie Williams and Oasis have both played to audiences of over 125,000 in the grounds. The distinctive style also means that Knebworth is much in demand as a popular backdrop for films: it has featured in everything from *Batman* to *The King's Speech*.[3]

It was certainly not a comfortable family home when they returned from India. Robert built a third storey on top of the house, where he and Edith and the older girls had their bedrooms, and the younger children had a series of nurseries. The nursery corridor was painted in colours that evoked their Indian garden. With a five-year gap between Constance and Emily, the children naturally divided into two groups, and at Knebworth that became more pronounced. Emily, Victor and Neville were young enough to spend all their time playing. They were outdoors all the time, playing cricket and climbing trees. The younger ones were supervised by a nurse, nanny, nursery-maid and governess and lived almost entirely within the nursery.[4] Betty and Constance were now expected to become young ladies. They lived separately, with their own rooms, governesses and maid. Their rooms were called 'the schoolroom passage', and much later became known as 'the bachelor passage', as it was where single young men would stay.[5]

Seventy years later, Victor wrote a memoir of his early years at Knebworth, and though 'my sister' appears frequently, this always means Emily. For much of the time, Betty and Constance may as well not have been there at all. They ate dinner in the dining room rather than the nursery and only saw the younger ones for an hour in the evenings. Sometimes they would formally invite their siblings for tea and then dress up as ghosts to entertain them.[6]

Their only shared interest was music: aside from Constance's piano, Betty played the violin, Emily the guitar and Neville the flute. (The family talent passed Victor by.) With her brothers soon off to school, they were almost strangers to Constance until they were grown up. Then they became firm friends: she talked about music and art with Neville and argued politics with Victor.[7]

The younger children looked back on this period at Knebworth with great fondness, but Constance was rather less happy. She disliked the memory of her grandfather and did not enjoy being reminded of him constantly; she found the atmosphere at Knebworth rather oppressive. Though her parents were now much less busy, the children still rarely saw them as they were often away. Victor missed Robert's valet more than he missed Robert himself.[8]

Constance would look back at her younger self scornfully. 'An overmastering laziness and a fatalistic submission to events as they befell were guiding factors in my existence … so far as I know, I was an average ordinary human being, except perhaps for an exaggerated dislike of society and of publicity in any form.'[9] That shyness and nervousness was her defining feature even into adulthood. Sylvia Pankhurst recalled that the grown-up Constance suffered from 'a morbid self-deprecation and fear of giving offence'.[10] One on occasion, she was having breakfast alone when Lord Salisbury came in and she was obliged to talk to him, casting desperately around for a suitable subject; she could only come up with jam. In her early twenties she remembered this as the most terrible moment of her life.[11]

Unlike many shy girls, Constance wasn't much of a reader and actively disliked studying (she and Edith agreed that Dickens was 'so dreadfully vulgar, and the people seemed to do nothing but drink'). She didn't need to be prepared for a career and was expected to aspire to nothing more than being a dutiful helpmate to a suitable husband. She could talk knowledgeably about art, architecture and sculpture, but also enjoyed making up wild facts and opinions on these subjects, just to amuse herself.[12] Emily and Constance grew out of their childhood rivalry and became good friends, but Betty was still Constance's closest confidante. According to Emily, Constance was the family misfit, quite a badge of honour in this family of eccentrics. Her shyness made her lonely. Betty made friends easily and rather than finding friends of her own, Constance tagged along with them.[13]

Her most notable physical feature is very clear in surviving photographs: her height. She carried this height awkwardly, too self-conscious to be elegant or graceful, and was constantly stooping. She was thin, too, with sharp and refined features. Her hair was dark, worn swept up and back with combs and curling a little in wisps around her face.

She did have two close confidantes among her relations. One was her cousin Adela Villiers. Three years younger than Constance, Adela was the daughter of her mother's brother Ernest. The second of three sisters, Adela was a thoughtful, sympathetic and tender correspondent. Constance's other strong supporter was her mother's strident sister, Teresa Earle, always known as Aunt T. Constance and Aunt T were very different in temperament and outlook but the two were great friends. Constance's accepted Aunt T's unsolicited advice and forthright opinions with good humour. She didn't see these women often, which gave her a certain freedom to be open and honest, secure in the knowledge she would not actually have to discuss her private feelings in person. All the Lyttons were prodigious letter writers, and all became writers who drew on their memories and experiences and committed their personal histories and identities to print.[14]

Constance also kept regular diaries and, with a couple of

exceptions, these still exist for the years 1893 to 1907.[15] They are a series of uniform, fragile black date books, printed with morals at the head of each page and filled with notes in her tidy handwriting. They are a record of lunches and dinners, letters written and books read. 'Accounts' is a regular entry; perhaps they troubled her. 'Hospital' is noted once or twice, as is 'In bed', without further comment. Her memories and feelings are not recorded, and with one or two poignant exceptions, these books contain facts, not emotions.

Constance preferred spending time with her pets to spending time with people. She loved arranging flowers, but her favourite hobby was cleaning, which annoyed her family, as she was perpetually shining door knobs and indulging in other such demeaning activities. She cleaned all her copper coins with relish. Her birthday treat was to clean the lavatory.[16]

Constance was a believer, in a quiet, authentic sort of way; a 'true Christian', Neville called her.[17] She disliked what she saw as the hypocrisies of the church and instead cultivated a direct and profound relationship with Jesus Christ. Allied to this was a strong sense of justice and determination. 'What a mistake it is to allow oneself to care for little things, or to care for things a little,' she wrote to Betty in her early twenties. 'If one only cares enough, there is strength enough to overcome every obstacle, or at least to endure every martyrdom.'[18] Both by nature and inspired by her religious belief, Constance was extremely sympathetic to the needs of others, even to the point of rubbing her more forthright brothers and sisters up the wrong way. Constance was desperately good, and found her greatest happiness in catering to other people, especially if she could go without in order to do so. 'Con is such an angel and seems to make everyone happy,' wrote the sixteen-year-old Emily enviously, and 'when there is someone very good near me, it seems to make me feel extra bad.'[19] Neville said that she 'went through life full of mercy, pity and sympathy, and by a wise dispensation of her gentleness and sweetness, she relieved countless cases of hopeless suffering'.[20] Edith was the main beneficiary of this selflessness. Constance could anticipate what her mother would need and then quietly address that need, unnoticed and unrewarded.

Luckily, Constance was also blessed with a tremendous sense of humour, which saved her from becoming totally unbearable. She had a knack for grave asides and a strong sense of the ridiculous. She would break into a serious conversation with a witty observation and completely transform the mood. When she laughed, 'there would be a few seconds of absolute silence, and then a long shrill note, increasing in loudness, would draw everyone's attention to the fact that she was overcome with merriment'.[21] She was constantly giggling and making her siblings laugh with her. Emily remembered this as 'delicious', though, while at school, Neville pleaded with her not to embarrass him in front of his friends.[22]

She appears to have been periodically laid low with depression. 'She was never strong in health, but she had no serious illness – certainly nothing that could account for such a look of sorrow which was her normal expression,'[23] Neville said. Depression was a family complaint and, interestingly for a family of this time and situation, their shared experience appears to have been openly acknowledged and discussed. Emily describes her grandfather, father and the children as all being, to varying degrees, prone to 'moods of black melancholy'[24] – Robert himself called these his 'blue devils'. This family tendency was most marked in Constance.[25] Neville remembered her, albeit clearly influenced by the knowledge of how her life had turned out, as having 'a destiny of sadness that surrounded her'.[26]

Like all the Lyttons, Constance was shaped by a strong sense of family. But while it is impossible for the modern reader not to draw links between Anna's feminist thinking, Rosina's suffering and Constance's campaigning, the reality was that this generation of Lyttons was defined by Edward and Robert, their famous male relations. This didn't mean they always met with approval. Constance was scathing about what she saw as the moral failings of her grandfather. According to family legend, as a child Constance, sensitive and attuned to suffering, vowed to seek out Bulwer-Lytton's illegitimate children and help them. It certainly seems in keeping with her character, but it does not appear that when she became an adult, she actually carried out those good intentions. Perhaps the obstacles seemed too difficult or the responsibilities too great, or her natural shyness held her back. But the problem bothered her occasionally. At a family dinner towards the end of the century, as she wrote to Aunt T,

> One of the waiters was the living image of Grandfather, his picture at least, and another younger one looked like Lytton-stock, some ten times diluted. I kept on meeting their eyes and it was all I could do not to relieve Grandfather of the salmon … I thought p'r'aps these are stray bits of illegitimacy who, but for the fluke of circumstances, would be sitting here instead of us, and we going round with the plates.[27]

Meanwhile, Robert's carefree happiness was gone forever and he became increasingly weighed down with regret. His personal life also grew more complicated. Shortly after he returned home, Rosina published *A Blighted Life*, which described her treatment by Edward and her incarceration in the mental institution. Her portrait of Robert was also less than flattering. Robert was horrified and cut off the additional allowance he had been making to her.

In the past, Robert had always found solace in poetry, but he was unable to settle and instead spent months writing his maiden speech for the Lords. This turned into an epic 22,000-word vindication of every decision he had made in India. When Disraeli caught wind of this, he was appalled. Robert was forced to ditch his 54-page draft and instead make a much blander statement to the House. Having missed this opportunity to put his side of the story, he would find that his opponents' account of his supposed failures hardened into fact and then history.

Rosina died in March 1882. There had been no reconciliation, and Rosina was buried in an unmarked grave. But Robert was not yet free of her. He began work on a biography of his father but found it impossible to deal with his parents' complicated feud. The published biography ended when his father was just twenty-nine. But Rosina still had friends and allies and they objected to Robert's portrayal of her. They retaliated by publishing their own life of Rosina in 1887 and then a collection of her letters in 1889. Robert could do nothing about this perpetual raking over the past except ignore it.

His life became sadder and more desperate. He suffered from bronchitis, rheumatism and sciatica. His periodic depression became more frequent. But, rather surprisingly for a distant Victorian father, he discovered and liked his children. If Edith had hardly seen Robert during their years in India, then the children had seen him even less. They barely knew him. Now he began to enjoy their company. Betty was a particular favourite and as Robert began to travel Europe in search of poetic inspiration, she became his travelling companion. She remembered this time with fondness: 'He was often ill … often melancholy, but always intimately loving, indulgent and the object of my unqualified adoration.'[28]

Betty began to take on many of the formal hostessing duties that Robert's position required, allowing Edith to take a back seat. Charming, gracious and confident, Betty adored an active social life. Betty's increasing closeness with Robert put distance between her and Constance. Constance loved Betty dearly, but found her friends incomprehensible, her literary interests dull and her general zest for life draining.[29] Betty and Constance 'came out' at the same time, in 1887, at the ages of twenty and eighteen. For Constance the experience was predictably painful, but Betty enjoyed every moment. One of the most important reasons for 'coming out', of course, was to find a suitable husband, and Betty was very quickly snapped up. Gerald Balfour, MP for Leeds Central and nephew of the former Prime Minister Lord Salisbury, was the lucky man. Gerald was extremely handsome and very intelligent. His political career promised to be significant (though it never lived up to this early promise) and Betty was ideally suited, by temperament and training, to the match. She easily fitted into 'The Souls', the social set who clustered around Gerald's brother Arthur – known as 'King Arthur', and another future Prime Minister. Gerald's family welcomed her with open arms. Unfortunately for Victor, his classmates noticed the engagement in *The Times* and decided to call him 'Betty' for the rest of his time at school.[30]

Betty's marriage to Gerald brought Frances Balfour into Constance's circle of acquaintances. Frances, married to Eustace, another Balfour brother, is an important figure in this story. She was already, very unusually for a woman of her class, an active campaigner for women's suffrage. She never became a militant suffragette, and represents the acceptable face of suffrage campaigning: the path Frances chose is the path that Constance rejected. At this time, though, Frances was simply the young woman who became Betty's best friend. Frances described Betty as:

> By common consent one of the most delightful girls alive. She is just 20 but with a mind very much older than her years. She is not pretty but with such a good & charming expression that she makes up for everything. She plays the violin & is very clever ... she is very deeply religious & with such a bright unworldly mind.[31]

Constance had made up her mind to dislike Gerald but soon warmed
to him, and decided to look on the situation as gaining a brother
rather than losing a sister.[32] She found the enormous Balfour tribe
rather cold and their collection of Souls overwhelming. She felt the
Balfour brothers were very lucky in their wives: Betty, of course, but
Frances too. 'Hers not the nature that can lie down with either the
lion or the lamb,' Constance wrote admiringly to Betty.[33]

Gerald was alarmingly ill before the wedding and Constance
wished fervently that she could sacrifice her health for his. Fortunately, he recovered, and the wedding was held at in the upstairs
drawing room at Knebworth in 1887. Theirs seems to have been the
happiest of the Lytton marriages.

Meanwhile, Robert was on a romantic adventure of his own, with
an American actress named Mary Anderson. While she was more
muse than mistress – she was a devout Catholic, as well as being
only half his age – Robert's feelings for her seem to have been serious. He developed an obsession with finding the perfect play to
show off Mary's talents. She was a frequent visitor to Knebworth.
'We children adored her and thought her – as indeed she was – the
most beautiful woman we had ever seen,' Victor remembered.[34] For
the first time, Edith was genuinely hurt by his behaviour.

Later, there was another intimate relationship, this time with a
writer, Marie Louise Rame – known by her pen-name, Ouida –
which he soon regretted. Nevertheless, it was Mary Louise Rame
who suggested to the Foreign Secretary's wife that Robert would
be ideally suited for the vacant post of ambassador to Paris. Robert
was ashamed when the story got out but was pleased to accept the
offer. The family left for Paris immediately after Betty's wedding.
Constance's beloved dog, Punch, died around the same time. She
was bereft. She felt Punch was the only creature who loved and accepted her for who she was; he was the repository of all her secrets
and confessions, and always comforting.[35]

Robert wanted to recapture some of the ease and glamour of his earlier career in Europe – which he did, and made a great success of this last post. This was his natural habitat and the four years he spent in Paris offered him a chance to redeem his career and his reputation. In Paris he was once more able to enjoy the company of artists, writers and musicians, and he had a thoroughly good time. 'He used often to say that he worked himself almost to death in India and got nothing but abuse; in Paris he only enjoyed himself and got nothing but praise,' said Victor.[36] But he was increasingly ill. He wrote to Teresa Earle from Paris, 'My health is not good just now and I feel very depressed and weary, and all the long dinners through which I have to eat my way like a caterpillar don't improve the state of my peptics.'[37]

In Paris, Constance was naturally expected to step into the breach and fill the gap left by Betty's departure. She makes her first appearance in the social pages of *The Times* at Robert's introductory reception in Paris, in January 1888. She hated every second of this new life. But she interpreted her sacrifice as the price she had to pay for Gerald's recovery; this was the bargain with God she had made. Where Betty was easy, graceful and sociable in company, Constance was awkward, halting and silent. Nevertheless, she did her best at 'trying to talk when I had nothing to say, trying to please without wishing to be pleased'.[38] 'Her life … was one of uncongenial duty uncomplainingly performed,' said Emily.[39] Constance found solace from unremitting family duty in playing her piano. Her instrument was the one thing that brought her to life. Neville remembered her as being 'all on fire with passion for music',[40] and this is striking because of the contrast with the quiet docility her family otherwise remembered. She practised for hours each day, as many as could be spared, and used a silent keyboard with stiff keys to exercise the muscles of her fingers. She was encouraged by her music teacher, Fräulein Oser, whom she worshipped and adored. But her talent, passion and dedication were entirely her own. 'Her interpretation of music was so personal and so successful that it is impossible to listen to other renderings of the same music,' Neville recalled with sadness. She began to harbour dreams of studying music seriously, perhaps even becoming a professional, and told Aunt T:

> When I was alone and playing, I felt as if my body couldn't and didn't contain the spirit that was in me, but seemed to get out and be everywhere, so happy was I in the dream of the artist I would one day be, or better still in the actual joy of the music itself.[41]

Music was the way she could transcend the trivialities and troubles of her everyday life.

It is impossible to judge how realistic her dreams of becoming a serious musician were. Betty, for example, remembered her playing as beautiful, 'but never professional in accuracy and faultlessness of execution', and suggested that Constance's talents were better suited to accompaniment than solo performance.[42] But a move to Austria for intensive study was certainly discussed. Surely Robert, remembering how Edward had poured cold water on his poetic ambitions, could not have repeated this so heartlessly. At the same time that Constance was immersing herself in music, Neville was discovering art by watching students painting at the Louvre, and Robert could not do enough to help nurture this talent.[43] But then, a career for a young man was a very different prospect. In Neville's view, the reason that Constance never went to Austria was not that life as a professional musician was unsuitable, or even unobtainable, for her, but that her parents could not bear to part with her.[44]

In the autumn of 1891, Robert's illnesses became worse. He was suffering from a painful bladder inflammation. Edith's support became more important than ever; he deeply regretted the sorrow he had caused her over the Mary Anderson affair. Constance looked at Edith with new admiration for her quiet, unwavering loyalty. He was in a great deal of pain in these last weeks, as the infection reached his kidneys. Constance went in to see him on what would be the last day; he said he wouldn't talk as he wasn't sure if it would be a good or bad day, but scribbled away at a poem quite contentedly. When the end came, it was unexpected and painless, from a blood clot.[45]

Robert Lytton was sixty years old when he died. So much more sensible and mild-mannered than his father, he was amiable, good-humoured and delightful company, with friends across all artistic fields. One was Oscar Wilde, who dedicated his play *Lady Windermere's Fan* to Robert's memory. Robert was always sorry that his poetry had taken second place in his life to diplomacy. His children loved him deeply, while acknowledging his flaws. Constance in particular felt that Edith had tolerated the intolerable during the Mary Anderson affair. Many years later, Constance wrote a foreword to a new collection of Robert's work which tried to convey 'the magic of a personality in which gloom and radiance, the perfect and the imperfect, had their part and yet the whole was deeply revered'. Constance acknowledged that she had been hard on him at the time of his death: 'Being of a somewhat puritanical turn of mind, I was out of sympathy with several of his theories of life.'[46] In a family of strong and opinionated personalities, this is only natural. She also commented on his hatred for hypocrisy, even when it got him into hot water; his generosity; his unconventionality. These were qualities she only admired more as she became older and more open minded.

Robert's financial affairs had serious repercussions for his wife and children. He had entrusted his money to a man who went bankrupt eighteen months later. Edith, Constance and Emily returned home from Paris – the boys were at school – to tremendous uncertainty. Victor was only fourteen, not old enough to assume the responsibilities of running Knebworth and they could not afford to move back in and maintain it anyway. It was let for a decade, and the Lyttons moved to London. Their lack of money became one of the defining features of their lives. Emily could not 'come out', as Betty and Constance had, because of the enormous associated expenses, and had to be presented privately at court. This is, of course, relative poverty. No matter how bad things got, they always had several servants and didn't have to do much for themselves.

The girls did not take their situation seriously at all. They had been long used to Robert's extravagance and trusted that some solution would present itself. 'Con and I are finding so much amusement out of the smash that it is quite dreadful considering how miserable mother is,' Emily reported, with a trace of guilt. At first, they proposed that Edith should go and live at Hampton Court while Constance, mocking her own situation in more ways than one, decided she would go into flats specially designed for 'poor spinsters of the gentry class'. A couple of days later, their plans had escalated. They would let their home and take off round the country in a gipsy cart. Edith was to become a fortune teller and Emily would dance to the music of a hurdy-gurdy, which Constance would play. Constance took pleasure in selling off old jewellery to the pawnbroker and found she had quite a talent for striking a bargain. At this time, Constance was giving her eccentricity free rein. She and Edith decided that 'to breathe very hard through the nose is as good a form of exercise as you can have. So when they have nothing better to do, they both begin snorting violently for exercise, which is terrible to listen to,' Emily complained.[47]

But Edith was spending most of her time worrying rather than snorting. She knew only too well how uncomfortable genteel poverty could be. In her married life she had been totally dependent on servants – she did not even put up her own hair – and she was totally unprepared for a widowhood spent scrimping and saving.

A widow at just fifty years old, Edith's life now bore an unpleasant resemblance to her mother's: precarious, impecunious and dependent on her male relations for protection and advice. But she was determined the make the best of the situation for the four children still at home, particularly so the girls could marry well.

Just before Robert died, Betty had commented that Constance would 'never fall in love while she has Mother at her side and her best chance of its coming to pass is that she should be allowed here and there to go about independently by herself'.[48] Betty believed marriage was in Constance's best interests, as a way to loosen her ties with Edith. But Constance, all awkwardness and shyness in public, didn't seem likely to find the right man in the social circles that the Lyttons moved in. She didn't like balls, as none of the men she knew seemed to want to dance with her. Neville remembered her trying to dance with the men who were being left on the sidelines so that they would have a better time.[49] She found the men at country house parties dull and dim-witted. As they never seemed to remember her, no matter how many times she met them, presumably she did not make a favourable impression either. 'What would they do if I suddenly unbuttoned and shook up Deborah upon them in one of her maddest moods?' she asked Emily, Deborah being the family name for Constance's eccentric side.[50] To find the right man, she would need to be in a different environment altogether, where she could relax, be herself and find someone who could see beneath the awkwardness to the genuine qualities that lay beneath.

CHAPTER THREE

THE PONSONBYS

'This is a different Con to any Con you have ever known.'[1]

Towards the end of 1892, Constance and Edith went to South Africa. They were to stay with Edith's twin sister Elizabeth and her husband, Henry Loch, who was then the High Commissioner. In South Africa, Constance found herself liberated and almost giddy. Though it lasted only a few short months, her time here would be the most unconditionally happy period of her life. She wrote home to Adela that she was not only enjoying the company of men, she was actually flirting with them. 'You wouldn't know me if you could look on me here,' she told Adela airily, 'lazy beyond description, bumptious, forward, and self-asserting, gay to silliness, almost flirtatious, talkative to a fault, generally noisy and boisterous.'[2] She enjoyed discovering and indulging this more liberated side of her personality.

In South Africa, Constance began two relationships which would have a profound influence on the rest of her life. The first was with the author Olive Schreiner.[3] Olive was one of twelve children from a strict missionary family, named Olive Emilie Albertina after three dead elder brothers. As a governess in her late teens, she had the time and inspiration to write novels; later, she joined some of her brothers in England, and had one published. *Story of an African Farm* (1883) was an instant hit. Its arguments in favour of women's rights meant it was required reading among progressive people, and it was controversial enough to attract a much wider audience: Robert Lytton read it during one of his convalescences.

Olive was naturally drawn to the literary circles in London and confident enough in herself to form unorthodox relationships. In 1884, she and her partner Havelock Ellis went on a joint 'honeymoon' with leading socialists Eleanor Marx and Edward Aveling, though neither of the couples were married. Eleanor and Olive enjoyed a very free and frank relationship in which no subject was off limits: Eleanor's biographer Rachel Holmes tells us that they discussed 'sexual desire, periods, premenstrual tension, the effects of their monthly cycle on their work and moods'.[4] Olive's relationship with Havelock Ellis did not last and settled into friendship. She continued to write but was often unsatisfied with the results and only published her next work, *Dreams*, in 1890. Olive travelled extensively around Europe but could not settle, always homesick and never feeling like she belonged anywhere. After eight years away, she returned to South Africa, still searching.

Constance and Olive were drawn to each other despite a fourteen-year age gap and vastly different backgrounds. It is impossible to imagine the two of them sharing the same discussions about their bodily functions as Olive had once held with Eleanor Marx, but Olive was now older, a little less hopeful and exuberant, soon to be married in a conventional, bourgeois way, to Samuel Cronwright. She did not want only bohemians for her friends and responded to Constance's sincerity, generosity and earnest naivety. Constance thought Olive ugly and badly dressed, but articulate, dignified and incredibly impressive.[5] Perhaps too, Constance admired Olive for her progressive thinking and unorthodox life as well as her writing. Like Constance, Olive was somewhat eccentric, and had been brought up in a way which was far removed from the stifling politeness of English drawing rooms.[6] Olive may have represented a way of living that Constance lacked the courage to try herself, just as Robert had once lived vicariously through Wilfred Scawen Blunt.

Constance and Olive professed lifelong friendship and devotion to for one another and Olive regularly wrote to her correspondents about Constance's exceptional qualities. Olive was also close to Constance's cousin Adela and admired Edith. The feeling was mutual. After Edith saw Olive again in London the following year, she came home and told Constance how much she wished Constance could find a man just like Olive to marry.[7] Edith's love for Olive is another sign that she was not quite as stuffy, conventional and unimaginative as Robert's biographers seem to have believed.

Meanwhile, Constance had already found a man to marry, and he was nothing like Olive. His name was John Ponsonby and he was working for her uncle Henry Loch. John came from a family of aristocrats and military generals. His great-grandparents were Frederick and Harriet Spencer, the sister of Georgiana, Duchess of Devonshire, whose own love life was equally colourful. Frederick and Harriet had four children. (Harriet had two more with her lover.) One was Lady Caroline Lamb, who would give Byron the label 'mad, bad and dangerous to know', and was disastrously married to William Lamb, who as Lord Melbourne would become Prime Minister and tutor to the young Queen Victoria. Another was Henry's father, Frederic (sometimes more conventionally Frederick), who had a distinguished career in the army and eventually became Governor of Malta.

Henry Ponsonby was the eldest son, and followed his father into the army, serving in Ireland and the Crimea before becoming a private equerry to Prince Albert. While at court, he met Mary Bulteel, where she was a maid of honour to the Queen.[8] Mary was deeply religious but also clever, artistic, progressive and liberal. She later helped to found Girton College, Cambridge, and was interested in a variety of women's issues, including employment for married women, and the controversial Contagious Diseases Act. Mary was a great patron of writers and, like Edith, she was a friend of George Eliot's. Unlike Edith, though, Mary was inclined to passionate relationships with women, most notably Ethel Smyth. Ethel and Mary first met in the early 1890s. Mary was much older (and married), and Ethel continued to have other affairs, but theirs was an intense and passionate relationship which, even if it may not have been wholly sexual, defined Ethel's life for over a decade.[9] She called it 'the happiest, the most satisfying, and for that reason, the most restful of all my many friendships with women'.[10] Constance first met Ethel Smyth at Lady Ponsonby's house: fifteen years later they would come together again under very different circumstances.

Henry and Mary's relationship did not suffer from her involvement with other women: on the contrary, it seems to have been fulfilling and affectionate throughout their lives. Henry was appointed private secretary to the Queen in 1870 and the family moved to the Norman Tower in Windsor Castle. He was an out-and-out Liberal while the Queen became increasingly Conservative, and this often caused difficulties, but he nevertheless held this post for a quarter of a century.

Born in 1866, John was the third of five children, with two older sisters and two younger brothers. He had chosen the military for his career. One brother, another Frederick, served at court like their father. The other, Arthur, went into the diplomatic service and then politics. John, though, was hampered by a slight disability: he was born without a palate and with a hare lip. He grew a moustache to disguise the physical impairment, but his speech was always rather difficult to follow for those who did not know him well.[11]

This made no difference to Constance. There was an attraction, and an understanding was reached – or at least that's what

Constance believed. They were not formally engaged when she sailed for home, but she thought she only need wait until John had risen in the ranks and was earning enough money to make them a comfortable home.

In the meantime, she relied on letters from South Africa to keep their relationship alive. There were never enough – perhaps one every several months – and she was thrilled when she received one unexpectedly. 'Cape Mail in' is sometimes noted in her journal and marked with a cross. Aside from her correspondence with John, Constance also began to develop a relationship with his sister, Maggy. Five years older than Constance, Maggy was outgoing, vivacious and fun and, like her brother Frederick, moved easily in royal circles: she was friends with Victoria's daughter Princess Louise.[12] Maggy was 'an absolute angel and a delightful companion', Constance told Aunt T enthusiastically, and Lady Ponsonby (who was soon just 'Lady P') 'an unusually clever and cultivated woman'.[13]

To Constance, John seemed ideal in every way. 'I have never yet told you of any of his good qualities, or of any of those characteristics which make him to my mind adorable,' she told Adela, with all the exuberance of first love. Sometimes she called him by his own family nickname of Swift, as in Jonathan Swift. More obscurely, she sometimes referred to him as Shelley Plain. There is a Browning poem which reads in part:

> Ah, did you once see Shelley plain,
> And did he stop and speak to you?
> And did you speak to him again?
> How strange it seems, and new!
> But you were living before that,
> And you are living after,
> And the memory I started at –
> My starting moves your laughter.

In the summer of 1893, Maggy and Betty talked the situation over. Maggy's 'eyes often filled with tears, and she kicked her legs in the most ungainly but delightful way', Betty reported back to Constance.

> The hopelessness of the situation lies in the absence of money ... money is the sole impediment and objection. I feel sure in my own mind that he did love you that he would love you still if there was the smallest ground for hoping he could ever tell you so ... For God's sake therefore don't torture yourself by thinking that you are not worthy of him.[14]

For the moment, this was enough to give Constance hope.

Throughout these years, Constance became more closely entwined with John Ponsonby's family. Though the letters no longer exist, if her diaries are anything to go by, in the mid-1890s she was writing to 'Lady P' and 'Maggy' almost as often as she wrote to Aunt T and Adela. It seems rather unfair that, by taking her into their midst, the Ponsonbys encouraged her, unconsciously or otherwise, to cling onto her hopes and believe that she might one day become a Ponsonby herself, even while telling her that it was impossible. In October, she went to stay with them at Windsor, and was so paralysed with fear whenever she caught a glimpse of the Queen that she could barely remember what Victoria looked like. She was forced into an amateur theatrical performance with Princess Beatrice, Maggy and Frederick Ponsonby. The experience was excruciating, and Constance tried to escape by sneaking away. Some of the guests thought she was ill, others that she was sulking, so she screwed up her courage and participated, until the last night when she could take no more and ran away to hide in a bedroom.[15]

In the meantime, Constance was in the difficult, though fairly common, predicament of struggling upper-class women: she had no money, but society – and, more particularly, her immediate family – frowned on women of her class working. It was not done, no matter how desperate the situation. The need to keep up appearances was greater than the need to bring in money. Her illnesses and shyness made being a maid of honour out of the question. But towards the end of 1893, she made an unusually bold decision and began writing and reviewing for the *National Review*, run by Leo Maxse.[16]

This new venture went down extremely badly at home. When Edith made a fuss, Emily felt bound to stick up for Constance out of sheer perversity, though she was just as horrified.

> To think she has come to this! … I think I should prefer the workhouse … I don't think that even were I starving, and certainly not before, that I could descend so low as to write articles for a miserable paper. I cannot myself understand how she can bring herself down to such a level.

'I wish', Emily continued in disgust, 'she would remember that our name is the same, and that we are in a measure dragged after her.'[17] Emily could be just as much of a snob as Edith. But she was overreacting. Among Constance's fellow reviewers in January 1894 were Frances Balfour and Margot Tennant (later, Asquith): she was in impeccable company. She was also characteristically modest and dry in her debut review:

> If we have braced ourselves to read a review of a book, it is generally with one of three objects: to find out whether the book be worth reading; to agree with the reviewer at the expense of the author; or, it may be, for the purpose of ridiculing the review. In this instance, the name of the author … suffices to dispose of the two first, and there remains but the last reason, if there be any, for scanning this notice.[18]

Despite this self-deprecating tone, Constance took her work extremely seriously and profoundly enjoyed it. Her journal for 2 January 1894 notes her payment for this review twice: £3.3s. Her journal entries till this point are often sparse, with days and weeks left empty. Now they suddenly spring to life, and are full of business-like entries. She was prolific. She would generally receive a book one day, read it the following day, and then write on it.[19] This outpouring of creative energy and productivity suggests that her illnesses were at least in part psychological. When she had fulfilling work, she was happy and her pain was forgotten, or at least no longer seemed important. All the money she earned was spent on presents for Edith or treats for Emily.[20] Perhaps this way she could pretend she was doing it for them, not for herself.

Constance's new career caused all sorts of ripples in the family dynamics. While Constance was working, she 'neglected' Edith – at least, Edith saw it that way – and Emily had to fill the gap. Emily did not have Constance's unselfish nature and didn't take kindly to Edith's constant demands. Edith made it very clear that Emily wasn't up to scratch. Emily, in turn, took her feelings out on Constance. 'She has grown perfectly unbearable, there is no other word for it, since she took to reviewing … she reads on average one volume a day and sometimes more. Is life worth living on these terms?' Emily complained. Constance's only supporter in her new profession was Betty, who thought it was a better use of her time than darning socks.[21] Betty herself was an aspiring writer and was currently compiling a new edition of Robert's poetry; Constance helped her with the proofs.[22] Olive was also in England during this period, and Constance must have enjoyed the sense that they were both professional writers.

In 1894, John came back to England from the Cape and, at the end of May, came to the Danes for lunch. 'We didn't have a moment alone,' she told Aunt T. 'I was very shy and hardly dared look at him for fear of living up to my reputation concerning him.'[23] Soon afterwards, there were more talks about money. 'Swift, Maggy and the parents have plainly stated that there is no money and no hope of money in the way either of allowance, or inheriting from them. That being the case they feel S., (and he feels) is not in a position to ask, much less claim anything,' she told Betty.[24] She and Edith reached a compromise: nothing would be 'done', but she would be able to see him when the opportunities arose, and she could write to him. Edith was being cautious in guarding Constance's reputation. Her feelings for John were obviously clear to both their families, but it was important that any alternative suitors should not be put off.

In the meantime, John visited several times during the summer, and in September there was a flurry of letters as he pondered his next career move.[25] He would soon be returning to South Africa, but 'it is really very difficult to say what will happen to me afterwards … the hopeless fact remains that I can't afford to live even in my own battalion'. Planning months if not years abroad and not asking her opinion about it, as well as mentioning his lack of money again, is not a strong indication that he was thinking of a shared future with her. But she wrote back telling him that 'the lifting of the yoke of restrictions would remove all burden and false position, misunderstandings etc', and he responded with 'some things which I feel have insured me a foundation of happiness for life'.[26] It was enough to give her hope, even after he went back to South Africa with the Lochs in October. She was determined to try to keep all their relations out of their relationship in the future. They were telling her that it was in her best interests to give up and cut off all contact. She refused, and was obstinate enough that Edith eventually gave up and allowed Constance to write. She was desperate to keep up her bond with his relations. She wrote to Maggy with such emotional honesty that it was an instant cause of regret, saying she had created 'an impossible situation between her and me'. Maggy could not treat Constance as John's fiancée because her status was ambiguous and uncertain.

Early in 1895, Constance began writing for a journal called *The Realm*, where she earned £20 a quarter: her first regular salary.[27] Priced 3d, *The Realm* covered the week in politics and the arts alongside 'miscellaneous' essays and 'personal recollections'. Constance's job, once again, was reviewing novels, though the real work was in the reading, with every article covering several volumes, each briskly dispatched in a few hundred words. She wrote to Aunt T:

> I feel so invigorated by this new work. The first day I sat up till 2 am doing the work and letters, accounts, etc. Got up 7 next morning, walked to station, lunched off brown bread and butter and three gingerbread nuts, walked home from station, same lunch, no tea either day, walked home from station. Felt rampantly well.[28]

Her articles in *The Realm* were unsigned, so perhaps Constance felt valued for her skills rather than her name, and at least this would give Emily less cause for complaint. But Constance soon gave up her new profession. 'She found it took her too much from home,' Betty wrote: both Emily and Edith believed that all Constance's time was best spent with Edith.[29] Perhaps it was too much to argue with her family over her work and her faltering relationship at the same time. After her summer holiday, mentions of *The Realm* and references to reviewing peter out in her journal; by the following year, they have disappeared.

On holiday in Florence in May, Constance met John's cousin Maurice Baring. His mother was Lady Ponsonby's sister; his father was part of the Barings banking family. Then only twenty, he would become one of the country's best-known writers, as a journalist, poet, novelist and playwright; he was also a close friend of Ethel Smyth.[30] At first, Constance was only interested in Maurice for his associations. 'He has gestures, tones and looks that betray his line-age. Result ... desperate flirtation at once,' she told Betty. 'I grew loud over this, and ended up with one of my worst giggles ... to the alarm of everyone else.'[31] Then Maurice let her down by going to Naples instead of taking her on a promised excursion.

> Oh! so aggravatingly like the family his writingless way of doing it. I know if ever my matters run smooth and banns are published, wedding arranged etc. that I shall be waiting at the church, (as the bridegroom generally does ... I can see myself hovering about the Altar) and that the other person will never turn up.[32]

Despite this early hiccup, Maurice and Constance spent much of the rest of the holiday together, becoming lifelong friends and regular correspondents. Sadly few of their letters have survived – in fact, Betty says they were 'destroyed' – and one wonders if this was because of what they may have revealed about the John Ponsonby relationship.[33]

When they returned home in June, Edith received an unexpected letter from Balmoral. The Queen, 'having a grateful sense of yr husband's distinguished services, as well as a sincere admiration of the way in which you have borne yr sorrows & trials', asked her if she would become a lady-in-waiting. Edith fretted over the decision. Being a lady-in-waiting was no great hardship, requiring just a few weeks' service a year. It came with a salary of £300. Now the family income was just £1,900 a year, that was a very significant sum. Yet Edith hesitated. She had got used to a quiet life and was reluctant to go back into public. She tentatively suggested that a maid of honour post might suit Emily instead, but Emily turned this down indignantly, declaring that she was a republican. It was Gerald, Betty's husband, who persuaded Edith to accept the offer – not least because otherwise she might not be able to keep Neville at Eton.[34]

Edith's four years as a lady-in-waiting to Queen Victoria were uneventful. Her diary of her time at court is not very interesting and mostly comments on the weather, the dinners and the drives. She spent two fortnights with the Queen each year, sometimes at Osborne, sometimes at Balmoral and sometimes at Windsor, which she liked most as it enabled her to see Neville. These interludes were a welcome break for Constance: she enjoyed being on her own sometimes. She went to stay with Betty in Ireland, where Gerald was now the Chief Secretary. She appears in the court circular pages of *The Times* during the late 1890s, attending state concerts or balls in the London palaces; not very often, but almost certainly more frequently than she would have liked.

John returned to England after about six months in South Africa and came for a short stay in August. Whatever Edith saw on this occasion, it was enough to set alarm bells ringing again and she banned Constance from writing to him. On 26 October, Constance wrote in her diary with evident relief, 'Decree lifted, alright again!' John's father died on 21 November, but he sent her a telegram telling her not to come to the funeral. She saw him with his siblings and Lady P after Christmas.[35] By now, she was marking all her journal entries relating to John, his letters or his relations with a cross, making it easier to find them when she went back over her notes.

The next time Constance saw John was in April 1896 when he came to stay for a weekend. Constance was in raptures, but the visit was not a success. He was ill and tired and seemed sad, but given the fact that she tried not to talk to him when she saw him, for fear of family scrutiny, she did not really know why.[36] The uncertainty was terrible, and brought on a bout of depression. 'I've been having the most sickening time with myself,' she told Adela.

Can't think what it is that suddenly lets me down to the lowest depths without a word of warning ... I now seem to have slipped to

the very bottom of the pole and know that the inducement which
led to my climbing it is gone, worse still perhaps was never there, and
the power to imagine it again won't come back either.'[37]

John came again in August and Constance did her best not to be
awkward, or give away anything of her feelings, or even to have a
minute alone with him. 'Hardly talked to him and never looked till
one last moment on the last day,' she told Adela.

All I did, and didn't do, must have helped to lift me off his conscience. Of course the moment he had gone I began to wonder if
I need have been quite as wasteful of diamond moments, and wise
still to wonder if he could have thought me a fraction unkind. But
he never 'sees', and never thinks anything, so I only consoled myself
with the knowledge that he couldn't have repented at the time or
afterwards, 'What a bore that she sticks so!'[38]

In November, he came again, which was cause both for complete
elation ('the most dreamlike true thing almost that my life has
known') and total despair ('the woeful realisation ... of how hopelessly ugly I've grown lately, and that I don't possess a single garment of any kind that isn't acutely hideousifying [sic]'.) He was
– as usual – late. The next morning, he proposed that he might
stay after breakfast. But the rest of the family were going out, and
Edith said he must go with them. Had he planned for the two
of them to be alone for a reason? Was this a moment that was
missed?[39] If so, it was an opportunity which never came again. 'For
three years she fed on hope; for another eleven years she continued
to cover up a volcano of feeling with no hope,' Betty wrote sadly.[40]
This unsatisfactory encounter, so longed-for and so disappointing,
dragged her down through 1896. It was not until January 1897 that
she was able to tell Adela: 'Suicidal mania gone. No self-deception,

no nonsense.'[41] Her birthday entry in her journal that year reads: 'Cleaned. Darned … Did flowers. Played.' These are what passed for birthday treats.[42]

Though she had given up journalism, working for her aunt was a different matter. It was exactly the sort of dutiful task that appealed to Constance and was acceptable to her family. Throughout 1896, Constance helped Aunt T to write the book that became *Pot Pourri from a Surrey Garden*. It is a mixture of instruction and anecdote; half-diary and half-guide to household management; the upper-class and scatty offspring of Elizabeth von Armin and Isabella Beeton. The tone reflects what Aunt T was: a lovely, but undeniably batty, aunt, with fixed and eccentric opinions, who careered through life and expected others to catch up. On 28 May, for example, she extolls the benefits of gravel paths, then instructs the reader on the best way of packing flowers, then offers advice on making fish sauce and risotto. Aunt T had personality in spades, and it shines all the way through the book. 'Weeding!' she exclaims. 'What it means to us all!' Her class is very evident: 'Get the village blacksmith to make you some flower-pots – he will understand that,' she says; but so is her worldly practicality: 'Celeriac is an excellent vegetable, not very common in England, and when carefully cooked, with a good brown sauce, forms a valuable contribution to the winter supply.'[43] Though she herself was a vegetarian, there are plenty of recipes for omnivores: chicken ravioli, roast hare and oxtail soup. Once the year in the garden and the kitchen has been dealt with, Aunt T turns to more general topics, such as how to raise children. 'The longer I live, the more I believe that a woman's education … should be awakening and yet superficial, teaching her to stand along and yet not destroying her adaptability for a woman's highest vocation, if she can get it – which is, of course, marriage and motherhood,' Aunt T opines. 'Marriage should not be a woman's only profession, but it should be her best and highest hope.'[44] How much might this have affected Constance, still no nearer to realising her best and highest hopes.

Unexpectedly, *Pot Pourri from a Surrey Garden* was a bestseller. It went into twenty-eight editions – it was still being reprinted after the First World War – and there were to be three sequels. Constance's work is acknowledged in the preface: 'These Notes would never have been extracted from me without the encouragement I have received from all my dear nieces, real and adopted, and the very practical assistance of one of them.'[45] The appendix, on the art of Japanese flower arranging, is directly attributed to Constance; it was a particular interest and hobby of hers. Apart from that, it is impossible to disentangle exactly what Constance's contribution was, but she appears to have been a kind of amanuensis, cajoling and patiently keeping Aunt T on track until it was complete. Constance received £75 for her work.[46] Later, she regretted taking the money, turning what should have been a family duty into a professional transaction, and decided to try to pay it back.[47] The book is dedicated to Edith. Their shared delight in the publication was short-lived, though, as Aunt T's husband died in an accident soon after; Constance went to visit and comfort her.[48]

But her main preoccupation was John and their lack of contact. She saw him for the day in April and then there was total silence. On 28 June, she wrote in her diary, 'Three months since seen JP,' and then every Tuesday for the rest of the year, she added to the list: three months and one week; three months and two weeks; three months and three weeks. By August, she was reduced to writing, 'Heard JP lost cigarette case and wished for it.'[49] Neither Emily's marriage to Edwin Lutyens nor Victor's twenty-first birthday celebrations that month – at which Edith wore the same outfit, perhaps reminding her children that money was still in short supply[50] – could distract her from her obsession. Emily's wedding was notable mostly because

John sent a present. Shortly afterwards, Constance wrote in her diary despairingly: '10 times seen, 7 times a letter by this time since April 5 last year. This year not once nor one letter.'[51] A visit to Ireland that autumn with Edith did not cheer her up.

Constance had to hear it from a friend that John was planning to go to Niger with his regiment – only to hear from Maggy and Lady P that this was off. When she saw them in November, their attitude gave her a renewed glimmer of hope. The way that 'Lady P' talked over the situation made Constance feel sure that they both wanted the same thing, and it was wonderful. 'Oh … that a real live someone else to whom I haven't talked should turn and talk to me as if it was all something real and still alive. Instead of the feeling of a stale me more of something that praps [sic] never was,' she told Adela.[52] It is odd that Lady P was encouraging Constance to cling on if there was still no prospect of John inheriting or earning enough money and still no formal understanding, to say nothing of the fact that he had been ignoring her for months. Perhaps Constance was reading too much into whatever Lady P actually said, for soon after came the only letter from John which seems to have survived.

Dear Lady Conny,

… I have just been offered a post in the Uganda Rifles, which after family deliberations I have accepted. It means a two years job, and I shall be seconded from my regiment … Two years rather a long time but I hope to save a bit out there although I have to provide myself to start with, with jams and potted meats to last two years … I hope you will think it a good thing as it may get one on a bit, and perhaps it may lead to getting a nomination for the Staff College out of it…

Yours very sincerely,

S.[53]

Was she supposed to wait? Would this salary be enough to support married life when he got back? Nothing was clear to Constance. These words, as she reported to Adela, 'may mean something although they also may mean nothing'. Constance was hopeful they meant something, saying, 'When I think of these things I can't believe my own happiness.' But he had not written to her in over a year, nor seen her in nine months, nor consulted her on his plans. He doesn't even wish her a Merry Christmas. His noncommittal attitude was all too clear to Edith, who was extremely upset by this letter. She didn't want him to come and say goodbye. 'Wished I'd "set him free", "give him up", not see him before he went, etc etc. That he didn't care for me one bit, never came to see me or took any trouble to be nice, only warmed me up just before he went away, etc etc,'[54] Constance told Adela. She saw this as Edith being obstructive and annoying. She did not contemplate the possibility that Edith was right. Eventually, since Constance said that if John wasn't allowed up to the Danes she would simply go down to London and see him, Edith relented.

This visit seems to have given Constance further cause for hope, as she told a friend that 'the rasping thumping groaning pain of questioning whether he cares a rap about me and only getting "No" for answer has ceased'.[55] That didn't mean that they were any nearer to getting married. Constance seems to have taken an almost masochistic pleasure in pining after a lost cause. She would not tell him how she truly felt and tried her best not to be an obligation, a bore or a stain on his conscience. She told herself that all that mattered was that he loved her, whether or not they ever got married. But he left for Uganda in January 1898 and there was still no engagement. Her journal for this year records his movements as well as hers. When she had letters or news, she would go back and note where he had been on a particular day.

In February, she went to visit Maggy and Lady P. They obviously loved her, particularly Lady P, 'who talked to me as if I had almost a share in the family circle'. It was wonderful not only to have news from John in Uganda, but to hear anecdotes and stories about his character and his childhood. But it wasn't enough when 'he has been dead lame for a time'. She began to feel that it was silly to try to be a part of a family where she didn't really belong. She decided to try to loosen the ties between them. Still, when John's younger brother Arthur got married at Easter, 'after years of seeming quite impossible', she must have wondered whether her own seemingly impossible situation would end the same way. She was asked to be a bridesmaid, but had to decline as she was going to Venice with her family for a month.[56] Neville's friend Edward Marsh came with them. He was a civil servant and in 1905 became private secretary to Victor's great friend Winston Churchill; as such, he will recur in this story.

John wrote once in a while from Uganda, but with neither the frequency nor the tone that Constance hoped for. Letters took weeks to arrive; she began predicting when he might receive hers, and then calculating when she might have one back. He signed the letters 'ever yours' but didn't respond to any of the 'special bits' in her own letters.[57] For more substantial information, she had to rely on the letters home to his family, which they forwarded to her and she copied out. Her desire to hear news overcame her resolution to put some distance between herself and the family, partly because she was so worried about him. The regiment was caught up in fighting throughout the second half of 1898; his movements were uncertain; and he was periodically laid low with fever. Once or twice he wrote unprompted, which only encouraged Constance's imagination more, especially when he said he was 'hoping for another letter from you which will buck me up considerably'.[58] He seemed lonely and he was certainly uncomfortable, with only goat to eat and warm water to drink during his illnesses.

In October 1899, the second Boer War broke out. 'It knocks me bang up against reality in the midst of so much that's sham and hypocritical, and hysterical,' Constance told Aunt T. 'The thought of war doesn't grate on my nerves as family quarrels, female jealousies … do.'[59] It is rather surprising that she didn't take a more critical approach to the war, given that Olive was an outspoken opponent and was even interned for a period. Constance was primarily concerned about the consequences for her friends and relatives who went out to fight – especially, of course, what it might mean for John. His regiment was far away from the fighting for the moment, and he was due home in January, but there was still the possibility that he and his comrades may be drawn into the conflict. Aunt T, like Edith, suggested to Constance that she tell John she didn't love him anymore. It was rather a heartless thing to do in the circumstances, and Constance refused, though it was now four years since they'd even breathed a word of marriage. She had, though, given up seeing the Ponsonby family, and told both John and his family that she had done this 'so that when he comes home there may not be the shadow of an expectation on the part of my people'.[60] She was often ill this year. She felt terrible for almost the whole of January, had a 'sick headache,' in April, rheumatism in her shoulder in September, and lumbago in December. 'Felt rather slack', 'dead tired' and 'very exhausted' were also noted.[61] These illnesses were surely connected to her constant worrying. This only got worse when Aunt T's son Syd was killed in the fighting; her cousin Edward Loch was also injured. But Edith was angry that Constance seemed to be escaping family duties and wasting her time on an impossible dream, and burst out in frustration that if Aunt T had lost a son she had lost a daughter.[62]

John did not come home in January as expected and instead went to Rhodesia with his regiment. Once again, months went by with barely a word, and even when a letter did finally arrive it only made her wonder, 'Does he ever think of the past or the future in connection with me?'[63] She became terribly depressed. 'My life today seems like an inland stagnant pool,' she told Adela. The news from the war was bleak. His regiment was now engaged in the fighting and there were daily reports of officers being killed. But was it worse to wish him safe away from the battlefield when John so wished to distinguished himself on it? Like thousands of wives and fiancées around the country, she tracked the progress of the war in great detail; wished, hoped and prayed.

On holiday in Derbyshire, Constance stared and stared at a couple in their hotel, so obviously in love, and wished fervently that she could experience the same with John. They set her imagination on fire. On the train home she confessed to Adela that she would go to bed with John, even if there was no prospect of marriage, even 'if I should have given away all that makes the position of a single woman decent, socially speaking; that I should be for ever more beyond the pale and shunned by all my relations etc; that I should have no right to self-respect'.[64] It is the most extraordinary declaration to make for a woman of her time and position. But it shows something of the martyr in her nature. She would be prepared to sacrifice everything, even if she got nothing in return. The only thing that put her off was the prospect of having children outside of marriage, and the thought of Edith. 'It would be impossible to do anything which would give her moral pain,' she concluded. Still, the wild lengths that her thoughts had run to, imagining all sorts of unlikely prospects and theoretical circumstances, show that she was firmly in the grip of an obsession.

But what was the alternative? Only her empty life with Edith, and this wasn't enough. 'From the no-roots of my own life I long so desperately to have any life I'm interested in,' she told Aunt T in desperation. 'I have nothing to offer in return for whatever show I'm given in other people's lives. This makes me a debilitating kind of lap-dog. Every night when I go to bed I feel a fearful kind of hunger in my arms for something to belong to of my own.'[65]

Though she loved her mother, she found her almost impossible to live with. In Neville's careful words, 'They were intensely fond of one another, and yet their natures and temperament were entirely different, and, had their tempers been less sweet, there must have been some friction as the result of such radical differences.'[66] Edith enjoyed being a grand lady. She knew her place and encouraged others to keep to theirs: she liked a well-ordered world. She preferred to dispense charity from above, as was proper; she did not have Constance's intense empathy for the sufferings of others. Constance tended to go along with Edith to keep the peace, but she still had her own wishes and desires, and the frustrations seethed inside her. She was over thirty but treated like a child. She deeply resented being treated 'as a semi-maniac; my wishes studied only to oppose them, it being a kind of accepted thing that if I want a thing it's bad for me and therefore to be refused ... it's the kind of attitude behind everything which gets on one's nerves at times'.[67] It's easy to imagine the awkwardness and tension, the deliberate misunderstandings and the unspoken accusations, thinly veiled by politeness, that characterised their lives. But there is no doubt that while they found each other exasperating, they genuinely loved each other. Edith was always 'Angel Mum' in Constance's letters. It's probably fair to say they would have loved each other more if they had spent less time together.

The Ponsonby family did not understand or accept Constance's wish to have some space. They continued to write, to forward on his letters and to invite her to visit. Eventually, Constance gave in. In January 1901 she went to visit Lady Ponsonby '& talk with her as to why not see her and Maggy ... sick head,' she wrote in her journal, and then told Adela, 'She was too beloved for words.'[68] The final illness and death of Queen Victoria occupied her thoughts for the following weeks. Edith had been due in attendance but was asked not to come; instead she went to view the lifeless body of the Queen at Osborne. Edith rode in one of the carriages in the funeral procession; Constance went to see it and reported that it 'was the most choking and impressive public thing I've ever seen'.[69] The new Queen, Alexandra, asked Edith to stay on as a lady-in-waiting. Edward Marsh's dog died around the same time and Constance wrote an effusive note of consolation, describing the death of her own beloved dog fourteen years earlier. The letter is edged with a black border, perhaps for the Queen and perhaps for the dogs.[70]

On 24 March, Constance had a letter from John, but also noted cryptically in her diary, 'arraignee du matin, chagrin'. It is a French proverb, about a spider in the morning meaning bad luck. 'JP 35 today (born 1866 March 25),' she wrote the next day. '2 years 46 weeks older than me.'[71] In May, she read in the paper that he had been promoted to Major and was commanding the 5th New Zealand Regiment. Maurice Baring came for a visit in June and, though she liked him for himself, she liked more the features and the voice that recalled his cousin.[72] But then in June there was 'unhoped for goodness' when she had the news that John was coming home, via New Zealand. She had been writing 'what by now?' in her journal and, on 24 June, she was able to report back to herself, 'Wonderful things.' She then started asking herself, 'What by this time next week?'[73] His ship docked in Southampton on 8 July, and on the 9th he wrote to her, asking whether he might come for a visit and saying, 'Shall look forward immensely to seeing you again.'[74] More ominously, he also wrote to Edith to say he was still no richer. Edith, however reluctantly, invited him to stay. In the meantime, John's brother Frederick presented him to the King and he was honoured with a South African War Medal.[75]

At the end of July, just after Adela's wedding, John came to see her at last. The relief of seeing him alive and well was tremendous. He was just as wonderful as ever, as she told Adela:

All the imaginings and memories seemed stale and full and unen-
chanting compared to the real. Best and least looked for of all, I'd so
rehearsed the lesson 'He doesn't care for you or realise, except to the
extent of a small worry, that you care for him' that it was surprising
to find him kind and considerate and even seeming to like talking
to me.[76]

But, for once, John seemed to have made up his mind to act deci-
sively. They went for a walk and he ended things once and for all.
When he left the Danes on the early train the next day, Constance
believed it was for ever.

She had told herself for many years that there was no hope, but
it made the end no easier. Her imagination took a new and wild
turn and she began bargaining with God, as she had done years
earlier when Gerald Balfour's life seemed in danger. She considered offering her life so that Edith's friend Mrs Cory might get
better, but then decided this sacrifice would be too easy. Instead
she resolved to give up loving John, so that Adela might find true
love and happiness in her new marriage. The decision seemed right,
but did not make her happy. First she had 'a sort of rage storm
… a sort of fury against JP which nothing can describe'. Then she
was plunged into depression. 'All happy things seem far off … and
there clouds through the gloom, war horrors and cases of misery,
stories of broken lives, broken limbs and broken hearts, and feeling
of heavy load that no-one can lift all around me,'[77] she told Adela;
while to Aunt T she wrote, 'Tho' this inevitable has … been obvious
to outsiders from the first, and I myself have realised it and stared
at it for the last three years, yet the actual happening of this break
has been different and worse than I expected.'[78] She gave up writing
in her diary, unless it was to mention him. In June, in the midst of
her excitement about John's homecoming, she had turned ahead
to her diary for 12 August and asked her future self, 'How about

JP now? Will he be in England?' Now she answered tersely: 'Yes he's in England & I've seen him & I shan't see him again.'[79] She dreamed about him and his family and was reduced to recording those dreams instead of actual letters or meetings. She could not stop thinking about him. She tucked a press cutting into her journal called 'Songs of a Plain Woman No. II'.

> There's little I wish for, just taking
> The goods the gods give
> With a fate to be marred in the making
> A life I must live;
> Through desolate space,
> Yet blessed in remembering only
> Your blessed face
>
> …
>
> I crave not your love, nor your notice
> This thing will suffice;
> To be near you on earth, to be with you
> In God's Paradise
> To have loved you – to love you for ever,
> My glory shall be
> And this – precious possession can never
> Be taken from me![80]

John was awarded a Distinguished Service Order in October. Before the end of the year he wrote to her, 'which seems to show he would like present things altered to better', though she was realistic enough to conclude that this was probably his family leaning on him. Still, even his pity was better than nothing, especially if it would mean he would write when he next went abroad. She knew that a clean break would be better for all concerned, yet she couldn't make one. John was due to return to South Africa in February 1902 and she desperately wished to see him again before he went. Then a letter arrived from her cousin Edith Earle, who was married to Aunt T's son Max. As Edith Loch, she had known John well in South Africa. She asked to meet Edith Lytton for lunch, and Constance fervently hoped that it meant John was indirectly reaching out to her. It turned out the opposite was true. John was in love with someone else. Constance barely slept for three nights, collapsed into sickness, and only collected herself enough to write a final letter to John before he departed England again. Then he wrote to say that he would be in touch when in South Africa. Perhaps the break was not to be clean at all. She took to reading his old letters, over and over, to prove to herself that there had been something there and she had not, as her family seemed to believe, simply imagined the whole thing. She even read bits out loud to Edith to prove it.[81]

Her diary for 1902 is missing. The following year, 1903, makes a poignant contrast with the diaries of a decade earlier. Then, she had enthusiastically noted all the books she had read and reviewed; now she has shrunk to commenting on her illnesses and the weather, as well as the birthdays and visits of her increasing tribe of nephews and nieces. 'I don't mean entirely to live in the past,' she told Aunt T, but she couldn't help herself. She made clippings from the newspapers whenever they mentioned John, or his regiment, or his family. She even tried to make the best of John's new love affair, which did not seem to be going well. 'She sounds a perfect and ideally suited sort,' she told Betty magnanimously, 'and it makes me wretched that his family and friends should take the line of saying he must keep away entirely from a short-sighted view of his happiness.'[82] This is her inner martyr talking. Surely she must have been just the slightest bit pleased that he was now experiencing what she had endured for so long. In 1906 she heard that the object of John's desire had married someone else. Her diary entry for Christmas Day that year says, 'Left off wearing the ring.'[83]

The intervals between scraps of news became longer and longer. (Though that didn't stop the family gossip. 'From Adela via Aunt T – via Gerry – via Betty – Montgomery heard that family perturbed that I still care for JP – feared this would prevent his marrying,' she wrote in her diary in 1903.)[84] Her contact with Maggy and Lady P shrank and then disappeared, though one year she had a Christmas card from Lady P which said, 'Si l'espace nous separe la Pensee nous raproche.'[85] ('If it is space that separates us, it is Thought that brings us together.') After 1900, Maurice Baring was her main source of information about John. She saw Maggy and Lady P again in 1907 and they didn't mention John once. She knew though, that his regiment was being sent to Egypt, and fretted over the impact the climate would have on his health. Later that year, she wrote to Adela that she simultaneously wished for a glimmer of hope and knew that if the past came back it would only be more painful. She tried to be grateful for what she had had: meagre as it was, it had taught her what joy was. Yet 'there remains something incongruous within me that doesn't grow old and experienced with the rest … but turns round now and then on its starved bed and shrieks out for food and drink with a strength all useless and uncanny coming from I don't know where'.[86]

Constance never got over her disappointment with John Ponsonby. Because the letters between them have not survived, we may never know for certain why they did not get married early in their relationship. Lack of money may have been important, but it cannot be the only reason: it did not stop either of his brothers marrying well. Arthur had married Dorothea Parry, daughter of the composer Hubert, as far back as 1893, while, as we have seen, Constance was asked to be a bridesmaid at Frederick's wedding to Victoria Kennard in 1899; and John was the oldest son, who might fairly expect a reasonable inheritance. Nor is it fair to blame Edith for getting in the way (though Maggy once called her 'the

Ogre').[87] Many years later, Victor wrote to Betty, 'I wonder if poor Mother realises how much suffering she caused all unknowingly through want of sympathy.'[88] Edith also disapproved of Edwin Lutyens at first, but through persistence and patience, Edwin and Emily would eventually get married. Constance thought that Edith was being selfish and difficult, but Edith seems to have seen clearly what Constance did not: marriage was never realistically on the cards. Constance got carried away with her infatuation and John didn't know what to do about it. His family may have wanted him to marry her, but that doesn't mean that he wanted the same. If John had really cared for Constance, he surely would have made more of an effort. He hardly ever wrote, and when he did the letters were usually unsatisfactory. But it's not fair to blame him for this either. The conventions of the time and the fact that there had never been a formal agreement may have made it more difficult to extricate himself. It was a hopeless situation.

But if Constance didn't marry John Ponsonby, why didn't she marry someone else instead? Perhaps because, as the cliché goes, she wasted the best years of her life waiting for the wrong man. Presumably, though, a woman of this class, attractive if not beautiful, would not lack for alternative suitors if she made herself in the slightest bit available. In 1897, Emily wrote to Edwin about another prospect who was 'anxious to marry Conny'. Unfortunately, 'he is crass and idiotic and anything he does is wrong. He is to deal with exactly like a jibbing horse and it does tire me getting him along … Darling Conny! It is delicious the idea of brilliant Conny marrying such a foozle headed old bore.'[89] But Constance never seems to have sought out anyone more suitable. Looking back with a quarter of a century's hindsight, Neville suggested that she was so gentle, merciful and kind that she inspired adoration among women but was unlikely to prove attractive to potential husbands. 'Men fight shy of women who are saints,' he concluded.[90]

Perhaps, too, she may have looked at her siblings' marriages and thought she was better off out of the whole business. With the exception of Betty, her siblings all had extremely complicated relationships. Between 1893 and 1896, when Constance's relationship with John was the most promising and hopeful it would ever be, Emily was playing a dangerous game with her father's womanising friend Wilfred Scawen Blunt.[91] Constance could see the direction this was heading and warned Emily to make it clear to Blunt that they could only ever be friends. But Emily, perhaps out of innocence, or perhaps enjoying the drama, failed to keep the situation under control.[92] She fancied herself in love with him. There were late-night rattlings at her door. There was even a mock Arabic wedding ceremony. This was playing with fire. He was married, nearly thirty-five years older than her, and had been a close friend of her father. Blunt's daughter Judith was also Emily's best friend: Judith seems to have been half in love with Emily herself.[93] Through her mother, Judith was descended from Lord Byron and his daughter, Ada Lovelace. Her life was all but destroyed by fury at her emotionally manipulative father's constant bad behaviour. While carrying on his flirtation with Emily, Blunt also fathered a child with Mary Elcho. Judith was made to act as a go-between between Blunt and his mistress. When Emily confessed to her friend that she was thinking of eloping with her father, Judith told Emily what he was really up to.

With Blunt out of the country, Emily met the architect Edwin Lutyens – Ned – at Hatfield. She very quickly determined she would marry him. There was a genuine spark between these two, but each also had ulterior motives. A connection to the Souls through Emily and Betty would do Ned's career no harm at all. Emily simply wanted to escape, both from Blunt and from her mother. This meant both overlooked their fundamental differences and ultimate incompatibility. Edith was not in favour of the match, though perhaps she might have approved more strongly if she had known about the narrow escape with Blunt. Ostensibly, she objected to Lutyens because she was worried about his finances. More to the point, Edith was also snobbish about his background. But her brother, Lord Loch, now nominally head of the family, resolved the issue and Emily married in 1897.[94] Emily's wedding night and honeymoon were apparently an unmitigated disaster. Her daughter Mary recalled her mother's ineffective advice to always keep a pot of cold cream by the bed, and the alarming, unexplained suggestion that 'whatever happens to you, it's happened to me too'.[95] It is rather surprising that Betty didn't enlighten Emily about the facts of life. But it is inconceivable that Emily didn't drop some extremely alarming hints in Constance's direction. Emily never got over her honeymoon nightmare. She put up with Edwin long enough to have five children, but eventually banned him from her bedroom entirely. The Lutyenses found it very difficult to get on with each other in person but they were extraordinarily prolific and often affectionate correspondents. Emily had spent her teenage years pouring out her heart and soul to an elderly vicar; now her letters flew back and forth to her husband, wherever he was working. This correspondence still exists and runs to thousands of letters.[96]

Meanwhile, Judith Blunt spent several years unhappily in love with Victor Lytton. Despite an apparent attraction, he did not pursue her. She had the impression that this was because she was a Catholic, a connection that would be bad for his career. Judith was extremely eligible and had frequent offers of marriage. Many of these were from Neville Lytton, who had been pining for Judith for almost as long as she had wanted Victor. Eventually, realising that the situation with Victor was hopeless, she gave in and said she would think about it. Her father Wilfred seized on this chance and put a notice in *The Times* as if it were a done deal. Judith was twenty-seven; Neville was just nineteen and barely out of school:

they shared a birthday, 6 February. 'It maddens me that nobody sees how false this whole thing is,' Judith wrote bitterly.[97] Neville did not follow Victor to Cambridge, but went instead to Paris to study art. Constance visited them soon after they got married, and was impressed with their lifestyle, as well as Neville's talent and his evident dedication to make a living as an artist.[98]

Later, Neville and Judith would come back to England to live at the famous Crabbet stud, where Judith's parents had been breeding exquisite horses. But, predictably enough, this marriage, built on broken dreams on one side and unrealistic expectations on the other, would be no more successful than Emily's. Judith did not want children, but their makeshift attempts at contraception failed, and their three children were acutely aware of Judith's lack of maternal feelings towards them.[99]

After leaving Cambridge, Victor married Pamela Plowden in 1902. She was the daughter of the Mrs Plowden who had been romantically linked with his father in India. Pamela's childhood was unhappy: her mother died and her father remarried a woman she disliked. When her sister also married, Pamela felt completely alone in India and returned to an England she barely knew; her only hope being to find a suitable husband. Winston Churchill proposed to her, but was short of money; in the meantime, she met his friend Victor and accepted him instead. Pamela was thought to be one of the most beautiful women of her generation, with elegant manners to match. But the Lytton sisters were snooty about her. She was formal and had a conventional way of looking at things that bored Betty and Emily. Constance, though, was her usual kind and gentle self, which Pamela appreciated. Their marriage, at least in the early years, also had its fair share of difficulties. There are strong suggestions that the youngest son may not have been Victor's child, though Victor, to his great credit, never treated him any differently. Victor and Pamela could not afford to live at Knebworth for many years, and they lived in London until 1908, when there was a homecoming party. Photos of this occasion show how large and sprawling the Lytton tribe had become. Victor and Pamela kept up the family tradition of extensive renovations, aided by Edwin Lutyens, who is responsible for much of the current garden layout.

Lutyens was also commissioned to build a home for Edith and Constance. Built in 1901 a mile away from Knebworth, this was known as Homewood, and it would be Edith's home for the rest of her life. According to his biographer, Edwin 'imagined it as a doll's house where the architect would suddenly remove the front and reveal at each end two women employed after their own hearts'.[100] The reality was rather less picturesque. Homewood is a contrast between the vision of one of the country's foremost architects, paying close attention to tiny details on the windows and doorknobs, and the execution of that vision, as cheaply as possible. As money was so tight, nothing was finished properly and the doors were second-hand. There was only one bathroom, and this was in the servants' quarters: there would always be a live-in cook and housekeeper. Constance and Edith had hip baths in front of the fire, though this surely must have been out of choice rather than economy. But most noticeable of all was the cold. The front door led onto a long passage down the house which carried the wind straight through the house. Edith's room was the coldest in the house: it wasn't until many decades later that it was discovered that the wall inside her wardrobe hadn't been built properly, allowing the cold to seep in. With little money for maintenance and upkeep, the house almost immediately began to decay.

Life at Homewood with Edith was quiet, punctuated only by visits from Constance's siblings and their growing families, and bouts of rheumatic fever which kept her in bed for weeks at a time. She was not, as she would later say in *Prisons and Prisoners*, 'more or less a chronic invalid for the greater part of my youth',[101] but by the time she came to write this, illness had become the defining feature of her life. The first serious attack was in 1902, with another one the following year. She probably could no longer imagine a time when she had really been well. 'Oh! King Pain and his kingdoms! What a king and place they are. Autocratic, tyrannous – if power is a fine thing, they are magnificent,' she told Betty in 1908, when she was well accustomed to this new ruler.[102] Her health problems were vague but persistent and often serious. She had a 'weak heart' and debilitating rheumatism. Her belief that she was an invalid now became central to her sense of self and the way she lived her life. Trapped in bed, she turned to books, sometimes making surprising choices. For example, in 1907, probably at Olive Schreiner's suggestion, she was reading Edward Carpenter's book *Love's Coming of Age* – after which Olive wrote to Edward calling Constance 'a born socialist'.[103]

It's probably not a coincidence that she became more frequently ill after she had finally given up on John. It seems almost certain that her illnesses were, at least in part, symptoms of her psychological troubles. She brings to mind famous nineteenth-century invalids like Elizabeth Barrett Browning and Alice James, with their vague and mysterious complaints, their tiredness and lethargy.

In her vast history of women and mental illness, Lisa Appignanesi has described how the cultural conditions which confronted Victorian women shaped their illnesses. When women's lives were so entirely circumscribed, it might be a relief – it might even be a conscious choice – to escape onto the sofa. Becoming an invalid let women off the hook from the endless round of family and social duties and, for some, this was irresistible.[104] It was all the resistance they could muster. Indeed, Appignanesi sees 'the escape into illness' as 'the mirror image of rebellion'.[105] Women who had no recourse to action withdrew entirely, defeated. This seems to have been part of Constance's strategy. Family obligations piled up once her siblings embarked on their large families. It was taken for granted that

Edith and Constance would be ready at a moment's notice to help out. Constance was good natured about this, and did like being surrounded by children (though she said to Betty, 'It's lucky nieces came first in our tribe, and nephews followed after, for nice as nieces are there's no comparing them with man-cubs.').[106] Nevertheless, once she had nothing to do but look after other people, regularly hiding herself away must have seemed extremely appealing, especially because she never overcame her shyness. This is not to say that her illnesses were invented, because at certain points they were obviously debilitating, but it does mean that sometimes she used them to escape. Whenever she really needed a burst of energy, she summoned it up from somewhere.

In the meantime, Aunt T persuaded her to become a vegetarian, then an extremely faddish and unconventional choice. Always willing to humour others by following their advice or giving in to their suggestions, Constance found it actually made a difference. She felt stronger and healthier as a result.[107] Being a vegetarian also suited her kind and sympathetic nature.

Constance resigned herself to remaining unmarried and settled down at home, becoming that Victorian stereotype, the maiden aunt. There were legions of spinsters – by the 1890s, one in every six women would remain unmarried – but in popular culture they were viewed with suspicion. Celibacy was thought in medical circles to be potentially damaging, while women who remained unmarried were considered abnormal in some way.[108]

On the surface, Constance was the very model of an Edwardian dutiful daughter. With her half-begun relationship and thwarted career, she had once or twice hesitantly tapped at the limits of what was appropriate, but each time obediently retreated at the slightest hint of maternal disapproval. Her family believed Constance had accepted her personal disappointments and was resigned to a quiet, uneventful life. 'For aught you or I know, I may become an electioneering propagandist woman … or anything else, before the next 10 years run out,' Constance told Betty in 1899. 'But this is unlikely, and I've reached that place in the lane of life when the probable alternatives of the future are fairly visible. I can't honestly say they please me much, but how few people are really pleased?'[109] Nevertheless, Constance felt her losses more deeply than she was prepared to let on. 'It seems like waiting, not like actually living,' she continued to Betty. Though no one noticed, each disappointment and failure – music, writing, love – was locked away inside her. They were no less painful as the years passed. Outwardly, she was docile and compliant. She filled her days with routine domesticity and derived her own happiness by making other people happy. But, inside, Constance craved much, much more. In fact, she was quietly seething. She told Aunt T that 'the first symptom of robustness with me is to lose my temper, and long to hurl stones at windows or break something with my hands'.[110] She only needed a spark to set her off.

In the summer of 1908, Constance saw John Ponsonby at a production of a Maurice Baring play in London. It was, she told Adela, 'just plain real joy with no effort and no sham and no alloy. Just plain wonder joy.' Then the Ponsonby family invited her to visit them, like old times. John would be there. 'It's such Paradise temptation!' Constance exclaimed. Precisely because of this attitude, Edith didn't want her to go. Fearing old wounds being reopened, she said it would be better if Constance and John did not meet until he was married. Victor persuaded Edith that it would be fine, and Constance was allowed to go. It was beyond her wildest dreams. 'All more divinely natural and easy than I had dared hope … He is simply exactly the same. The whole thing is like magic. I feel a wee bit dazed but immensely happy. He is most dear, and easy and charming to me,' she told Adela.[111] It seemed as though she was in danger of falling for John Ponsonby all over again. Instead, she met the suffragettes.

CHAPTER FOUR

THE CAUSE

'There was a call from far off, something inevitable as the voice of fate.'[1]

There is a famous and lovely – though sadly probably apocryphal – story that one day, Emily Davies went to visit her friend Elizabeth Garrett and Elizabeth's younger sister, Millicent, and the conversation turned to the embryonic struggle for women's rights. These three young women – Millicent was only thirteen – decided to put the world to rights between them. Emily was given the task of tackling women's education, Elizabeth would open up the medical profession to women, and thirteen-year-old Millicent would win women the vote. That is almost exactly what happened. In 1865, Elizabeth became the first woman qualified to practise medicine in England and three years later, Emily founded the first women's college at Cambridge. Millicent dedicated her life to winning the vote and became the leader of the National Union of Women's Suffrage Society (NUWSS). She would have to wait a lot longer to see her dream realised.

In the Victorian era, the rise of the middle classes meant the rise of a new bourgeois ideology which divided the world in half: public/private; male/female – an ideal historians have called 'separate spheres'.[2] In theory, men and women had equally important roles: men had to take on the burdens and responsibilities of public life, while women were supposed to nurture the home and the children, ideally as the patient, submissive, devoted 'angel in the house'. In reality, women were very much second-class citizens, dependent on husbands, fathers and brothers.

But as the nineteenth century progressed, the role of women in society began to significantly change. Women (and their supporters) began, tentatively and one step at a time, to challenge the limitations and constraints that shackled their lives. Judicial reform gave women new legal rights over their money, their property and their children. Divorce, though still time-consuming and expensive, was becoming accessible. Some middle-class women went to university, though it was still out of reach for the working classes and unthinkably déclassé for the upper classes. A few pioneers joined the professions. Thousands became teachers and nurses. Some women joined the chorus of late-Victorian concern about poverty and inequality and began to push for social reform. One notable success was the repeal of the Contagious Diseases Act in 1886, which allowed police to arrest and inspect women in certain areas suspected of prostitution. Led by Josephine Butler, this campaign was particularly notable for the way in which 'respectable' women were prepared to risk that respectability by standing up for prostitutes, showing how women from extremely different backgrounds could work together in a common cause.[3] (Lady Ponsonby, for example, was interested in this issue.) Campaigning women rejoiced in these successes. They were increasingly confident, with a growing belief in what they could offer, what they might do and what they might achieve.[4]

But there was one glaring omission from women's advance into public life: they could not vote in national elections. As a result, the struggle for the vote came to preoccupy the women's movement. Historian Susie Steinbach suggests that 'nineteenth-century feminists focused their efforts on suffrage because it was the one battle they were losing; from the 1850s to the end of the century they won astonishing victories in almost every area'.[5] The vote became a talisman for progressive women. It had both symbolic importance – for the first time, acknowledging women as equal citizens – and tremendous practical importance. It would give them power and influence over political decision making and be a means to achieving other goals, whether that involved improving conditions for working women, supporting family life or changing the sexual double standard.

As we have seen, Constance's great-grandmother Anna Wheeler had been arguing for female suffrage in the 1820s. The first petition to Parliament on this issue was presented by Henry Hunt in 1832, on behalf of Mary Smith of Stanmore, who stated that since she paid taxes she should have a representative in Parliament. In 1867, John Stuart Mill presented another petition, signed by 1,499 women, asking to be enfranchised, but the Reform Act brought in that year by Disraeli did nothing for women. In 1868, a Miss Lily Maxwell was named on the electoral roll by mistake. Supported by the campaigner Lydia Becker, she duly voted and was duly knocked back in court. The vote was, and would remain, the preserve of men. Lydia Becker was the driving force behind the campaign for the vote until her death in 1890. The struggle was then taken up by a new generation of reformers: Esther Roper, her partner Eva Gore-Booth and, most significantly, Millicent Garrett (now Fawcett) stepping up to fulfil her destiny.[6] The demand for the vote was also taken up by working women in Lancashire, whose experiences in mills and factories made them simultaneously independent, vocal and acutely aware of the disadvantages they faced as women, paid less than their male colleagues and disregarded by male-dominated trade unions.[7]

The campaign united women who otherwise had very little in common. It was not just class that divided the women, but also geography, religion, party; whether they were married or not; whether they worked outside the home or not.[8] Yet 'most appeared to have felt that they had a unique contribution to make as women, and that their authority in moral affairs enabled them, at times, to transcend customary affiliations and to join hands with women across political and ideological divides,' writes the historian Kathryn Gleadle.[9] Supporters said that the vote would be good for women: it would make them better, more engaged citizens.[10] Women and men were thought to be different, which meant that gaining the vote was essential to protect women's unique interests. Further, women's participation in political life would change it for the better, bringing new issues into the political arena and changing the tenor of debate.

On the other hand, opponents had any number of reasons why women should not be able to vote. Some pointed to biology, arguing that menstruation, pregnancy and breastfeeding would all apparently get in the way of women from voting. Others saw difference as a sign of inferiority, arguing that women were more emotional and less intelligent than men, lacking the logic and common sense needed to make political decisions. Some said that because women couldn't defend the state in wartime, they did not deserve the vote. Others – though by the end of the nineteenth century, their numbers were dwindling – thought the whole issue too stupid even comment on.[11] Still others were afraid of what women might want next.[12]

Nevertheless, by 1900, a million women could vote in certain local elections: for councillors, poor law guardians and school board representatives.[13] None of the catastrophic consequences for their families or communities predicted by apocalyptic commentators came to pass. Some women were even elected to serve as Poor Law guardians – one of these was Emmeline Pankhurst – and they helped make workhouses more humane, especially for disabled or 'delinquent' children.[14]

So why did the struggle for the franchise become such an epic battle? Part of the reason was disagreement about which women should be enfranchised, because significant numbers of men still could not vote. Campaigning women themselves were also divided. Some believed that, tactically, it would be more sensible to give single women the vote first, since it could be argued that without a husband, they did not even have indirect representation, despite the fact that as householders they were paying taxes. Others, though, believed that married women with family responsibilities had a greater stake in the nation's affairs and needed a voice.

But even more significant was the lack of political leadership. In the general election at the end of 1905, Arthur Balfour's Conservative Party was punished for the controversial Boer War and the Liberals, led by Henry Campbell-Bannerman, were returned to government in a landslide victory. Liberal Party members were generally in favour of the vote. But Liberal leaders took the position that giving the vote to women on the same terms as men would not be in their interests: they saw such women as natural Conservative supporters.[15] In any case, having been out of power for a generation, the Liberals had other, 'more important', business to get on with. Meanwhile, the labour movement, now represented in Parliament with twenty-nine MPs, was no more enthusiastic about women's suffrage, believing that attention should be focused on universal suffrage. This was hugely frustrating for the women who had campaigned to get them elected in the first place. An exception to the rule was the labour leader Keir Hardie, but he had little success in persuading his colleagues to take the women's demands seriously.

Most women were resigned to many more years of campaigning. Without government support, their only option was to sneak electoral reform in through the back door, by encouraging a friendly MP to sponsor a Private Members' Bill. It was very unlikely, but it was their best shot.

For some women, though, this wasn't good enough. They had been politely asking for the vote for over forty years. It was time to start demanding the vote. The most outspoken of these women belonged to the Women's Social and Political Union, led by Emmeline Pankhurst and her daughter Christabel.[16]

Emmeline came from a family of campaigning reformers. Her husband Richard, a barrister, was a progressive in every sense: in favour of education for the working classes and Home Rule in Ireland, as well as the abolition of the monarchy and the House of Lords.[17] Richard had helped John Stuart Mill draft the original parliamentary proposals to give women the vote in 1867 and also drafted the bill which gave married women the right to their own property in 1882. In 1889, the Pankhursts were among the founders of the Women's Franchise League, a campaigning group that helped win the vote for women in local elections. But at this time, suffrage was just one of the Pankhursts' many causes. They were more closely aligned with socialism than feminism and their house in Manchester became a meeting place for radicals and progressives. The Pankhursts were active in the Independent Labour Party (ILP), formed in 1893, and friends with Keir Hardie. Richard stood, unsuccessfully, for election in 1895. But Emmeline was becoming increasingly aware that her relationship with the labour movement was one-sided. Socialist women were expected to be active campaigners for their male colleagues, but few men felt the need to repay them by supporting women's suffrage.

Richard Pankhurst died unexpectedly in 1898 and Emmeline opened a shop in order to make a living. Her eldest daughter, Christabel, reluctantly worked in the shop, while the next child, Sylvia, took up a scholarship at the Royal College of Art. The youngest, Adela and Harry, were still at school. But neither Emmeline nor Christabel were successful businesswomen and Emmeline soon found alternative employment as a Register of Births and Deaths. This work led her into closer contact with working-class women and the many problems they faced, from illegitimate children and early widowhood to large families they could not afford to feed. More than ever, she became convinced that women needed political representation to solve the problems in their lives. Meanwhile, Christabel had been attending lectures at Manchester University and had become friends with the campaigners Esther Roper and Eva Gore-Booth. Both Emmeline and Christabel were reaching the conclusion that not only was winning the vote for women increasingly urgent, but that women would have to do it for themselves, with or without the support of the labour movement.

In 1900, the Richard Pankhurst Memorial Hall was opened, built with money raised by prominent ILP leaders like Keir Hardie and Ramsay MacDonald, and decorated by Sylvia. Emmeline was furious to discover that the hall was going to be used by an ILP branch which refused to admit women. Sylvia and her sisters would not even be allowed in. Emmeline needed no clearer evidence that the male-dominated labour movement at this time did not take women or their concerns seriously. She was determined to develop an alternative.

On 10 October 1903, she held the first meeting of the Women's Social and Political Union in her living room. It was set up to be 'a new approach to an old problem', as Sophia A. van Wingerden, historian of the WSPU, puts it.

> They were to be entirely independent of political parties, to oppose all government until the vote was won, to organise women all over the country, to educate public opinion, and most significantly, to adopt 'vigorous agitation upon lines justified by the position of outlawry to which women are at present condemned'.[18]

'Vigorous agitation' was enshrined in the constitution, though no one yet could envisage just how 'vigorous' the suffragettes would become.

Early in 1905, a Private Members' Bill to give women the vote was squeezed out of parliamentary time by a Bill requiring carts on public roads to have lights at the back.[19] That showed how important the question was to the new government. The Pankhursts had had enough. In October 1905, Christabel and her friend Annie Kenney attended a political meeting at the Free Trade Hall in Manchester. The speakers, Winston Churchill and Sir Edward Grey, were both supposedly supporters of women's suffrage. The women had made a long banner which asked, 'Will the Liberal Party give votes for women?' At the last minute, Christabel decided that the wording was too complicated and the banner too big: they hastily printed a new sign which said simply said 'Votes for Women', and one of the best-known slogans of the twentieth century was born.[20] At the meeting, Annie stood up and demanded to know the answer to their question. The women were summarily thrown out and arrested. They refused to pay the fine and went to prison. This marks the beginning of what became known as the 'militant' campaign. Churchill sensed the danger and tried to pay Christabel's fine, recognising that she would have instant and invaluable notoriety. He was right. All at once, the issue of 'votes for women' exploded into the political arena. What on earth had made these nice young women – pretty ones, too – decide to go to prison for a political cause?

To capitalise on this renewed interest and to take on the new Liberal government, Emmeline decided that this was the moment to transfer the centre of operations from Manchester to London. Christabel was studying to become a barrister at a Manchester law college, so Annie was duly despatched to London and Sylvia was roped in – rather reluctantly – as well. While undoubtedly committed to winning the vote, Sylvia also had her own interests in art and her own cause in the plight of the working-class women in the East End. She was committed to broader socialist campaigning and so was reluctant to dedicate herself entirely to the WSPU, only doing so out of obedience to her mother. Her involvement meant that the early supporters of the WSPU in London were almost all drawn from the

East End slums where Sylvia worked. The most notable exception was Emmeline Pethick-Lawrence. She was from a wealthy Quaker family who felt a call to serve working women, and had spent many years working with her friend Mary Neal in the East End. Emmeline was captivated by Annie Kenney and, despite initial misgivings, not only became Treasurer of the WSPU but offered her house and resources to the cause. She was a gift to the movement, the practical counterpart to the Pankhursts' idealism, with a talent for everything the WSPU needed to get going – propaganda, fundraising, editing – and she gave up the rest of her social activism in order to devote her life to suffrage. Until the Pankhursts got involved, Emmeline suggested, 'The suffrage movement was like a beetle on its back that cannot turn itself over and get on its legs to pursue its path.'[21] Suddenly the beetle was scrambling all over the place.

The WSPU was different from other women's organisations from the start. Most women campaigning for suffrage were also working for other social reforms, but the WPSU expected their supporters to concentrate all their efforts on winning the vote. Members of the WSPU weren't content to stuff envelopes and collect signatures year after year with no results. They wanted action immediately, and took their slogan, 'deeds, not words', very seriously. Members of non-militant organisations campaigning for the vote were called 'suffragists'. In 1906, the *Daily Mail* coined the term 'suffragettes' as a derisory term to describe the militants: the WSPU used the label with pride.

The Pankhursts' trump card was their incredible personal charisma. Emmeline was the notional figurehead of the organisation, but Christabel was the leader and unashamedly ran the WSPU as a dictatorship. Sylvia, afterwards sharply opposed to her sister's strategy and tactics, nevertheless remembered with admiration the extraordinary devotion she inspired among her followers. 'Christabel had the admiration of a multitude: hundreds, perhaps thousands of young women adored her to distraction.'[22] This gave her something like a personal army, just waiting to follow her every command; Christabel herself drew an analogy with being the conductor of an orchestra.[23]

Through personality as well as politics, the Pankhursts attracted women who otherwise wouldn't have been interested in women's rights.[24] They were blessed with extraordinary gifts of oratory and rhetoric, with the power to move mass audiences and captivate individuals. There is just one recording of Christabel's voice, made in 1908, which gives some idea of her forthright determination, but it cannot give any sense of her impact. She was a fiery speaker, quick-witted and deeply impressive in her intelligence. Emmeline, on the other hand, had an incredible emotional appeal which moved her audiences tremendously, particularly as she grew older and visibly weaker.[25] Emmeline touched the heart, Christabel appealed to the head: they were quite the team. The Pankhursts were reinforced by other women who were equally as dynamic, inspiring and larger than life. As well as Annie Kenney and Emmeline Pethick-Lawrence, foremost among these leaders were Flora McDonald, known as 'the General' for her military forcefulness, and the secretary, elegant, graceful and ladylike, Mabel Tuke.

The WSPU directly challenged the notion of 'separate spheres' for men and women by taking their campaign to public meetings, out on the streets and into Parliament itself.[26] As Emmeline Pankhurst wrote in her autobiography, 'There would be no more peace until the women's question was answered.'[27] The suffragettes wanted the British people to see that their cause was not only just but urgent. They relished this task, especially in the early years, when, as Emmeline Pethick-Lawrence later recalled, 'the spirit of laughter and adventure, the spirit of youth had been dominant amongst us'.[28] They were imaginative, impatient and exuberant. They heckled Cabinet ministers, disrupted by-elections and deliberately sought arrest. A series of stunts, each more dramatic than the last, kept their campaign in the public eye. When the Prime Minister, Henry Campbell-Bannerman, was prevaricating over receiving the suffragettes, Annie led a group straight to his front door in Downing Street and jumped on his car. When Keir Hardie introduced a Private Members' Bill into the Commons and the suffragettes in the gallery thought the idea was not being taken sufficiently seriously, they showered the MPs with banners and literature. When the Prime Minister eventually agreed to receive the suffragettes in May 1906, expressing his support but advising patience, to his astonishment, Annie Kenney jumped on a chair to express her dissatisfaction. Another suffragette, Dora Montefiore, refused to pay her taxes and, when the bailiffs came, she boarded up her home. The suffragettes were putting on a show.[29]

But perhaps the most staggering step the suffragettes took was their willingness to go to prison. They would deliberately break the law in some way – increasingly as part of an organised event, like a protest march, often towards Parliament – and then were brought to trial en masse. When arrested, the women were always offered the alternative of paying a fine, but it was a badge of honour that they rejected this and went to prison.[30] At first, this was in ones and twos, but soon it was dozens and the women's prison at Holloway was stuffed with suffragettes.

Britain had never seen anything like this before. Often well educated, 'respectable' and articulate, these women were also, in the eyes of the law and of polite society, violent hooligans and moral deviants who disregarded natural order and shattered social customs as well as breaking laws.[31] People hardly knew what to make of them. The police certainly didn't know what to do with these unlikely criminals, so far removed from their usual charges. Neither did the magistrates, who struggled to know what punishment to impose when it was obvious that no sentence would deter them from further criminal acts.[32]

Some people were inspired and thrilled by the suffragettes' extraordinary energy and commitment. But they were not, even at this early stage, universally admired for their bravery. They were often ridiculed in the papers, painted as 'shrews, viragos, hysterics, unwomanly women who abandoned their children and lacked feminine allure',[33] and because they were now 'unwomanly' they were no longer treated with the respect and care usually afforded to women. Out campaigning on the road, they risked not only heckling but physical assault. Eggs were thrown. Cayenne pepper was hurled. Even 'mice, poor little creatures, were flung at us', Christabel remembered with a shudder.[34] The hostility of the crowd was often matched by the brutality of the police. Even older suffragettes could expect a rough ride and Mrs Pankhurst herself reported several narrow escapes from scuffles. The suffragettes shocked British society, but they in turn were shocked by the ways in which they were treated. They were genteel ladies, and though their upbringing had restricted them, it had also protected them from the harsher realities of life. But they were not to be put off. They responded with indignation and a burning sense of righteousness in the justice of their cause.

All the publicity garnered by the suffragettes masked the fact that their numbers always remained relatively small. Only around a thousand ever went to prison, for example, though many of these were repeat offenders who were incarcerated multiple times. This is not surprising. Becoming a militant required incredible reserves of dedication and extraordinary single-mindedness. On a purely practical level, women who couldn't afford to leave their job, women with children and women who couldn't risk family disapproval were simply unable to do what was required, however much they may have wanted to. This didn't especially matter to Emmeline and Christabel, whose strategy depended on a small number of women having a massive impact with astonishing levels of intensity. The suffragettes were not a traditional campaigning organisation or a political party: instead they were, in historian Susie Steinbach's words 'a kind of army or secular religion'.[35]

One consequence of the suffragette campaign, then, was that thousands of women joined the non-militant National Union of Women's Suffrage Societies: it had 13,000 members by 1909 and 42,000 in 1912.[36] Some were women who reluctantly concluded that they couldn't make enough of a commitment to join the WSPU. Many more, though, were women who decided they supported the ends but not the means of the suffragettes. Some of these women wanted to distance themselves from the antics of their militant sisters, but Mrs Fawcett, at least in the early years, was a supporter, saying, 'Far from having injured the movement, they have done more during the last twelve months to bring it within the region of practical politics than we have been able to accomplish in the same number of years.'[37]

But there were already hints of the drawbacks associated with the Pankhursts' policies. For example, their policy was to campaign against any Liberal government candidate standing for election until the government committed to enfranchising women: this helped ensure Winston Churchill lost his seat at a by-election, and a new one had to be hastily found. But campaigning against a Liberal candidate if it led to a Conservative victory seemed ludicrous and self-defeating to critics. This move brought condemnation from the Labour Party, which adopted its own policy of refusing to support 'votes for women' if the franchise was based on a property qualification: instead, their policy was to advocate for universal suffrage – however unlikely that may have been. Despite Keir Hardie's best efforts, Emmeline and Christabel Pankhurst left the party, dividing the suffrage and the labour movements for several years.[38] This was a profound concern to many women, who disliked having to choose 'sex' over 'class;' Sylvia Pankhurst in particular was very

uncomfortable with this position. Class was an increasingly sali-
ent issue for the WSPU. The first edition of the suffragette paper
Votes for Women demanded that 'if you have any class feeling you
must leave that behind when you come into this movement. For
the women who are in our ranks know no barriers of class distinction.'[39] But, in practice, it tended to attract women who were
already relatively well off. Their belief that other concerns were
secondary to the vote – because having the vote would help solve
other problems – could seem overly optimistic and hopelessly naïve
to working-class women faced with enormous practical difficulties
in their day-to-day lives. Such women could also be put off by what
could sometimes be seen as 'self-indulgent' antics.[40]

Another controversial element of the WSPU, which continues
to divide historians, was the perceived level of autocracy. This does
not mean that members just followed orders with unquestioning
obedience. Many ordinary members took action on their own initiative, including Marion Wallace Dunlop, the first hunger striker,
or Emily Wilding Davison, who started the craze for torching
postboxes. It was the ordinary rank-and-file members who kept
militancy on the advance with increasingly violent acts, only gaining approval from Christabel later. But Christabel and Emmeline
Pankhurst would not tolerate any woman whom they saw as a
threat to their own popularity or power in the organisation. The
suffragette historian Jill Liddington quotes a contemporary critic
saying, 'Mrs Pankhurst would walk over the dead bodies of all her
children except Christabel and say, "See what I have given for the
cause,"'[41] while Christabel is seen, in the words of her biographer
June Purvis, as 'ruthless, cold, ambitious, unscrupulous, autocratic,
snobbish, calculating, selfish, right-wing and unco-operative op-
portunist'.[42] While this ignores the realities of what they had to do
to survive, it is nevertheless astonishing how many of their friends
and loyal supporters the Pankhursts managed to alienate. Some of

these left in disgust or astonishment: others were acrimoniously ejected. The first split came in 1907, when Charlotte Despard and Teresa Billington-Greig left to form the Women's Freedom League, a more democratic organisation committed to passive resistance. Losing some of their most important personnel at the same time as they were severing ties with the labour movement shows just how confident Christabel and Emmeline were.

The suffragettes deliberately employed a two-pronged strategy, combining mass protest action with individual acts of daring.[43] In 1908, the Home Secretary, Herbert Gladstone (the son of Robert Lytton's nemesis William) made the mistake of saying that men had won the vote through large-scale protest 'but of course, women cannot be expected to assemble in such masses'.[44] The suffragettes set out to prove them wrong. In June, MPs were taking tea on the terraces of the House of Commons, looking forward to their summer break. Their peace was shattered by a boatload of suffragettes careering down the Thames. A gleeful Flora Drummond unfurled a banner informing the MPs of a mass march at the weekend. 'Cabinet members especially invited,' it read. Then suffragettes carried off their greatest propaganda victory to date: a march and demonstration in Hyde Park, which attracted half a million people. The suffragette colours of white, purple and green were out in force; the air was buzzing with excitement and goodwill. The suffragettes felt that, surely, with so much visible support, the government could not ignore their demands for much longer.

There were, though, hints of trouble ahead. Campbell-Bannerman resigned owing to illness in April 1908, dying a few weeks later. Herbert Asquith, a long-standing, implacable opponent of women's suffrage, was now the Prime Minister. Though the Hyde Park demonstration passed off without incident, afterwards, Edith New and Mary Leigh went to Downing Street and threw stones at No. 10. Later that month, arrested on a deputation, Florence

Haig told police, 'Mr Asquith has shown us that peaceful demonstrations are useless'.[45] Until now, the suffragettes had been loud, disruptive and a general nuisance. They had not, however, been deliberately violent.

Nevertheless, the general mood was optimistic and joyful. The suffragettes left London for their summer holidays alive with hope and energy. Emmeline Pethick-Lawrence headed off to the seaside in Littlehampton for her annual break with her friend Mary Neal. Every year, they offered sea bathing, boating and dancing to a group of working-class girls at a hostel they had set up called The Green Lady. One of their guests that year was quite different from their usual mill girls and factory hands.

In May 1905, Constance's great-aunt Georgina Bloomfield died, leaving £2,000 to her namesake niece.[46] Constance decided, with characteristic unselfishness, to spend it on improving life for the local village girls. But she shrank from established methods of charity and cast about for a better way of investing the money, a way which might make a genuine difference to their lives. Eventually, she decided upon establishing a Morris dancing club. Morris dancing had been undergoing a revival since the turn of the century. Neville was an early enthusiast and introduced Constance to the movement. Morris dancing appealed to Constance because it put her 'into touch with the village-folk ... free from churchiness or Lady Bountifulness or District Visitor Business or other terrors.'[47] In the summer of 1908, Constance, Betty and Neville attended a folk music event in Westminster, run by the Esperance Club, which was encouraging working-class girls to take up Morris dancing.[48] Constance enlisted their help to run the sessions for her and became friends with the club's founder, Mary Neal.

Like her friend Emmeline Pethick-Lawrence, Mary Neal was a relatively wealthy woman from a good family who had put aside her privilege in order to work among the poor in east London. The two women had collaborated on a series of projects, like a dress-making club which gave working-class girls a steady job and a fair wage, and the Green Lady Hostel at Littlehampton, which offered them much-needed holidays. After Emmeline got married in 1901 and began to work more closely with her husband, Mary became interested in Cecil Sharp's embryonic work studying English folk music and dance. She taught Morris dances to the Esperance Club girls, convinced of their many 'improving' benefits. In fact, though it is Cecil Sharp who is remembered for rescuing folk music and dancing when it was at risk of being lost entirely, it was Mary Neal and the women in her club who brought that music to life and convinced Sharp that his project was worthwhile.[49] Though their paths diverged, Emmeline and Mary remained very close and they joined the WSPU together. But the vote was never one of her main concerns. Constance liked Mary because she was 'the only practising philanthropist I have ever met who is sympathetic to me – one feels she does it all for her own fun, not for the good of her soul, and to join in with, and really appreciate the lives of those she befriends, rather than to "save" them'.[50] Constance was invited to join the club's holiday in the summer of 1908.

The holiday itself was not an unqualified success. There was singing and dancing and the girls threw themselves into all the activities on offer with unbridled joy, but Constance found herself on the margins. Emmeline Pethick-Lawrence spotted her awkwardness, and the two bonded over their connection to Olive Schreiner (Emmeline's husband Fred was one of Olive's friends).[51] But when it came to the working-class girls, Constance's shyness was exacerbated by her social position. She had nothing in common with these women and found it hard to know what to do with herself. Worse, she realised that she herself had unconsciously been trying to 'save' them, by bringing along 'improving' books. She was embarrassed. The only truly enjoyable occasion was a night when she dressed up as Deborah Jenkyns from *Cranford*. Only when pretending to be someone else could she be comfortable.[52]

Then, one wet evening, the young women gathered around the fire, looking for an enthralling story to pass the time. Jessie Kenney volunteered to talk about her time in prison. Prison! Constance was shocked at the very idea. Worse still was the revelation that Jessie had gone to jail for her part in a suffragette demonstration. Like many people, supportive of women's rights or not, Constance thought that the suffragette tactics were 'unjustified, unreasonable, without a sense of political responsibility, and ... a bad example'.[53] But, on the other hand, Constance was interested in prison conditions and here was a unique opportunity to hear from a recent prisoner at first hand. So, setting aside her misgivings, Constance listened intently.

After working in a cotton mill, Jessie had followed her sister Annie into the suffragette movement while still a teenager. She was now private secretary to Emmeline Pethick-Lawrence as well as responsible for organising the great processions and pageants in London. She was less voluble and demonstrative than her elder sister Annie, and not as polished a speaker as some of the other suffragette leaders; she was nevertheless equally capable of making an impression. Jessie had been in prison for a month following a disturbance in Parliament Square. Constance was profoundly moved by Jessie's tale of the grim conditions in Holloway: 'The tins in which the drinking water stood were cleaned with soap and brick dust and not washed out ... the want of air in the cells; the conduct of prison officials towards the prisoners.' Hearing this first-hand account went straight to Constance's heart. There was only one redeeming feature of Holloway, it seemed: the food was good.[54]

'Got knotted up with Suffragettes down at the club in Little-hampton; through them have come into personal first-hand contact with prison abuses. The hobby of prison reform has thereby taken on new vigour,' she told Adela.[55] Constance's 'hobby' is a frustrating 'fact' in her history which has been accepted and repeated but for which there is no longer much evidence. There is no record, for example, of her being part of any organisation campaigning for prison reform. Neither does she ever mention visiting any prisons or prisoners before she became one herself. Nevertheless, she was right to conclude that 'the fact of many educated women being sent to gaol for a question of conscience must do a great deal for prison reform'.[56] This became an important issue for those suffragettes, like Sylvia Pankhurst, who were interested in broader progressive campaigns. Some of the suffragettes saw themselves as following in the footsteps of the great Victorian social reformer Elizabeth Fry and, as one suffragette put it, 'like a flame the movement swept through the prisons, purging them and purifying them'.[57] The single-minded Christabel, though, always saw prison reform as a distraction from the main prize.

What happened next showed exactly the difference an intervention from the right sort of person could make. Constance wrote to Betty complaining of what she had been told: dirty clothes to wear and dirty socks to darn; humiliating inspections and vermin in the combs. Betty passed the letter on to the Home Secretary, Herbert Gladstone, who, while saying the account was 'obviously untrustworthy', nevertheless demanded an explanation from the prison governor. That seems to have been the end of that, but it's easy to see why the suffragettes wanted to recruit Constance, who could readily access the highest authorities in the land. She even intended to meet with Sir Evelyn John Ruggles-Brise, the Commissioner of Prisons, and Dr Mary Gordon, the first woman Inspector of Prisoners.[58] It does not seem that this plan came off, though Sir Ruggles-Brise comes into this story again.

Over the next few days, Constance began to consider Jessie's cause as well as her experience. Though she still took a dim view of Jessie's militancy, she could not help but be drawn to this quiet and plain-speaking woman. Constance was already as intrigued by the personalities as by the politics in the women's movement. Emmeline and Jessie seemed to represent 'something more than themselves ... their remarkable individual powers seemed illumined and enhanced by a light that was apart from them as are the colours and patterns of a stained-glass window by the sun shining through it'.[59] Annie Kenney too was remembered with striking intensity – and typically purple prose:

> Through Annie Kenney's whole being throbbed the passion of her soul for other women, to lift from them the heavy burden, to give them life, strength, freedom, joy and the dignity of human beings, that in all things they might be treated fairly with men. It was straightforward in its simplicity, yet there was inspiration about her.[60]

Constance had several intense heart-to-heart conversations with Emmeline and Annie but was still unconvinced. It took an animal, rather than a woman, to bring home the urgency of the suffragette cause. Out for a walk in the countryside, Constance came across a sheep that had been separated from the flock and become distraught. The handlers were trying to recapture it and a crowd had gathered to laugh at the scene. The sheep 'seemed to reveal to me for the first time the position of women throughout the world. I realised how often women are held in contempt as beings outside the pale of human dignity, excluded or confined, laughed at and insulted.' Constance began to see herself as utterly ignorant. 'My sympathies had been spontaneous with regard to the wrongs of animals, of children, of men and women who belonged to down-trodden races or classes of society yet hitherto I had been blind to the sufferings peculiar to women.'[61] She was ashamed of herself.

This moment of conversion is a common feature of suffragette autobiography.[62] It's easy to see why: it's extremely dramatic and has a huge impact. But it's hard to believe that's all there is to it. In the first place, there is Constance's friendship with Olive Schreiner, one of the most prominent feminists of the day. Secondly, during her brief journalistic career she had described to Emily a projected article on the problems women faced. 'She got very excited the other night, giving me a long account of what women had to complain of, and certainly they have a right to complain if all Con says is true,' Emily wrote in a letter. 'No doubt her article will give the solution to the whole question.'[63] Finally, there is the fact that her sisters were already involved in the campaign for suffrage. Betty, together with Frances, supported the non-militants and Emily was already a member of the WSPU. Constance was unusual for women of her class in having relations who were already active in the struggle. She cannot really have been as ignorant of what they were up to as she liked to pretend. Indeed, in 1907, she had written to Aunt T backing votes for women. 'I am for it. I am impressed by practically all the arguments for it, and I have never yet heard an argument against it which I thought convincing.' A few months later, describing her politics to Dolly Ponsonby, John's sister-in-law, she came up with 'advanced – radical – socialist – individualist'.[64] In truth, Constance did not suddenly 'see the light' in the summer of 1908. What changed was that what had been abstract and distant was suddenly given human form by Jessie and Annie Kenney, and by Emmeline Pethick-Lawrence.

These is also a completely different version of the story of how Constance came to join the WSPU. Emily claims that she was actually responsible for introducing Constance to the suffragettes.[65] She had been holidaying at Littlehampton for several years and through her friend Mrs Webbe had also met Emmeline Pethick-Lawrence. Emily, like Constance, was just the sort of woman the suffragettes, with their new interest in recruiting the well-to-do, were after. Jane Ridley, biographer of Edwin Lutyens, says Emily fell for Emmeline's charms 'like a ripe plum'.[66] Soon she was selling *Votes for Women* on the seafront with her children, much to her husband's disapproval. So why would Emily be left out of Constance's story? Perhaps because by 1914, when *Prisons and Prisoners* was published, Emily had left the suffragettes far behind. Utterly opposed to all forms of violence, she reluctantly dropped out as suffragette militancy escalated. Nevertheless, Emily was ambivalent about the decision: 'I know I am right, and yet it seems so contemptible to stand aside and criticise when these other women are giving their lives,' she wrote.[67] Emily had dedicated her life to theosophy instead and didn't want her former association to taint her spiritual purity. Edwin had always been against Emily's involvement and perhaps he encouraged Constance in this omission. Or perhaps it's simply because the sheep story makes for a more dramatic yarn than Emily's account. It allows Constance to paint herself as living in ignorant isolation before she went to Littlehampton, and to make the suffragettes her saviours.

Back at home, Constance threw herself into the issue of women's suffrage. She began studying the question earnestly and went to meetings to hear directly from suffragettes. At home, she was reading extensively: she subscribed to the suffragette newspaper *Votes for Women* and ordered back copies of the annual report. She could think of nothing but suffragettes and prisons. She called *Votes for Women* 'wonderfully thrilling' and wrote to Aunt T about her 'immense admiration for the devoted workers and martyrs in the cause'.[68]

Emmeline Pethick-Lawrence took Constance under her wing in these early months. Emmeline was genuinely attracted to this shy, awkward, earnest woman, but also acutely aware of the symbolic and practical value of having a women like Constance joining the WSPU. Emmeline tried to win Constance over by urging her of the importance of the mission and the role that she could play, telling her, 'You have been led to us, for the fulfilment of your own life, for the accomplishment of your destiny and for the working out of a new deliverance for humanity.'[69] (She was not given to understatement.)

When suffragettes were released from prison they were given a reception to honour their service. Emmeline believed that these breakfasts were the best opportunity to make 'converts and enthusiastic adherents to our cause ... the sight of the women who have suffered so bravely, and their words of greeting to the heart of everyone present'.[70] She took Constance along accordingly, and was certainly proved right. These breakfasts, with their extraordinary outpourings of emotion, could have been designed exactly to appeal to Constance's profound sense of empathy. Driving to Holloway, Constance was taken through another world, defined by poverty and hopelessness, peopled by 'grim despairing faces'. But at the prison gates, a dozen prisoners came tumbling out, 'looking like children, some of them with their arms outstretched. The mixture of extreme joy and heart tugging for those still left inside was very overcoming,' she told Aunt T.[71] Almost in spite of herself, Constance was being steadily drawn in.

But though Constance now believed in the vital importance of winning the vote and was prepared to back the campaign, she still held back from total commitment. She had 'one or two serious disappointments with the policy of the Union'.[72] Betty and Frances had lunch with Margot Asquith, husband of the Prime Minister and one of the Souls connected with the Balfours. Margot railed against the suffragettes: she had been spat at and received a letter which wished her husband and children dead. Betty and Frances spoke up for the suffragettes, but it was not difficult to see why this sort of behaviour would alienate Margot, and many women like her.[73] Militant tactics were, at this point, beyond the pale.

CHAPTER FIVE

THE PANKHURSTS

'To consciences stirring uneasily with the thought: "Ought I to help?"
the militant movement appealed insistently: "Here is action! With us
stagnation and quiescence under the sufferings of women are no more.
It is your duty and your privilege to help us in the cause of your sex. You
can go to prison and win the laurels of immortality."'[1]

In February 1908, a Private Members' Bill to enfranchise women had passed its second reading in the House of Commons by a significant majority. But by the autumn it was clear the government was not going to give the Bill more parliamentary time, which meant it had no chance of becoming law. Christabel was determined to lead a new protest on the House of Commons. But what should they do to Parliament? Raid it? Storm it? Besiege it? Mabel Tuke considered the problem and came up with the idea of a 'rush' on the House of Commons.[2] The day was set for Tuesday 11 October 1908. On Monday, Christabel, her mother Emmeline and their chief organiser, 'General' Flora Drummond, were summoned to Bow Street Magistrates' Court for 'inciting the public to do a wrongful and illegal act'.[3] They refused to go. Instead, they cheekily informed the authorities that they would be available for arrest at 6 p.m. the next day, giving them time to finish preparing for the rush. The police searched the WSPU's headquarters at Clement's Inn but failed to track down the fugitives, who were hiding in the flat above. As promised, at 6 p.m. on Tuesday the leaders emerged triumphant, in full view of the press, were arrested and were taken to Bow Street.

The show went on without them. Spurred on by the thought of their beloved leaders in prison, thousands of women marched on the Houses of Parliament that evening. They were met by 5,000 policemen and 60,000 spectators. There had been a march against unemployment earlier in the day and many of the protestors had stayed on into the evening hoping to see some fun. Two women threw stones at the windows of 10 Downing Street. Another, Mrs Travers Symons, actually made it to the floor of the House of Commons, where she howled at the MPs to stop their debate until the women's question was answered. One paper wrote that 'the scene in Parliament-square was extraordinary – perhaps the most astonishing scene ever seen in this place of history',[4] but the coverage was, in general, dismissive. These were women 'doing their best to destroy their own cause', said the *Mail*, while the *Express* said that 'the cause of women's suffrage has been put back a generation by the freaks of Mrs Pankhurst and her silly followers'.[5] Thirty-six people – including twelve men – were sent to prison for three weeks following the scuffle.[6]

Constance did not take part. Earlier in the day, she had arrived at Clement's Inn and declared to Emmeline Pethick-Lawrence that although she couldn't support the deputation, she wanted to help in some way. Emmeline asked her to try to secure 'first division' status for the prisoners. This had practical advantages – since first division prisoners had more privileges – but was also symbolically important. It would mean that the suffragettes were recognised as political prisoners and not treated as common criminals.

Constance took this mission extremely seriously. It is unlikely that there was another woman in the entire movement who could have done what she did. She simply marched down to the House of Commons to find Arthur Ponsonby, who, in one of those strange coincidences of history, was now private secretary to the Home Secretary. He carried a series of notes between Constance and Gladstone back and forth, but to no avail. Gladstone said that he couldn't intervene before a sentence had been passed and still wouldn't intervene afterwards. Undeterred, Constance decided to track down the magistrate responsible for sentencing the three prisoners and appeal to his better nature.

She went first to Bow Street Magistrates' Court. The magistrate had left for the day, but a kind policeman asked if she would like to see one of the prisoners; and so Constance found herself face to face with Emmeline Pankhurst herself. She never forgot her first encounter with the 'guardian protector of the women's movement'.[7] Mrs Pankhurst appeared almost regal, despite her physical frailty, evident weariness and grim surroundings: Constance called her 'the friendly Great One'.[8] She wanted more clothes. Constance offered hers, before the wardress politely pointed out that she would probably need them in order to leave. Mrs Pankhurst then asked if Constance would try to get the three released for the night so they would be fully rested for the trial.

Constance set off again in search of the magistrate. She tracked him down through a gentlemen's club phone book and traipsed halfway across London to find him. But she accidentally had found the address for the magistrate's son. He was able to put her on the right track, but more time was lost. When she eventually found the right address, it was very late in the evening. She asked if he would see Lady Constance Lytton. 'I own the family name was dragged in here,' she told Edith later, 'but I can't think it was in a disgracing way.'[9] Of course, the magistrate refused to listen and sent her packing back to Clement's Inn where she regrouped with Emmeline Pethick-Lawrence. By now, it was very late in the evening. Emmeline was struck by the change in Constance, seeing that 'she had become since some hours earlier in the day, a transformed person. All the caution, all the mental reserve which hitherto she had maintained, had gone.'[10] The two women returned to the magistrates' court to see whether anything could be done to make the prisoners more comfortable. They were too late. The Pankhursts and Flora Drummond were enjoying a beautiful dinner from the Savoy, sent over by a friendly MP, complete with silverware and servants and comfortable beds for the night.[11] 'They don't let 'em starve,' shouted one of the crowd outside. 'No need to let them starve until it is necessary,' Constance replied.[12]

Constance had genuinely believed that a well-meaning request from a well-placed person would be enough to bend the strict rules of the English legal system. Ironically, this was the sort of abuse of social position and privilege she would soon find abhorrent. As Constance herself later admitted, it was obvious that she was 'altogether new to the rules of the game'.[13]

'We believe in Emmeline Pankhurst – Founder of the Women's Social and Political Union. And in Christabel Pankhurst, her eldest daughter, our Lady, who was inspired by the passion for Liberty – born to be a leader of women. Suffered under the Liberal government, was arrested, tried and sentenced. She descended into prison; the seventh day she returned again to the world. She was entertained to breakfast, and sat on the right hand of her mother, our glorious Leader, from thence she went forth to judge both the Government and the Antis.'[14]

The Pankhurst trial caused a sensation. Christabel had earned her law degree in 1906, but was prohibited from practising as a barrister because she was a woman: this was the first time she had been able to put her legal training to use, acting as defence lawyer as well as defendant.[15] Her defence rested on two central points. First, the word 'rush' was a mild term which could not be interpreted as incitement to violence. Second, the Liberal government itself had positively encouraged women to take these sorts of steps, just as men had done in uprisings which had preceded the Reform Acts in the nineteenth century. It is difficult to exaggerate the courage it must have taken to stand up for herself in this courtroom full of men: in those days, the magistrate, prosecutor and police were all male. Many people have criticised Christabel's leadership, her strategy and her position on everything from the First World War to sexually transmitted diseases, to religion and even to all men. But despite her questionable opinions, it is sometimes impossible to do anything but admire her exceptional bravery, and this trial was the first time the public really saw her in full flight.

With extraordinary audacity, Christabel called both the Chancellor, David Lloyd George, and the Home Secretary, Herbert Gladstone, as witnesses, and then proceeded to skewer them so precisely that the magistrate had to remind her that she was not actually allowed to cross-examine her own witness. Lloyd George, who had been in Trafalgar Square, was made to admit that he had not heard any calls to violence; in fact, he had taken his six-year-old daughter along, and eventually said that he was 'not competent to express an opinion in the witness box'. Gladstone, who had witnessed events in Trafalgar Square, was made to listen to his own words, and quotes from his famous father, used as evidence that the government encouraged the suffragettes to behave as they did. Taken to pieces by this uppity young woman, the Cabinet ministers were evasive, bad-tempered and non-committal. They were not used to being questioned by women. Christabel, in contrast, was impassioned, impressive and lethally effective. Her bold move guaranteed extensive coverage in the newspapers, which covered their trial and reported their speeches in great depth, cementing the Pankhurst name in the popular imagination. Christabel planned to call more than fifty witnesses but the magistrate, irritated that she had turned the courtroom into her personal political circus, refused to let her. This was the first time Christabel and Lloyd George would directly cross swords and she said that his rebellious, troublemaking career had actually been an example to them.[16] In the future, Lloyd George would become one of the suffragettes' main targets; they were so disruptive that he eventually banned all women from his public events.

The press fell in love with Christabel. She was described as 'Portia in the dock'[17] and Max Beerbohm wrote in the *Saturday Review*:

> Her joyousness is one of the secrets of her charm ... she is a most accomplished comedian ... she has all the qualities which an actress needs ... her whole body is alive with her every meaning ... she was like nothing so much as a little singing bird born in captivity.[18]

Constance, sat in court with rapt attention, was transfixed, and called Christabel 'the sunrise of the women's movement'.[19] She herself was called as a witness and testified that the crowd had been orderly, peaceful and well-behaved. She had been in a cab in Trafalgar Square: progress had been slow but the traffic was still moving.[20] She had not been afraid. Edith was in despair at the Lytton name appearing in the press associated with this circus. 'Of course I did not give my name to any press man, nor make a bid for publicity. I have done nothing that you need be ashamed of,' Constance wrote, but then continued, 'Wild things are like me. I shall probably do them.'[21] It's unlikely this reassured her mother much.

On the last day of the trial, Christabel faltered for the first time. Worn down by the immense strain of the past few days, she seemed on the verge of tears, and instead of her usual theatrical performance, she read nervously from a prepared script. 'Though a pale gleam of sunlight touched her face and hair, it was evident that the shadow of the gaol was already creeping into her heart,' said one paper.[22] Emmeline Pankhurst rose to the occasion instead, and gave the performance of her life. 'We have tried every way,' she told the packed courtroom.

> We have presented larger petitions than were ever presented for any other reform, we have succeeded in holding greater public meetings than men have ever had ... We have faced hostile mobs at street corners ... because we have done this, we have been misrepresented, we have been ridiculed, we have had contempt poured upon us ... we are here not because we are law-breakers; we are here in our efforts to become lawmakers.[23]

She spoke of her experiences as a guardian, of her contact with innocent women treated appallingly under existing laws and of her belief that female participation was needed to shape those laws to the realities of female experience. The *Telegraph* was impressed. 'The powerful and impassioned speech addressed to the Bench by Mrs Pankhurst will linger in the memory of all who listened to it. Anything more earnest, more intense, more appealing, in its own particular way, it would not be easy to imagine.'[24] The papers were united in their admiration of the women and only wished they were putting their considerable talents to better use.[25] Constance was likewise deeply moved. 'It was obvious to all who listened to the case that they were fighting against evil and were in all things most essentially good, so that one was awed by them,' she wrote later in *Prisons and Prisoners*.

It was not obvious to quite everyone. The magistrate found that the 'rush' handbill was likely to cause a breach of the peace; he sentenced Christabel to two months and Flora and Emmeline to three. Showing just how much he had misunderstood the dynamics of the relationship and how much prejudices about acceptable behaviour came into play, the elder women were given longer sentences because they had, in the magistrate's view, led Christabel astray. In the event, Flora served only nine days of her sentence when it became obvious that she was pregnant.

Though the Pankhursts ended their trial in prison, they emerged from the experience as national celebrities. More importantly, the press were at last taking them seriously, and detailed coverage of their arguments enabled them to reach an audience of millions. Millicent Fawcett, though, felt they had gone too far, and wrote to a friend:

> The House of Commons, with all its faults, stands for order against anarchy, for justice against brutality, and to overcome it and to invite others to endeavour to overcome it by brute force of the lowest ruffians in London was in my opinion the act either of a mad woman or a dastard.[26]

For the first time, the NUWSS distanced themselves from the militant suffragettes.

But Constance was absolutely won over. She wrote to Aunt T, 'I go deeper and deeper in my enthusiasm for the women, and even for their "tactics" as I understand it more and more – not only what they do but what has been done to them.'[27] She had seen women attempt to exercise their lawful rights in lawful ways only to be brutally rebuffed. She blamed the authorities for forcing them to behave like outlaws. She couldn't understand why men like Gladstone and Lloyd George, who, as Liberals, theoretically supported votes for women, were not doing more to achieve that end and instead had joined forces with those trying to silence the women. They made a stark contrast with the WSPU leaders. As she wrote later,

Mrs Pankhurst was the most noble, Mrs Drummond the most practical, Miss Christabel Pankhurst the most clever. She appeared to me to be the most far-seeing, the least depressed by wrongs although she would work day and night for their redress ... She saw far off the attainment of that for which we in darkness strove.[28]

Constance was not content to simply support the suffragettes with her money, time or title. She had to become a suffragette herself. 'I needed no converting now,' she wrote in *Prisons and Prisoners*, 'and my only wish was to convince my mother.'[29]

This would prove impossible. Edith was horrified by Constance's choice and remained implacably against it. It was difficult for Edith to understand and accept her daughter's new cause when Constance had spent forty years acquiescing to her every wish with barely a murmur of dissent. She might perhaps have understood such a rebellion from Emily, but not her beloved, obedient Constance. 'Poor Mother talked of the disgrace to her name and you would have thought Con had done some real crime. She was quite ill over it and is still very seedy and upset. I am truly sorry for her, but I feel more sorry for Con that at her age she may not follow her own principles,' Emily wrote to Edwin, with generosity, and perhaps even a hint of regret that she wasn't sharing in the drama. Edwin, though, would clearly not have allowed it: 'I do feel mightily sympathetic for angel mother, Connie being mixed in print with such a crew of notorious rioters – and I sympathise Connie [*sic*] too, but Mrs P. Lawrence is so very very second rate and I suppose they are all like it.'[30] (A recent arrival to the upper classes, Edwin could not afford the Lytton unconventionality and as a consequence always seems much stuffier than his in-laws.) There is no doubt that Edith had made many emotional demands on Constance, and Constance had, until this point, let her. But it is too easy to make Edith into the villain of Constance's story. Few mothers would react well to the news that their middle-aged daughter had suddenly taken to political protest, provoking the police and jaunting off to prison (unless they were Emmeline Pankhurst). Yet Edith always welcomed Constance back home after her suffragette adventures and was deeply worried about the impact on Constance's frail health. She was uninterested in votes for women but did care about women's rights and fervently wished to see women ordained in the church.[31] She wrote to Constance:

> You don't realise one bit what I feel of real misery at the work of your leaders, which I feel is really wicked and wrong, and leading to murder being done as a noble duty, which is against all my principles and beliefs and I see it is all spoiling my beloved perfect child.[32]

Constance had frequent fits of guilt about the impact her behaviour had on her mother, though none were strong enough to make her change her mind. She did not, however, give up hoping that her mother would not only accept her decision but support it. 'My hope has been all along that I should be able to take you into my confidence, that I should have the perhaps all undeserved yet heaven-like joy of knowing that though you could not share my views yet that you would understand why I had them,'[33] she wrote, pleadingly, to Edith. For the first time, she believed that she had a duty which transcended her obligations to her mother. But Constance would never have that heaven-like joy. Her decision remained incomprehensible to Edith. Even now, at first sight it seems baffling. After nearly forty years of genteel inactivity, why should Constance suddenly become, 'a whole hogger',[34] as she called herself? Why not, as her sisters did, simply collect signatures, host tea parties and stay on the right side of respectability?

At the time, Constance's actions seemed to many reading the papers to illustrate the dangers of being a single woman. Without a

man to keep her in line or children to keep her occupied, it was unsurprising that she was drawn to the suffragettes. Even her brother
Neville said she was 'ripe for conversion, for she had not the cares
of a family and she wanted an object in life'.[35] The spinster had once
been a benevolent and kindly figure in popular culture; now, she
became something sinister and even threatening.

In fact, it does not take much imagination to see why Constance
should have become attached to the suffragettes, despite her shyness and diffidence, despite incredible differences of class and background, despite her illnesses and ailments. Constance always committed herself wholeheartedly to whatever she did, even if, until
now, she had done very little. When her father died, she set aside
all her own needs to devote herself to her mother in a way that
made her siblings a little uneasy. There was no need for her to do
so much. 'She adored to serve,' wrote Neville. 'The more thorough
her service, the more happy she became. It was obvious from the
first that she would become a militant, because militancy involved
a greater degree of sacrifice.'[36] As Constance herself wrote to Adela
in 1900, 'What I hunger for most is to be able to serve those I love.
I don't want their respect, but that they should need me, whether
as a servant or a toy or a wife.'[37] Ray Strachey, one of the first historians of the struggle for the vote and herself a devotee of Millicent Fawcett, was always scornful of the suffragettes, arguing that
they attracted drama queens, hero-worshippers and martyrs.[38] The
WSPU demanded everything, but Constance was prepared to give
everything. It was what she had always been waiting for, though she
had not realised it till now. At last, there was an alternative to the
quiet life at home and the retreat onto the sofa.

What is more difficult to explain, perhaps, is the apparent
transformation in her personality. She was universally admired for
her kindness, sympathy and gentleness: now she would become a
self-proclaimed 'hooligan'. Too crippled by her shyness to speak

to people, now she would be thrust into the spotlight, speaking to huge crowds and regularly written up by the press. But was it really so out of character? Two decades before joining the suffragettes, she wrote to Aunt T, 'I am often at my happiest when I am doing what is thought to be disagreeable.'[39] The only way to explain this is to understand the sense of duty which was impressed into every fibre of her being: indeed, as she once said, her family had been 'founded on chivalry without social distinction'[40] and she was simply following this Lytton tradition. Her notion of public service may have been very different from her father's, but it was no less important to her. Yet her siblings could never accept or endorse her commitment to violence, and it was to separate and isolate her from them in the coming years. Constance completely accepted what Christabel believed: that every possible course of action had been exhausted and the suffragettes had no choice left but violence. Her siblings saw alternatives; Constance did not.

In the WSPU, however, she had the friendship, admiration and support of hundreds of other women: a ready-made family to replace the family she was leaving behind. The suffragettes had extraordinarily strong ties of sisterhood which were more than compensation for the hardships they suffered in prison or the humiliations they were subjected to on the streets. If Constance had been set on pursuing music, journalism or her relationship with John Ponsonby, she could perhaps have done so, but she would have been entirely alone. Now, for the first time in her life, she had friends. The profound ties of allegiance, so deep and binding, went far beyond the realms of ordinary friendship. This was a revelation for Constance. Until that time, her understanding of friendship had been limited to the superficial relationships she had made with Betty's friends. She was too shy and awkward to make a friend of her own: 'Every attempt to make a friend failed; the rebuffs I received seemed to turn one part of me to stone.'[41] The suffragettes made Constance realise just how lonely she was, at home with only her mother for company. Their presence filled the void she barely knew existed. The suffragette leadership gave Constance something above and beyond even this exquisite friendship: something to believe in, someone to follow. Her spiritual side responded powerfully. 'My life was literally transformed by contact with the four great leaders,'[42] she said, counting Mabel Tuke alongside Emmeline Pankhurst, Christabel Pankhurst and Emmeline Pethick-Lawrence.

The suffragettes gave Constance an entirely new way of looking at her life. She had never before connected her personal frustrations and disappointments to the political oppression of women. Joining the women's movement made her see that she could hope and strive for something better, grasp at new possibilities and fulfil her potential.[43] In this, she was like many women who, as Ray Strachey described, 'read into the Cause not only what lay upon the surface, but all the discontents which they, as women, were suffering; their economic dependence; their conventional limitations, and all the multitude of trifles which made them hate being women'.[44]

The suffragettes also offered Constance a sense of purpose and excitement. 'If you could see the look in the eyes of the shop-women when I gave my name recently in London!' she wrote to Aunt T in exultation.[45] Constance was by no means the only woman who found her calling in the suffragette movement. 'What the movement did was to make me think and then to believe that I could do things for myself,' recalled one suffragette. 'And I did!'[46] Many came to see their time in the WSPU as the turning point in their lives, a transformational experience that defined them. These years were long, dangerous and uncertain, but for women who had lived hemmed in on all sides by convention and restraint, they were also unbelievably exciting and rich with possibilities. This quote is typical of the revelation which suffragettes experienced:

The militant suffrage was the very salt of life. The knowledge of it had come like a draught of fresh air into our padded, stifled lives. It gave us release of energy ... the sense of being some use in the scheme of things ... it made us feel that we were part of life and not just outside watching it.[47]

The WSPU was liberating for Constance, but she was good for them too. Though the union had its roots in the labour movement and many of the members were either sympathetic to or members of the Labour Party, Christabel and Emmeline had long since decided – to Sylvia's consternation – that working women would not win the battle for them. Instead, they deliberately sought out and courted women with money, power and connections, believing – rightly, if cynically – that these women would attract attention and publicity. In *Votes for Women*, Christabel argued that 'it is especially the duty of women of distinction and influence to show their earnestness and devotion to this cause by taking part in the militant movement'.[48] 'The political and geographical heartland of such a campaign,' says the historian Martin Pugh, 'was not Lancashire or the East End but Chelsea, Kensington, Holland Park, and, increasingly, the Home Counties.'[49] Constance was by no means the only well-connected woman who was drawn to the suffragettes: another was Frances Parker, the niece of Lord Kitchener, and still another was Mildred Mansell, a cousin of the Liberal Chief Whip.[50] Constance was, however, the biggest 'name', and hence the biggest prize of all. Hooking Lady Constance Lytton was a masterstroke. Edith always felt that Constance was being used and certainly Constance fell completely under their spell. But Edith could never come to terms with the idea that her beloved daughter would choose to join these outcasts and outlaws voluntarily.

'My sister knew perfectly well that the publicity value of her name was considerable, and she herself saw to it that her public conduct should be courageous and honourable, so that by it the cause should be advanced,' Neville stated.[51] The suffragettes were mistresses of propaganda and public relations, and having the Lytton name, with all its aristocratic associations, was akin to a celebrity endorsement for a brand today. Constance absolutely knew what she was doing and she well understood what being a Lytton entailed. She was not hypnotised nor duped nor even gently persuaded into anything. She made her choices with her eyes fully open to the consequences.

Once convinced that the suffragettes were on the side of righteousness, the next step was to start working for them. She eased her way in gently, going to London to help gather signatures for a petition to the King asking for suffragettes to be treated as political prisoners. For the first time, she encountered women who were unenthusiastic, lukewarm or even positively opposed to suffrage; finding 'people who either couldn't [sign] because of their official position or their husbands wouldn't let them, or merely refused with shocked faces'. More significantly, perhaps, Victor made his first speech on women's suffrage. He had sat in the Lords for several years but had not yet made any particular mark, unlike his friend and contemporary Winston Churchill. Now, under Constance's influence, he began tentatively to fight this most unpopular of battles and to impress those who heard him speak.[52]

At the end of December, Constance was at WSPU headquarters to welcome Mrs Pankhurst home on early release. She wrote to thank the Home Secretary, Herbert Gladstone, for this delightful Christmas present. 'I have seldom seen so many beaming countenances or experienced such a sense of bubbling happiness as I found there,' she told him.[53] But this event also sharpened her sense that she lacked credibility. 'I got in with the two Miss Brackenburys and another girl, ex-prisoner too, who said she could not go in again, as it would cost her livelihood,' she told Aunt T ruefully. 'I felt an awful fraud amongst that truly serving lot.'[54] If Constance was going to become a militant suffragette, she felt she would have to do more than the ordinary suffragette, to compensate in some way for her privileges and advantages. In the meantime, she sent a copy of Robert's poetry to Annie Kenney as a Christmas present, and said, 'When I look back – over all that has happened since – to our Littlehampton days together I feel that years must have gone by.'[55] She signed herself Sister Conny. Emmeline Pethick-Lawrence was called 'Sister Emmeline' by the women in the Esperance Club, but Annie and Jessie were too conscious of Constance's nobility and it never caught on.[56]

In January, Constance wrote her first pamphlet for the cause, dismantling the arguments of those who were against votes for women. She was keen to point out that she doesn't believe in the superiority of women, merely that without women's views being represented, especially on questions which primarily affect them, the issues cannot be satisfactorily addressed.[57] Interestingly, both in view of her own background and the Pankhursts' views, Constance puts her faith in the 'working women, unshielded by social privilege' who 'see with more directness than those in the leisured classes'.[58] She was already questioning the established social hierarchy and the privileges of her own class, believing that women who know more of real life and real hardship should direct the future. This is a more radical viewpoint than most women of her class, even those who were in favour of the vote, would be prepared to countenance. It is worth remembering that many of the 'working women' Constance so championed would not actually benefit from the policy that the suffragettes were pursuing: the right to vote on the same terms as men. Many would be excluded by the property qualifications. Either Constance had not fully thought through the implications of the policy, or she took an optimistic view of the numbers who would qualify, or else she saw a partial franchise as a step towards full suffrage. It is also noteworthy, given Constance's interest in working women and their living conditions, that she was drawn to Christabel and not Sylvia Pankhurst. Sylvia's politics were far to the left of Christabel's, and she would spend many years among the working women of the East End of London, striving alongside them for a better life. Nevertheless, for Constance, it was Christabel and Emmeline who were the heart and soul of the women's movement. They were the leaders to be followed, at any cost.

Constance had already been given a taste of some of the anti-suffrage sentiment in the country, and quotes an anonymous letter she has received, which describes suffragettes as 'common scolds and viragos, who are fortunate to live in an age which has forgotten the use of the ducking stool'.[59] But what comes across most strongly in this booklet is her admiration for the suffragettes.

> The women in this movement are pledged to it by their belief in it, by their devotion to it, by their service for it. The greater the call for their labours and their heroism, the greater their response. The more the sphere of legitimate action is narrowed for them, the greater the pressure of their cramped enthusiasm, and, whatever the cost, they do not yield.[60]

Constance was impressed and inspired by the suffragettes; and felt enveloped by the warmth of their welcome. She could not wait to truly become one of them. But when she offered the pamphlet to Leo Maxse, her old editor at the *National Review*, he wrote back to say that he 'thought female Suffrage would be worse than German invasion in the way of national calamity'.[61] It was a small foretaste of what they were up against.

CHAPTER SIX

HOLLOWAY

'The poor prisoner, when she entered Holloway, dropped, as it were, into a tomb. No letters and no visitors were allowed for the first month of a sentence ... kept in solitary confinement in a narrow, dimly lit cell, twenty-three hours out of the twenty-four.'[1]

Constance was ready to take the next step and become a militant herself. On 28 January 1909, she wrote to Emmeline Pankhurst, offering herself up for the next deputation of women who would attempt to petition the Prime Minister. She was accepted and did not have long to wait. The King's Speech, on 16 February, made no mention of women's suffrage, and Christabel immediately wrote to *The Times* to announce their intention to pay Asquith a visit. 'Upon his attitude to this deputation the future policy of the Union will depend.'[2] In the meantime, Muriel Matters hired an airship emblazoned with 'Votes for Women' and sailed over London, while Jessie Kenney, discovering that postal regulations allowed people to be sent through the mail, posted two 'human letters' to Downing Street. There was still room for a sense of humour and a sensational gesture.

Elsewhere, Constance was making her first faltering attempts to become a speaker for the cause. Speakers were sent all around the country to address meetings of assembled suffragettes, to inspire them on to greater service. Sometimes opponents came along to heckle them, but Constance didn't mind this, since it sharpened her sense of the just righteousness of the cause and of the suffragettes as David fighting a Goliath of public hostility. Those who came out of the meetings as converts or even recruits made it all worthwhile. Constance was not a natural orator, unlike the Pankhursts or even her brother. But she screwed up her courage, and was determined to practise. 'I always "perorate" on origin of "nobility", and spirit of suffragette motto "To defend the oppressed, to fight for the defenceless, not counting the cost", and that always unites the audience in loud approval,' she told Betty.[3] Back at home, there was an awkward encounter with Margot Asquith in which she tried to prove 'I was still same-as-Con – not a maniac, or wild'un'. Both of them were nervous, and made difficult small talk before getting down to business. 'She most civil and sympathetic ... but I felt she did not really want to hear.'[4] Adela's infant son died of meningitis at this time; Constance represented her at the funeral as Adela could not bring herself to go.[5] She was also arranging the English publication of Olive Schreiner's latest work, which came out as *A Closer Union* in 1909.[6]

On 24 February, Constance headed for London without breathing a word of her plans to her mother. Her letter home makes clear how much her mother depended on her for all things practical: 'The account papers, tradesmen addresses, wages paper are in the lift-up place of desk on dining-room writing table,' she wrote. 'I expect I shall be away from you a month. The others will cling round you. If I were going on a trip abroad you would not resent the separation. In my little warm nest in Holloway my only thought of the outer world will be of you.'[7] It's a curious mix of reassurance and wilfulness. She cannot have thought for a second that Edith would be mollified by the idea that a prison sentence was anything like 'a trip abroad'.

This was the dramatic evening described in the preface. It wasn't an especially violent night by suffragette standards, though for the innocent Constance it was yet another eye-opening experience. Her new-found sense of solidarity with working-class women permeated even the tumult of her first protest. From among the jeers in the crowd, one remark cut through to her: 'Go home and do your washing.' That has echoes even today in the way that women who get ideas above their station are told to get back to the kitchen. Constance, of course, had never had to work in her kitchen or do her own laundry. But she loved cleaning, as we have seen, and she was fascinated by washing. 'If there is one single industry highly deserving of recognition throughout the world of human existence and of representation under parliamentary systems, it is surely that of the washers, the renewers week by week, the makers clean.'[8] That was enough to keep her fixed on her goal throughout the evening.

After her arrest, Constance's emotions were in turmoil. She was filled with pride, with a sense of unity with her sisters and a belief in the importance of her work. On the one hand: 'For the first time in my life I felt of some use; since we were all so different from each other, it seemed we could each contribute something to the general solidarity of experience, of opinion, of conduct.'

And yet, on the other:

I felt, for about the fiftieth time that I had come in touch with the WSPU, ashamed of myself in their presence ... some had to face a situation in their homes more distressing even than my own. My little share of difficulty and sacrifice, of risk and dread, which had completely filled my horizon for so many weeks, seemed insignificant enough now.[9]

What lengths would she have to go to in order to truly feel she was one of them?

Constance was allowed to return home before her trial and sentence but she had been so caught up in the excitement, she hadn't organised a place to stay. The only place she could think of was Betty's house and towards midnight, dropping with exhaustion, she made it to safety. Betty was out, having gone to a play, but Emily was there and reported Constance's state to Edwin.

> I said jokily 'Are you arrested?' and she said yes. She was in an awful state of exhaustion and collapse with a racking headache, but happily we got her hot water and bottles, and she recovered ... how she did it all I can't imagine. Betty came in at 12 o'c. and we had a good talk till about 1, when I went to bed, and we put Con to bed, but I am afraid she got no sleep, but Bets rubbed her and was with her, and we were so happy we could be together.[10]

The next day, Constance returned to Bow Street Magistrates' Court to be sentenced, accompanied by Betty. She was one of a dozen suffragettes on trial, including Emmeline Pethick-Lawrence. One or two others, including Daisy Solomon and Rose Lamartine Yates, would become comrades and correspondents in the future. Constance stood in the dock, utterly unashamed, and triumphant. She said that she 'was more proud to be able to stand by her friends ... than of anything else she had done in her life'. She said that the suffragettes must have an opportunity of making their case, however much the government wanted to ignore them.[11] Constance got her reward in the form of a blessing from Christabel Pankhurst herself.

> She said 'thank you,' and seemed grateful for my share in the day's work. This was a most unlooked-for honour and joy, from that moment I felt a very privileged and happy person. The sound of her voice and the look in her eyes remained stamped upon my mind, and played the part of a sort of consolation whenever the trials of imprisonment weighed upon my spirits.[12]

There was no keeping her name or her face out of the paper now. The photo of her in the *Daily Mirror* took up half a page. Beatrice Webb saw her and was moved to write to Betty:

> It is magnificent and it is war. That is what I felt when I saw that Lady Constance had been taken up. She has done emphatically the right thing, because she is the right person to do it, with her charm and refinement, and also her delicacy, and last, but not least, her name.[13]

Emily and Betty were determined to stand by her, as was Neville. 'Her action is one of real courage and courage is the rarest and noblest of all human qualities. I am sure father would have been proud of her as no-one knew better than he the value of courage,' he wrote to Edith.

> I think also that her action, in view of the natural timidity and delicacy and horror of publicity, will do a great deal for the cause which she has at least. She is so little like the typical tub thumper that her strength at this moment will astonish her friends and enemies and will prove what a splendid thing faith is which overcomes all difficulties.[14]

Betty also wrote to *The Times*, challenging their coverage of the deputation. Their reporter said the women had been scratching and pushing the police, as well as doling out 'a vigorous if totally ineffective and unimpressive lashing of the tongue of sarcasm and abuse'; none of this had come up in court and in fact the police had testified that the women were quiet and orderly after arrest.[15] Given that Constance always stressed her isolation, it is important to remember that, in fact, her siblings did their best to be loyal and supportive: they only disagreed with her on the necessity of violence.

Having committed herself to going to prison, she was as excited as a child going on a school trip to finally get there. She was thrilled to discover that she was able to indulge her love of cleaning. What the other women dreaded or accepted as inevitable, Constance embraced as a treat. Her biggest concern during these first few days was that she would have to get up early, because she was not a morning person. Constance enjoyed making fun of herself and her naivety at these moments, but as the academic Marie Mulvey-Roberts points out, her use of humour may well be a way of keeping trauma at bay; making light of an experience means that she can contain it, not be consumed by it.[16]

Despite her determination to avoid special treatment, she sometimes gave in to temptation. The brutality of her arrest was still affecting her health, and she asked to be allowed to follow her vegetarian diet and wear flannel underwear to keep warm. Outside the prison, Victor had demanded to see the head of the Prisons Commissioners and then insisted that she also be allowed flannel bedsocks. Constance also allowed herself to receive a letter from Edith and a visit from Betty. Her response to that visit gives some sense of the utter loneliness and uncertainty that she could barely allow herself to acknowledge lest it defeat her. 'The joy of it' – seeing Betty – 'seems so exaggerated, I cannot trust myself to convey it,' she wrote in *Prisons and Prisoners*.[17] But Constance was in so much emotional confusion that instead of conveying her delight she somehow managed to tell her sister off. Her inability to put this right caused her great anguish in the many silent hours ahead.

Constance was unpleasantly surprised to find herself at first in the prison hospital instead of the ordinary cells. This was not part of her plan at all. The hospital patients were waited on hand and foot by other prisoners, whereas Constance 'wanted to share the lot of the bulk of my Suffragette companions … to know from my own experience the routine life of ordinary prisoners'.[18] It seemed to be an effort on the part of the authorities to keep their aristocratic inmate away from the routine degradations of ordinary prison life. The one advantage of being kept apart was that she shared the hospital wing with Emmeline Pethick-Lawrence, who took the opportunity to instruct her disciple, telling stories of suffragette heroism and derring-do. Emmeline wasn't ill either: she was being isolated from the other suffragettes so that they didn't rally around her and use her as a focus for rebellion. One night, Emmeline recited some of Olive Schreiner's *Dreams*, attracting a rapt audience and reminding Constance not only of her beloved Olive but also her father: *Dreams* had been one of Robert's favourites.[19]

But Constance was determined to prove to the authorities that she was well enough to be sent to ordinary prison. She refused the extra food offered to hospital patients and stubbornly slept on a mattress on the floor instead of a bed. When that failed, she decided on a more dramatic course of action. She would scratch the words 'Votes for Women' across herself.

The first problem was to find something to do it with: she decided she couldn't spare a hairpin. She managed to squirrel away a blunt needle and began her work. She managed a 'V' over her heart and then eyed it dubiously. 'I remained in doubt as to whether my evil deed had been sufficiently impressive.'[20] Eventually she decided, with 'a craftsman's satisfaction', that it would do: she demanded a plaster and some action. If she was not released to join her comrades in the prison itself, she would continue to scratch at herself, ensuring that when she was released her face would be scarred and she would tell the world why. The prison authorities gave in and discharged her from the hospital. They had not listened when she had tried to reason with them: they only responded to violence. Constance believed the same principle would apply to the broader struggle.

Though it pales in comparison to her later acts as Jane Warton, and though she executed it poorly, this act of self-mutilation was an extraordinary thing for Constance to do. This was a woman crippled by shyness, who hated to be the centre of attention, and here she was, demanding to be looked at. It was also, I believe, a unique act: I have not found any other references to suffragettes who cut themselves in this way.[21]

Prison was an anthropology experiment for Constance. It was a chance to become immersed in the lives of some of the most wretched women in society. The suffragettes were not kept apart from ordinary prisoners. These prisoners were nothing like the working-class women who lived around the estate at Knebworth: they were from slums where the poverty was beyond anything Constance had experienced or could imagine. 'Their faces wore an expression of extreme dejection; the lifeless, listless way they walked, enhanced the lack of entire detachment of one from the other; in spite of being so closely herded each seemed in a world of her own individual sorrow.' She was moved both by their sheer numbers and their accumulated weight of misery and also by a few individuals with particularly heart-breaking stories. By and large, Constance saw these women as victims of circumstance who needed 'the opportunity to mend their own lives, better conditions of work, fairer payment, and above all a more honourable recognition of their service as women' – in short, everything that they lacked because they could not vote. The suffragette cause was vital to helping these women. 'I thought of them as beads of a necklace, detached, helpless and useless, and wondered how long it would be before they were threaded together by means of the women's movement into a great organised band.'[22] Her ability to empathise with, rather than judge, these women is striking. But there is also some truth to Neville's view that 'Conny believed there was no such thing as a genuine criminal; she thought that all imprisonment was the result of miscarriage of justice, or defective education, or the vicious constitution of society'.[23] She could not see their flaws as well as their strengths, and so failed to see them as real people.

Nevertheless, Constance believed that working-class women were worth much more than women of her own class. Their experience was authentic, their problems were genuine and they needed a political voice much more than she did. Compared with them, the women of her class lived 'futile, superficial, sordidly useless lives, quarrelling in their marriage market, revelling in their petty triumphs, concerned continually with money ... they are the dross, the dead fruit ... they act upon the social organism in a way that is almost wholly harmful'.[24] This is strong condemnation for her friends, acquaintances and even her sisters.

But she did not, and would never, condemn the individual wardresses who worked in the prison. She did not blame them for their unkindnesses or abruptness: she understood that these were women who were a product of a brutal system. Unlike nearly all the other prisoners – Emmeline Pethick-Lawrence being, perhaps, the only other exception – Constance was from a class far above the wardresses: in different circumstances, they would have been taking her orders and this influenced the way she treated them. One wardress suffered from a constant, hacking cough, and Constance, sympathetic to nagging illnesses, proposed to help by rubbing the woman's chest. She saw nothing wrong or inappropriate in her suggestion. She also made elaborate and secret plans to meet with one of the wardresses once she was free. This came to nothing, perhaps because the wardress was scared of discovery.

While prison was as grim and bleak as Constance had expected, she was not prepared for the mental and emotional toll that the experience took on her. She usually enjoyed silence and solitude, but now talking was entirely forbidden and conversations were conducted in hurried whispers. She fell prey to a 'morbid depression of spirits' and found prison 'gave one the feeling of belonging to a race apart, something degraded and imbecile, despised not only for the particular crime one had committed but as an all-round inferior being'. She was saved from being overwhelmed by remaining outside her own experience. 'I in no sense regarded myself as a criminal, and was aware of a detached spectator's commentary running through my mind,'[25] she wrote in *Prisons and Prisoners*. She had to maintain this sense of herself as an observer, a stranger gathering notes to report back to the outside world, in order to survive.

What she experienced was much worse than she was prepared for. Constance came to see the prison as a 'hive of hideous purpose from which flows day by day into the surrounding city a stream of evil honey, blackened in the making and poisonous in result'.[26] There was no thought given to rehabilitation, no attempt to address either criminal behaviour or its causes. Instead, everything about the prison system seemed designed to infantilise the women. They were treated like children, not expected to respect the wardresses, just obey them. It was almost unbearable. But Constance knew her time behind bars, however gruelling, would only ever be temporary. Most of the other prisoners would be in for years and their lives outside prison would scarcely be better than their lives inside.

On 24 March, Constance and twenty-five other women were released. Five hundred supporters came to their breakfast and Constance gave her first reported speech to a rapturous reception. She told the crowd that the worst that had happened to her in prison was the thought of giving that speech. She said she had been forbidden ink and so had made her notes in her own blood; even at the most serious moments of her life, she still kept her sense of humour. Otherwise, though the prison system was 'ghastly', she had been treated with 'every consideration' and had 'an exceptionally good time'.[27] Mary Neal was in the audience to see just how far Constance had come since their Littlehampton holiday. 'For nearly an hour 400 people were kept spellbound,' she told Betty.

Without the slightest self-consciousness, or self of any sort, and in
her particularly charming voice she gave her acct [sic] ... I could
not help feeling that the spirit which was in her words must eventually be too strong for any Government. I do not think Conny's
physical health will suffer; she has something beyond mere
physical strength.[28]

With the applause echoing in her ears, Constance must have been
flushed with pride. For the first time since joining the movement,
she felt credible. She had earned her 'Holloway degree',[29] a term she
coined that gained currency in the movement. She could now take
her place among the suffragettes. 'Holloway has been the greatest,
most wonderful experience of my life. How I long to tell you things
that have burnt into my brain and heart forever,' she told Aunt T.[30]

Constance was becoming ever more radicalised. She doesn't ever
use the words 'socialism' or 'socialist' in *Prisons and Prisoners* – perhaps this would have been the final straw for Lady Lytton – but
with her profound sense of empathy, it is unsurprising that this is
where she ended up. Constance was now in self-imposed exile from
her class.

Her apparent transformation was difficult for her family to com-
prehend. Betty took her two eldest children to meet Constance and
found her unrecognisable. 'I realised that she no longer belonged to
us. She belonged to her union, and nothing else really counted.'[31]
This radical change, of course, had the greatest impact on Edith.
Judith told Betty, 'She is lost to your mother for ever, just as a tamed
hawk which has shaken off its hood and flown away into the sky.'[32]
Even Frances Balfour said to Betty, 'I have tea with them tomorrow,
but I hope I need not talk any form of Suffrage. I think it is boring,
and in my heart I am giving up hope of it.'[33] There is a family story
that after her release the family got together to hear her story.
Someone asked her about the biggest mark prison had left on her.

She said fiercely, 'I learned – to hate!' This must have been staggering to the family, who knew her only as gentle and kind. The object of this hatred was the prison chaplain, who seemed entirely lacking in empathy and understanding, lecturing the women on the wickedness of stealing, even when starving.[34]

Once released, Constance tried to rekindle friendships with some of the women she had met. One woman in the hospital had a broken leg which caused her undue agony for not being cared for properly; Constance lobbied the Home Office until she was granted £500 in compensation.[35] This act of kindness was typical of Constance, more so than the grander gestures designed to attract attention and maximise impact. Such acts came from the heart, without an eye on political strategy.

Her spell in Holloway gained her instant notoriety. Particular attention was paid to her claim that she had been badly affected by hearing the screams of a woman who was facing the death sentence. The point was even raised in Parliament. According to the Home Office, the child murderer was perfectly quiet and ordinary, though Constance might have heard an insane woman shrieking.[36] One woman's screams sound much like another.

This exchange bothered Constance enough to write to Gladstone about it. First, women sentenced to death for murdering their children were always reprieved, though this was not widely understood; she therefore thought it was inhumane that the women were not told this when they were sentenced. She would repeat this point on several occasions, which gained her an unfortunate reputation for being soft on child murderers.[37] She did not defend their actions, but she did understand the circumstances which might lead women to extreme solutions. This distinction was too subtle for some audiences. Second, she told Gladstone, the insane woman should not have been allowed to scream out her pain alone: she might be insane, but she was still a person. Finally, she wrote, 'I cannot help thinking that the information conveyed by the prison officials to the Home Office is not always correct.' This mistrust of the government's version of events would only intensify as she became more closely acquainted with official bureaucracy.[38]

Gladstone responded, and Constance wrote back gratefully: 'I have always heard from your friends of your keenness for reforms & of yr unlimited kindness of heart ... But I know something of the hindering handicaps which cling around the high official posts supposedly all powerful.'[39] He may have seemed kind at this moment, but soon Gladstone would represent to Constance and the suffragettes the worst excesses of government violence, brutality and abuse.

CHAPTER SEVEN

MILITANT

'The militant suffrage movement, which in its early days was like a
dancing singing mountain stream, became a raging torrent like the
Zambezi where at the Victoria Falls it hurls itself into a chasm, gathers
itself together and proceeds along a narrow defile with terrific and
overpowering momentum.'[1]

In the spring of 1909, Constance got more involved in the day-to-day business of the WSPU. Invigorated by her experience in prison, she gained in confidence and became one of the most prominent suffragettes. Christabel welcomed her deepening commitment and wrote to Betty saying 'how brave and fine your sister is to go on with her work without any timidity or hesitation, tho' she knows of her heart weakness'.[2]

Constance believed it was her duty to set aside her shyness in order to better serve the movement. That duty began at home. One of her first acts on leaving prison was to give a talk about her experiences to local women. It did not go well and she was embarrassed. She would need to raise her game if she was to become an effective speaker for the movement around the country. But her local listeners were forgiving of her shortcomings. The North Herts Women's Suffrage Association was established, replacing a Hitchin off-shoot of the London's Society. Victor became president, and Charlotte Bernard Shaw, George's wife, was a vice-president, though Constance does not seem to have done more than go to the first meeting.[3]

In April, she was at a breakfast of 500 supporters to welcome Emmeline Pethick-Lawrence out of prison; Emmeline was given a car. With Annie Kenney and Emmeline Pethick-Lawrence, Constance was one of the first women to plant a tree in the garden at Bath dedicated to commemorating the suffragette campaign, which would become known as 'Annie's arboretum'. This garden belonged to Colonel Blathwayt and his family, who were loyal supporters of the suffragettes. Their home outside Bristol became a place where the women could rest, recover and plot their next moves. It wasn't only the militants who were acknowledged in this way: Betty was later honoured with a holly tree.[4] In the photo taken to mark the occasion, Annie stands neatly, hands behind her back, turning her direct gaze straight at the camera. Emmeline is smiling, posing with a shovel full of earth, though the planting is clearly complete. Constance leans on the fence surrounding the new shrub, disregarding the photographer, lost in thought.[5] Annie and Emmeline remained her closest friends and mentors in the movement; she consulted them both on ambitious but vague plans to 'tackle Hertfordshire' and 'do something' in Ireland. Annie was the organiser for the west of England at this time, so Constance particularly wanted to campaign in Bath and Bristol, and regretted that she could not give Annie more of her time. She particularly admired Annie as a speaker and tried to emulate her style, instead of her own 'vague jumbly thoughts'. Standing on a stage and addressing a crowd was always a difficult experience for Constance, who never outgrew her shyness and awkwardness. 'I do wish I could feel some control over my speechifying instead of feeling it get on the top of me & grip me with terror-making claws,' she sighed to Annie.[6]

In May, Constance's first article in *Votes for Women*, 'Putting Back the Clock', was published. What mattered was not how

Robert's time as Viceroy of India was personally and professionally very difficult.

stance and her mother loved each other deeply,
heir relationship was emotionally complex: Edith
anded Constance's full attention.

Pretending to be someone else always gave
the awkward and shy Constance courage.

Constance shown here as Prince Charming to Betty's Cinderella.

The young Victor Lytton took this family photograph of Robert surrounded by – from left – Emily, Neville, Constance, Betty and Edith.

Edith was both a grande dame and a loving mother, shown here with Constance (left) and Betty.

An imposing view of Knebworth House, as Constance would have known it at the turn of the century.

... were always an important part of ...tance's life: she found them much easier ...ate to than people.

Constance's frequent illnesses are very apparent in this picture.

In 1908, Victor could finally afford to move back to Knebworth: this picture taken to mark the occasion gives some idea of how large the extended family had become.

Constance on trial at Bow Street magistrates' court: sentenced to one month for her part in a suffragette deputation. © *Mirrorpix*

Her imprisonment at Holloway was a transform experience for Constance. © *Museum of London*

re image with a smile: Constance is wearing the medal earned as part of her 'Holloway degree'.

Victor, around the time he was working on the Conciliation Bill.

Betty was a leading Conservative supporter of extending the vote to women.

Emily joined the WSPU before Constance but left the organisation when the women turned to violence.

Neville at work in his studio: he was less politically active than his siblings.

'Jane Warton' – the infamous disguise that Constance adopted to prove the government's double standards. Constance Lytton was not force-fed; Jane Warton was.

© *Museum of London*

Constance next to Annie Kenney in the suffragettes' procession to mark the coronation in 1911.

© *Museum of London*

Constance with Annie Kenney, Emmeline Pethick-Lawrence, Christabel Pankhurst and Sylvia Pankhurst, on their way to lobby the Prime Minister, in November 1911. © *Museum of London*

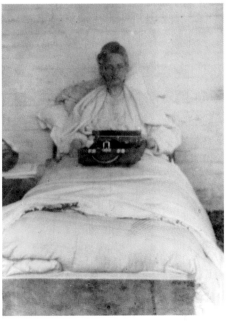

After her stroke, Constance was confined to bed and unable to write: her friends clubbed together to buy her this typewriter.

Rail: KNEBWORTH, G.N.R.
Telegrams: KNEBWORTH.

HOMEWOOD,
KNEBWORTH,
HERTS

In February 6, 1918 (4 years late from pubⁿ m
Ap. 191

By The Representation of the People

about 6, 000, 000 women of 30

years of age and over obtain

the Parliamentary Vote.

The European War August 191
To Armistice Day. Nov: 11 191

Constance's note, written in her left hand, to commemorate the Representation of the People Act 1918.

many women the movement could muster, but how strong their arguments were. 'Patience, the arch enemy of this movement!'[7] She was then one of the few women given the honour of opening a day's activities at the great Suffragette Exhibition. Held in the ice rink at Knightsbridge over a fortnight, entirely decorated to Sylvia Pankhurst's designs, this huge display was aimed at both fundraising and education. The other speakers were women who had made a mark in some way, in science or drama perhaps: Constance was distinguished only by her name but the leaders wanted to make sure that she was firmly on display. It lent legitimacy as well as publicity to the cause to have such prominent women supporting their efforts. Constance spoke about her experiences in the Black Maria on the way to Holloway, saying how alone and cut off from the world she had felt until she heard unexpected roars from the streets. One of the suffragettes was waving their scarf out of the window and the people were cheering for her.[8] Constance ran the flower stall with a comrade and offered prizes for 'the best bouquets and button holes' – a rare occasion when her interests in flower arranging and suffrage coincided.[9] Constance was feeling cut off from the world she had grown up in, and yet somehow didn't mind. 'I know there is much about me just now that must seem to you badly biased, excessive in concentration, and enthusiasm even to the point of falseness,' she told Betty. 'I don't of course feel that it is myself. But I do feel that one had got into a kind of other sphere, beyond some border line which separates from past life and non-sympathisers as much as death might do in a greater sense.'[10]

In another mark of her growing importance to the suffragettes, a picture of her proudly wearing her new suffragette medals was made into postcards. In one, she sits elegantly at a writing desk, presumably drafting an article on behalf of the cause, hair swept up, formal collar ending in a bow, the very image of an Edwardian gentlewoman except for the badge in a portcullis shape pinned to her breast, a memento of her time in Holloway. Suffragettes collected these postcards as mementos of their beloved heroines to inspire their sacrifice. Constance may have been only a new recruit but she was being quickly promoted to the suffragette leadership. The rank and file members of the WSPU accepted this: it seemed only natural that this woman from the top of the social scale would quickly rise to the top of the WSPU. Though she may not have had to make the same practical sacrifices that they did, they recognised the social cost to her actions and applauded her. She was at once 'one of us' and not like 'us' at all.

In June, Betty arranged a lunch for Constance and Herbert Gladstone to talk about prison reform. As part of the deal, Betty had made her promise not to talk about the suffragettes or their specific concerns unless she was asked. Constance felt she had fluffed the opportunity: she had got flustered and been unable to get her points across. 'At best, it is futile for an amateur like me to talk reform with an official, and I was brainless and unable to string my words or even my thoughts together,' she told Aunt T.[11] Later in the year, reading Gladstone's comments on the state of women's prisons, she felt the meeting had been a total failure. He seemed under the impression that they were clean and healthy places with excellent staff: she had obviously failed to convey anything of the realities in Holloway.[12]

Constance also began writing regularly to Betty's brother-in-law, Arthur Balfour. He was still leader of the Conservative Party, and Constance believed that the Conservatives as well as the Liberals should be paying attention to their demands.[13] Balfour already had strong supporters of women's suffrage among his close relations – Frances as well as Betty – while his sister Eleanor was president of Newnham College, Cambridge. Why Constance thought she might succeed in prompting him to action where his near relations had so far failed is not clear, but she did not have much of an effect. Balfour went on the suffragettes' ever growing list of politicians who supposedly supported them but did absolutely nothing to advance their cause.

Lady Lytton was increasingly alarmed at Constance's involvement with the suffragettes: not just because she disapproved but because she was genuinely concerned about the risks to Constance's health. Betty pulled some strings to get the doctor's report from Holloway Prison so they could make sure her treatment was appropriate. She wrote to the Home Secretary's wife, Dorothy, who replied:

> He says I may tell you in strict confidence, the information only to be used by you for medical purposes, in the interest of Lady Constance. The medical opinion was that there was well marked valvular disease of the heart, evidently of old date, and that she was very much underweight,

Oddly, though, 'her general health improved very much whilst she was in prison', perhaps because of the enforced rest.[14] Edith whisked her away to Austria to be near her old music teacher. Fräulein Oser had read Constance's pamphlet and told her that she was '*berühmt*' – famous.[15]

Back at home, her actions were splitting the family. Gerald's view, as relayed by Edwin, was that 'the suffragettes are engineering their cause very badly now [...] he had no sympathy with law breaking' and he suggested that Arthur 'would probably do the same as Asquith'. Further:

> If women had the great majority they might insist on a position or policy which they would not have the physical strength to eventually enforce ... He thinks Con is a saint upon earth and so say all of us,

but that she knows little of the world and wants judgment. Don't repeat this while we all know it.'[16]

After Edith, Edwin was the most opposed to Constance's actions. He was patronising and pompous, telling Emily, 'I had a talk with McKenna [a Cabinet minister] about Suffragettes and told him one or two facts he didn't know and which he would never have learnt or received if shouted at him through a press-gang-press or a megaphone.'[17] Aunt T also made no secret of the fact that she found the campaign boring and Constance's interest in it baffling.

Betty and Emily were more sympathetic to Constance's point of view, though not necessarily to her behaviour, and they were critical of what they saw as her increasing extremism. Betty remembered that Constance 'shook us all out of a normal conventional attitude, much as Francis of Assisi must have shaken his relations when he gave away the clothes from his back. We were all made to reconsider our fundamentals.' Emily was still selling *Votes for Women* on her seaside holidays, though she would soon leave the suffragettes, dismayed by increasing militancy. She told Aunt T that 'our old Con has gone forever … she has passed out of the lives of her family, except in so far as they can go with her into the new life and interest. I think she has ceased to have any private affection even.'[18]

But Victor proved to be her most loyal friend. He could see why the suffragettes had been driven to adopt militant tactics. In his view, the only course of action was to reach an agreement as soon as possible, before anyone was seriously hurt. In June, he spoke at a suffrage meeting to outline his support for militancy: the suffragettes had no other means of getting their complaints heard; constitutional methods of winning the vote had been exhausted; and they were fighting against the 'indifference and inertia' of the public as well as the government. It was a serious business for another Lytton to lend his support to the cause, and Victor was fully

conscious of what he was committing to. 'These militant tactics involve – I cannot shut my eyes to the fact – defiance of the law and a
species of revolution, and he who advocates or even sanctions revolutionary measures incurs a responsibility which it is impossible to
exaggerate.'[19] Afterwards, Constance reported back how impressed
Christabel and the Pethick-Lawrences had been: 'All quite overcome and awed at the absolute straightness and clearness of your
vision into the whole question, at the difference of your attitude
from that of any other "politician" they have come across.'[20] His
support for the suffragettes inevitably got him into trouble among
his peers. Pamela told a story of a house party they had attended at
Hatfield with the King; the guests all lined up at the end to wish
him farewell, but the King stopped when he reached the Lyttons to
give them the full force of his temper because of Victor's involvement with the suffragettes. She was humiliated, not least because
she too hated him being associated with the militants.[21]

Meanwhile, Mrs Pankhurst was increasingly agitated over Asquith's refusal to receive a deputation of suffragettes: she believed
it was unconstitutional. The Bill of Rights was quoted at every
suffragette meeting. 'It is the right of the subject to petition the
King, and all commitments and prosecutions for such petitions
are illegal.' They were not so brave as to imagine the King might
receive them, but they did expect that his Prime Minister should.
On 29 June, Mrs Pankhurst led the 'Bill of Rights' deputation to the
Houses of Parliament; the women were of course turned away once
more. In the fracas Mrs Pankhurst slapped a policeman and was
arrested. Constance wrote indignantly from Austria to *The Times*
to protest about their coverage of the incident. 'For some weeks
past I have been out of England, and have had the disagreeable but
enlightening experience of following the English woman suffrage
movement, not, as for the last nine months it has been my privilege,
at first hand, but from the position of the average looker on.' Given

the abusive press coverage, she continued, 'it has been difficult to explain to my Austrian friends that the leaders of this movement are not the feckless hooligans one would suppose from these accounts. The coverage was totally biased, she said: it professed horror at supposed acts of violence by the suffragettes, while totally ignoring both the contempt they received from the government and the brutality they suffered at the hands of the crowds. In her view, it wasn't surprising that Mrs Pankhurst had hit the policeman. It would save her and, more importantly, the elderly women accompanying her from the pain and indignity of being roughed up by the crowd. 'In defence of her companions she lifts her hands and strikes. It seems to me an action characteristic of this great leader … though the act required of her was one entirely alien to her own nature … yet she did not shrink from it or hesitate.'[22] Constance, like the other suffragettes, believed they had to be prepared to do whatever it took to succeed. Nothing was off-limits.

This became clearer still in July, when the suffragettes turned to smashing windows on a mass scale and more than a hundred women were arrested, along with fourteen men. This escalation of hostilities partly reflected their growing frustration at government inertia and was partly a new tactic to gain more publicity, but it was also a survival strategy. Like slapping a policeman, breaking a window meant immediate arrest, so that suffragettes could quickly escape from a hostile situation.[23]

But the most significant moment of the summer occurred almost by accident. At the end of June, Marion Wallace Dunlop, an artist, managed to gain access to St Stephen's Hall, the original debating chamber of the House of Commons. She was not armed with stones, but with a stamp and ink, with which she defaced the wall with words from the Bill of Rights, beginning, 'It is the right of every subject to petition the King.' She was sentenced to a month in prison and wrote to Gladstone demanding to be treated as a political prisoner. Receiving no reply, she spontaneously decided to go on hunger strike.[24]

'What are you going to have for dinner?' she was asked. 'My determination,' she replied. In one day, she threw 'a fried fish, four slices of bread, three bananas and a cup of hot milk' out of the window.[25] The prison authorities panicked and released Marion after ninety-one hours. Fourteen of the window breakers followed her example and they too were released. The suffragettes were jubilant. They had stumbled on a tactic that seemed to render the government powerless. Christabel wrote to C. P. Scott, editor of *The Guardian*, to say that 'the new policy of the hunger strike has given us the means of entirely baffling the government. They cannot now imprison us, whatever we may do, for more than a few days, unless, of course, they prefer that we should die in Holloway.'[26] It appealed to their sense of theatre and drama but also to their spirituality. Lisa Appignanesi points out that self-denial and even starving has a long association with religion; the more women could control their appetite, the holier they were thought to be.[27] The suffragettes themselves were already holding annual self-denial weeks, and donating the proceeds to WSPU funds. But hunger striking took self-denial to unprecedented heights, and was also evidence of their powerlessness and desperation. For the suffragettes, though it was a dreadful experience, with extreme courage it could be managed. They believed that the struggle itself would be won through endurance, that they could last longer than the government. Hunger striking put this belief to the test. 'The actual hunger pains last only about twenty-four hours with most prisoners,' Emmeline Pankhurst later reported matter-of-factly.

I generally suffer most on the second day. After that there is no very desperate craving for food. Weakness and mental depression take its place. Great disturbances of digestion divert the desire for food to a longing for relief from pain. Often there is intense headache, with fits of dizziness, or slight delirium. Complete exhaustion and a feeling of isolation from earth mark the final stages of the ordeal.[28]

When the hunger strikers were released from prison, they were given gold brooches studded with flint stones to acknowledge their exceptional service.[29]

The Liberal government was fighting on several fronts at this time. Irish Home Rule was once again causing political headaches and Lloyd George's 'People's Budget' threatened to spark a constitutional crisis. The government could not allow a few rowdy women to get the better of them, especially after the King wrote, via his private secretary, to demand why 'the existing methods which must obviously exist for dealing with prisoners who refuse nourishment should not be adopted'.[30]

On 17 September, Asquith was due to address a meeting in Birmingham and was assailed by a number of suffragettes. Two of them, Mary Leigh and Charlotte Marsh, climbed up on the roof of the building next door and tore off slates to hurl at his car. The police threw stones back and turned hosepipes on them but still they resisted. It took three policemen to finally get them down. Both women were sentenced to four months' hard labour. As was fast becoming the norm, they immediately went on hunger strike. Mary herself had already been on hunger strike twice and she thought she knew what to expect. She was wrong. After she broke the windows in her cell, she was taken to a punishment room, handcuffed and made to sit in a chair tipped backwards, while a doctor held her mouth open and a wardress spooned milk and brandy in. The next time was far worse: two doctors came in with a tube, two yards long, which was forced up her nose, and liquid tipped in. This continued twice a day, through alternate nostrils, from 22 September to 30 October 1909.[31]

When news of Mary's treatment got out, the suffragettes were appalled. The WSPU took legal action against the Home Secretary, the prison governor and the prison doctor on Mary's behalf, arguing that force-feeding was an operation and could not be performed without consent. They lost. According to the Lord Chief Justice, a person in prison lost their right to refuse an operation and the prison officers had a duty to prevent Mary from committing suicide. The suffragette tactics had backfired spectacularly. There were now ominous legal grounds for further force-feedings. But not every hunger striker was force-fed. In her exhaustive history of the movement, Sylvia Pankhurst gives Olive Wharry the dubious honour of the longest hunger strike: thirty-two days in all; Freda Graham would go without food and water for fifteen days.[32]

Gladstone was uneasy about the decision and consulted with Asquith before giving force-feeding the go-ahead. Force-feeding had long been used on the mentally ill in asylums – as the King clearly knew – but this was something quite different. The women were not mentally ill; they were making a political choice, and the doctors were inexperienced in carrying out the procedure. But the conclusion they reached was that 'for the present these women must be treated like the prisoners with defective minds who are not amenable to the prison regulations'.[33]

A hundred and sixteen doctors wrote to *The Times* to protest against the 'unwise and inhumane' treatment being meted out;[34] seventy-nine of these doctors were women. But public opinion was not wholly behind the suffragettes. Some felt they had left the authorities with no choice. Others thought they got what they deserved. Many other doctors wrote to *The Times* suggesting that force-feeding was essential in order to save lives: in other words, it was humane, not inhumane.[35] Keir Hardie asked questions in the House of Commons to a chorus of laughter and jeers. *The Times* summed up the general mood in an editorial on 29 September:

Most of us desire something or other which we have not got ... but we do not therefore take hatchets and wreck people's houses, or even

shriek hysterically because the whole course of government and society is not altered to give us what we seek. These notoriety-hunters
have effectually discredited the movement they think to promote.
Public interest in their proceedings is dying, and is being replaced
by public disgust.[36]

Constance's friends and acquaintances were horrified by this new
turn of events, and by her determination to stick with the suffragettes, even given this new tactic. 'Con is quite insane,' Frances told
Betty. 'She asks you to plead against a doubtful "torture" while they
are applying a great deal of very real torture to the Asquiths.'[37] A
family friend, Nellie Cecil, spoke for many when she said,

> I gratefully recognise the immense lift the Pankhursts have given the
> movement, but I think they are making a bad mistake now ... (sup-
> pose Margot, or one of her children, or some other innocent person
> were hurt one day?) ... These things I am convinced disgust many
> who might be won over otherwise.[38]

The authorities believed that force-feeding would act as a deterrent
as well as a punishment. This was a serious miscalculation: it actually had the opposite effect. Seeing the gaunt bodies of their comrades and hearing their horrific stories galvanised the suffragettes.
The outrage they felt at the all-powerful government inflicting such
punishment on defenceless women hardened their resolve.[39] If the
government was so naive as to think 'the nasal tube or the stomach pump, the steel gag, the punishment cell, handcuffs and the
strait jacket would break the spirit of women who were determined
to win the enfranchisement of their sex, they were again woefully
misled', declared Emmeline Pethick-Lawrence.[40] Their beliefs were
as strong as any religion and now women were actually being tortured for the faith. Suffragettes submitted to force-feeding as a way

to express solidarity with their friends as well as to further the cause. 'The thought that women were facing death in the cells painted life, for their friends and supporters, in heightened colours,' wrote Sylvia Pankhurst. 'Actions seemed right and necessary, which at ordinary times would not have been conceived. The spirit of adventure and sacrifice awoke in quietly mannered people, who hitherto had never stepped from the beaten track of conventional usage.'[41]

Constance, perhaps the most quietly mannered of them all, was sickened. In August and September, she made a series of visits around the country, including Birmingham, Liverpool, North Wales and even Scotland[42] and, while away, Christabel took her to meet a hunger striker. Constance found the experience intensely moving.

A beautiful red light lit up the window as we came in; against it was merely the shadow of a girl, sitting in an armchair. She did not look ill in an ordinary way, but young and fresh only so absolutely thin and wasted, it would not have surprised us if life had gone out.

The girl's 'ethereal' appearance reminded her of Italian paintings which illustrated 'the look of spiritual strength shining through physical weakness'. Just as before she went to Holloway, Constance believed that direct experience was the only way to truly under-stand and empathise with her fellow suffragettes. 'An angel had been in my presence, and I, who agreed with all she did, had left her and many others to go through with this alone.'[43] This 'angel' is not named in *Prisons and Prisoners* but the suffragette historian Elizabeth Crawford identifies her as Laura Ainsworth, who, like Mary Leigh, had been arrested in Birmingham for attempting to disrupt Asquith's meeting.[44] Laura seems to have been rather more robust than Constance gave her credit for. By the end of the month she had recovered enough to confront Asquith with a poster of force-feeding and demand of him, 'Why did you do this to me?'[45]

She also began (ultimately unsuccessful) criminal proceedings for assault against the government, which brought more publicity to the movement.[46]

Burning with outrage, Constance decided to join the ranks of the hunger strikers, even if it meant being force-fed herself. A train ride with Christabel finally made up her mind. Constance sought Christabel's advice on a series of papers and letters, and was deeply impressed by 'the wonderful character, the imperturbable good temper, the brilliant intellect'.[47] She was prepared to do anything to impress Christabel and demonstrate her loyalty. She began writing to Arthur Balfour again, trying to broker a meeting between him and Christabel. He was non-committal, saying that he did not approve of what had been going on lately with the suffragette movement. Constance replied saying that the suffragettes agreed with him 'if you refer to the action of the Government', which, of course, he did not.[48]

But the time had come for action – or rather, as the suffragettes would have it, deeds not words. The opportunity for Constance's next move presented itself in Newcastle, where David Lloyd George was due to make a significant speech promoting his People's Budget and attacking the House of Lords. Constance set out on his trail with a particularly dedicated group of women. They included Emily Wilding Davison, who would later die under the King's horse; Ellen Pitfield, who went on to become the first suffragette arsonist; Dorothy Pethick, Emmeline's sister; and Kitty Marion, who would eventually be force-fed 232 times. Yet still Constance felt she was 'the "hooligan" if there were one among them'.[49] One of the women, Jane Brailsford, was married to a prominent journalist, and her husband Henry was present as the women met to plan their upcoming ordeal. 'It is difficult for anyone without opportunities of personal observation to form a fair estimate of the cool and deliberate courage of these women,' he later wrote in *The Times*. 'For a week beforehand they had thought of all their acts would involve. On the eve of their battle they quietly discussed, without a sign of emotion, all the hideous details of the treatment they were about to receive.'[50] Another participant, Winifred Jones, was on her first mission. She was visibly rattled, asking question after question. Would she lose the tortoise-shell combs which held up her beautiful hair? Constance felt that Winifred, barely out of her teens, wasn't prepared for the ordeal ahead and tried to talk her out of it. She had forgotten that only a few months earlier she had felt the same mix of idealism and naivety. But Winifred was as strong-willed as Constance and determined to play her part.

The next day, 8 October 1909, the suffragettes carried out their plans with methodical precision. Despite Constance's misgivings, Winifred managed to throw a stone right outside the Liberal Club, where Lloyd George was due to speak. Kitty Marion and Dorothy Pethick threw stones at the Post Office windows. Four others smashed the windows of the Liberal Club. Jane Brailsford hid an axe in a bunch of chrysanthemums, sauntered up to the barricades lining the route and swung her weapon in full view of the police. Constance and Emily Wilding Davison waited by the side of the road, stones in hand, for Lloyd George himself to arrive, inwardly agitated though outwardly calm. Wrapped around their stones was a message to Lloyd George: 'Rebellion against tyrants is obedience to God.'[51] This was a passionate conviction of some suffragettes: they were justified in disobeying the government because they were carrying out God's will.

Then a rumour swept along the crowd lining the street: Lloyd George was going in by a different route. Emily and Constance hesitated. What should they do now? They decided to abandon the symbolic triumph of striking Lloyd George's car and simply get themselves into prison by striking any car that came their way.

A feeling came over me that I could not wait any longer, and that somehow or other I must throw my stone … One thing, however, I was determined upon – it must be more zealously done, more deliberate in its character than the stone-throwing at ordinary windows which had been done lately. I was determined that when they had me in court my act should inevitably be worse than that of other women.[52]

This was partly because her dedication had now reached such extreme heights that even throwing a stone must be done perfectly, with reverence, just as Christabel would want. But it also reflected more practical concerns: Constance would give the authorities no chance to give her favourable treatment or a lesser sentence.

She took careful aim at the next official-looking vehicle that passed, throwing her stone at the wheels to avoid accidentally hitting any spectators. That was all it took. The police descended immediately and arrested them both, 'and as they passed down Northumberland Street to the Central Police Station thousands of eyes were attracted to them', ran the report in *Votes for Women*, which described the day's events as 'the battle for Newcastle'.[53] To her chagrin, Emily didn't even get a chance to throw her stone and so was eventually acquitted. Constance was charged with assault, malicious injury to the car and disorderly behaviour in a public place. She was delighted. 'I felt very exalted to think I had done so much, and though that three months was the least they could give me.'[54] The press were equally pleased. 'Lady Constance Lytton, who recently wrote letters in her own blood from prison, has again been cast into the dungeon,' *The Times* reported with relish.[55]

The women regrouped in the magistrate's court and wrote a joint letter to *The Times*.

We want to make it known that we shall carry on our protest in our prison cells. We shall put before the Government by means of the hunger strike four alternatives: – To release us in a few days; to inflict violence on our bodies; to add death to the champions of our cause by leaving us to starve; or, and this is the best and only wise alternative, to give women the vote.

Constance also wrote her own letter, giving her address as Cell No. 2, Central Police Station, Newcastle, and imploring other women to follow their example: 'Our violence and our suffering will not always be linked with the symbols of shame. In the days to come it is not those who have fought in this good fight but those who have stood out from it that will be branded with disgrace.'[56] Imagine Edith's horror as her beloved daughter not only threw stones but encouraged others to do likewise. Nevertheless, she telegrammed immediately: 'We uphold you shall work for you God bless you,' as did her sisters, who wrote 'God Bless You I go to mother. Could I get to you in time tomorrow endless love Emily' and, simply, 'Wire if I can do anything.'[57] Constance wrote back to Betty to say, 'I quite understand all that the disapprovers feel. But to me the rightness and usefulness of our action seems to me so clear and sure.' To Edith she said, 'My darling Mummy need not feel ashamed nor afraid for me. All is well, and except for the thought of you I am Oh so happy.'[58]

Constance and Jane Brailsford, by far the best-known and best-connected of the suffragettes in their group, were given lighter sentences than the others, even though their actions had arguably posed a greater risk to the public. 'A sickening assembly of snobs defending snobbish action,' Constance wrote scornfully of the court.[59] They were sent to the second division. Winifred, who had caused only a pound's worth of damage to a window (and was a first offender), was given hard labour. They let this point go, since they had at least achieved their objective and got themselves into prison. They immediately went on hunger strike. Constance observed the prison activity through a light-headed haze, though she was alert enough to note that Newcastle

Gaol seemed more humane than Holloway. The prison staff were kind, and the prisoners were less downtrodden, almost more like servants than inmates. Conditions, though, were worse than in Holloway. The cells were dark and dirty and smelling; there was no bedding and Constance slept on a plank. In typical fashion, Constance wrote to the Home Secretary to complain that there were fleas in her knickers.[60]

After two days, when Constance heard footsteps approaching, she was sure the moment was at hand. 'I stood in the corner of my cell with my arms crossed and my fingers caught in my nostrils and my mouth. It was the best position I knew of for them not to be able to feed me by nose or mouth without a considerable struggle.'[61] Constance was puzzled when the doctor only tested her heart and left again. Later that day she and Jane were suddenly released, both on grounds of ill health. This set alarm bells ringing. Constance undoubtedly did have a weak heart but Jane was young and strong. What they shared was not physical illness but public profile and political connections. It seemed that the authorities were not willing to gamble on force-feeding prominent women who were well placed to kick up a fuss.

Having mentally prepared themselves for force-feeding, Constance and Jane found it hard to come to terms with being released. They felt extremely guilty about their comrades still in prison. In yet another letter to *The Times*, they asked:

> We left behind us in Newcastle prison several women much younger than ourselves, to whom, certainly in one case, if not in two or three, the risks from starvation are much greater than they were to us. Four of our friends who were sentenced on October 9 were already being forcibly fed; their cries of protest and distress reached us in our cells. What has a Liberal Government to say, what has public opinion to say, in defence of such glaring partiality and injustice?[62]

When their comrades were released and told their stories, Jane and Constance felt even worse. Dorothy Pethick had been horrified to find that the tubes were not even cleaned properly in between feedings.[63] Dorothy Shallard had been tied to a chair with a sheet and held down by three wardresses while she was fed through the nose. Kitty Marion had chewed through her pillow and set the contents alight with the gas jet in her cell, starting a fire. She was already unconscious when discovered. Each woman was told the other hunger strikers had given in and begun eating but they knew this was a lie: they could hear the screams and shrieks of other force-feedings through the wall.[64] Even Emily Davison, who had been so disappointed at missing out in Newcastle, had gone straight out and got herself arrested again so that she could complete her mission. Faced with the prospect of force-feeding, she barricaded herself into her cell, whereupon the prison wardens turned a freezing hosepipe on her and burst down the door, tore her soaking clothes off and fed her through the nose. Once out of prison, she sued the prison authorities for this shocking violence, but the judge ruled she was only entitled to token compensation since the incident had provided her with good copy for the papers.[65] All this had been endured while Constance and Jane were safe and well outside.

Progressive opponents of the government seized on this apparently blatant example of double standards. Henry Brailsford wrote to *The Times* to say that 'if forcible feeding is too horrible for some it is too horrible for all'. George Bernard Shaw also wrote to *The Times* on behalf of the Fabian Society, congratulating Gladstone on refusing to force-feed Constance Lytton and suggesting he do the same for all other women. If not, Shaw invited Gladstone to enjoy a delicious banquet with him: to be taken through the nose.[66]

The government refused to take the bait. Gladstone declared to Parliament that 'there is not the slightest ground for the insinuations which are being freely made that Lady Constance Lytton was released because she was a peer's sister. She was released solely on medical grounds.'[67]

Still suffering the after-effects of her hunger strike – shaking legs and poor digestion – Constance stepped out on the platform of the Queen's Hall to tell her story to the assembled suffragettes. 'I got hold of the audience, felt they were with me, and that something of all that is burning in my soul got out to them,' she wrote ecstatically afterwards. Emily was there, and told Edith, with some pride, that everyone had cried. Edith was pleased that the speech had gone down well, but was bitter about what she saw as the leaders egging on their innocent followers, and deeply worried about where this would all end. 'When the misguided ones take to shooting, besides trying to commit suicide, it will be misery and agony, no matter what forcing it brings on any government.'[68] Similarly, Margot Asquith asked Frances Balfour, 'Is Connie off her head? … Poor, poor Connie when I think of that fragile, excitable, unbalanced creature going in for this kind of life my heart aches for her.'[69] But what did this matter when her true supporters loved her more than ever? Olive Schreiner wrote to say how impressed she was with those fighting for their freedom: 'I am always so glad I didn't die before the Suffragette movement began, because now I know that my highest hopes for women on Earth will ultimately be reached.'[70] Constance also received this letter from an anonymous comrade:

> Women like ourselves who from force of circumstances are unable to take a place in the fighting line do very sincerely appreciate the noble self-sacrifice and devotion of those like yourself, Marie Leigh, [*sic*] and the other brave women who are ready to face even the barbarous tortures inflicted by the so-called Liberal Government.[71]

These were the women she was fighting for and she resolved to fight on. The last weeks of the year were spent criss-crossing the country: to Birmingham, Liverpool and Manchester, then finishing the year in Churchill's constituency, Dundee. 'It's the best possible practice for speaking to never stop,' she concluded.[72]

Betty went on her own tour for the non-militants, speaking to audiences 'of fashionable (at any rate large-hatted) ladies'. She reported back to Arthur Balfour – 'Dearest Chief' – on the sentiments she found, and encouraged him to let Conservative candidates speak their mind on the issue, even if he didn't make women's suffrage official policy. He did not respond. In Edinburgh, Betty made a moving speech on suffrage, saying that while she couldn't support militant tactics, 'they had made people like her feel that the time had come when those who were in favour of the enfranchisement of women could no longer sit with hands folded and let others fight the battle'.[73]

In early December, Constance met with a Liberal MP to discuss fair treatment for suffragette prisoners and was disgusted to discover just how afraid of the suffragettes he was, and how misplaced his priorities were. He asked whether Mary Leigh was likely to really kill anyone. Constance, instantly fired up, asked whether the government was likely to kill Mary, for that seemed to her far more likely. She described this angrily to Neville's old friend Edward Marsh, now Winston Churchill's private secretary.

> This and the like injury and torture to many other women, the over 400 other imprisonments of the last 3 years, the assaults and violent maltreatment by police … and all you have to ask or say when you see me is 'are we safe, d'you think, Winston and I – what degree of hurt might possibly happen to us?'[74]

On 9 December, there was a meeting at the Royal Albert Hall to celebrate Mrs Pankhurst's return from America. Medals were presented to those women who had been on hunger strike during the year. The women processed up in alphabetical order, so Kitty Marion, dressed in black, followed Constance Lytton, dressed in white. Kitty, as an artist, was pleased to note the aesthetic contrast she made, and said that 'it was an honour in itself, to walk in the footsteps of that great, noble soul'.[75] But walking up to the platform, Constance must have been aware that her hunger strike, lasting just a couple of days, paled in comparison to the efforts of the women around her. She was determined to truly earn her medal.

CHAPTER EIGHT

BECOMING JANE

'When great wrong is being done, when injury, harm, misery and death result from that fundamental injustice then no matter even if we can do nothing to effect a change, we should still make our protest.'[1]

A general election was held in January 1910 and Constance was sent north for the campaign. She began in Edinburgh, then went to Manchester and Liverpool to campaign against the government. In Manchester, Constance came face to face with truly appalling, grinding poverty for the first time. But the women she addressed were enthusiastic about the cause and the meetings were packed. Despite her undoubted empathy, Constance couldn't help patronising them. 'How eagerly and intelligently they listened, and what a wonderful light came into their eyes as the hope dawned in their minds!' Like Emmeline and Christabel Pankhurst, Constance saw suffrage as 'a woman's question, not a class question,' and she believed these women felt the same way.[2] She was dismissive of women with property who wanted the vote for themselves but were nervous about sharing the privilege with working women: she believed in votes for all women.

On 3 January, *Votes for Women* described in graphic detail the treatment of Selina Martin, a prisoner on remand in Liverpool.

She was kept in irons. Next day, her cell was entered, she was seized, thrown down, rolled over with her face upon the floor. In this position, face downwards, her arms were dragged up behind her till she was lifted from the ground ... She was 'frogmarched' up the steps to the doctor's room, her head bumping on the stone stairs. In the doctor's room the operation of forcible feeding was performed – causing intense suffering – and then this tortured girl, in a terrible state of physical and mental distress, was handcuffed again, flung down the steps and pushed and dragged back into her cell.[3]

Constance discussed the case with Mary Gawthorpe, the WSPU's Liverpool organiser. 'These women are quite unknown – nobody knows or cares about them except their own friends. They go to prison again and again to be treated like this, until it kills them,' Mary wept.[4]

This was exactly the sort of heartfelt emotional appeal that Constance could never resist. She was not 'unknown'. Her name and her testimony would automatically carry weight with the public. If she could bear witness to the horrors of force-feeding, perhaps she could win public sympathy to their plight. But how could she do this when the authorities refused to force-feed her?

The answer was obvious. She would have to go to prison in disguise. She could then experience force-feeding for herself, stand up for her suffragette sisters and expose the double standards which seemed to be rife in British prisons.[5]

Suffragettes often took action in disguise. Dressing up – or, like Constance, dressing down – became more common as the police got wise to their tactics. The suffragettes dressed as messenger boys, waitresses, cleaners and charwomen, which allowed them to slip into a meeting hall unnoticed before heckling an unsuspecting Cabinet minister. But Constance took this to another level.

First, she joined the WSPU again under the name of Jane Warton. 'Jane' was a nod to Joan of Arc, patron saint of the suffragettes. 'Warton' was a contraction of 'Warburton,' the name of a supporter who had written her a sympathetic letter. Then she set out around the shops of Manchester to find 'Jane' suitable clothes. She had her hair cut off, bought itchy woollen gloves and a scarf, and wrapped herself in a green tweed coat, topped off with an unfashionable cloth hat. Brooches with portraits of the suffragette leaders, and thick plain glasses which pinched her nose, completed her new look. Constance was always useless when it came to practical matters, but the stress of traipsing round an unfamiliar city on a furtive mission made her even more hopeless than usual. She bought the wrong dye for her hair, wasted hours on a fake eye test to get her glasses, and even had to hide from other suffragettes. Nevertheless, Constance/Jane was pleased with the result. It was not enough to become a different person: she wanted to become ugly and ridiculous too, as vulnerable and powerless as possible. She succeeded. The shop assistants could barely keep straight faces when they were serving her, and she was followed home by a trail of schoolboys jeering at her ugliness.

Her final task was to set her mother's mind at rest. She sent a breezy letter home, saying, 'We had the most splendid meeting yet had in Manchester. A large Town Hall simply packed, understanding and wildly enthusiastic,' adding in an offhand way, 'fear no time to write for several days to come but you will be on the move and will not miss my letters.'[6]

Jane arrived in Liverpool on 14 January 1910 and went straight away to study the prison walls and plan her actions. Somewhere beyond the anonymous grey walls, Selina Martin was still in jail. Perhaps even at that very moment she was being force-fed again. It gave Jane a sense of grim determination.

When suffragettes visited other towns to speak or campaign, they were usually hosted by sympathetic families to save valuable funds. Jane was being put up by the Ker family, two daughters and their mother, Alice, a doctor. There was a letter waiting at the Ker house from Ada Flatman, the Liverpool organiser. 'Just a line to welcome you to Liverpool, thought you would like to know we are holding a demonstration at Walton Gaol tonight at 7.45, if you can join us there, we shall be glad as we want our protest to be heard by the brave women inside.'[7] Dr Ker fed her a dish of stewed pears. Jane thought of those pears often in the days ahead. She selected some large stones from their garden in case they would come in handy later.

Back at the gaol, several hundred people were listening to passionate speeches by the local organisers. Most of the crowd were there out of morbid curiosity rather than outraged support, and Jane was afraid they would leave before she could get herself arrested. So she took over the protest, calling on the crowd to follow her to the prison governor's house, where they could demand the release of the suffragette prisoners. Rather to her surprise, people began to follow her. That would probably be good enough to get her arrested: just to make sure, she half-heartedly threw her stones at the governor's house. That did it, and she was taken to the police station to await her trial.

Jane had planned to go to prison by herself, unwilling to ask another woman to put herself through the torment ahead, but two women, Elsie Howey and Mrs Nugent, also had themselves arrested so that Jane wouldn't be alone. Jane noted that the policemen were as kind as they could be. The three women were kept in a cell together and were given sandwiches and a newspaper. Around midnight, Mrs Nugent's husband arrived, causing a stir among the officers because he was a well-known local magistrate. Perhaps the police were on their best behaviour as a result. At three in the morning, the women were lined up against the wall to report their details. When Jane stood up, her ridiculous appearance now wonky and dishevelled, the other prisoners began to laugh.

They were then taken to another police station. Elsie and Jane held hands in the police van as it thundered around the streets of Liverpool picking up drunks: some young and laughing it off, others yellowed with addiction. The suffragettes spent what little was left of the night together in one cell. The next day, Saturday 15 January, they were taken before the magistrates for sentencing. Mrs Nugent was let off, though Elsie was a repeat offender and got six weeks. Jane was sentenced to a fortnight.

Jane and Elsie were taken to prison and made to wait, lined up against a wall, before they were formally admitted. Elsie announced that the pair would be hunger striking and that they would refuse to obey the prison rules. She apologised if it would give the prison officials any trouble and made clear that their quarrel was with the government, not them.

Asked to undress and put on prison clothes, Jane suddenly realised she was carrying a reel of cotton and a handkerchief marked as belonging to Constance Lytton. Such a giveaway would destroy all her plans in an instant. She somehow managed to throw them in the fire unnoticed: the wardresses were too busy laughing at the way she looked. She was stripped of her own clothes and given a prison gown and boots that were much too small.

Then Jane was taken, alone, to her cell. Here she was neither Constance Lytton nor Jane Warton but simply prisoner 204. She was immensely tired.

The matron came to try to persuade Jane not to go ahead with her threatened hunger strike. This gave Jane the opportunity to rehearse her arguments about how the government had left the suffragettes with no choice. The matron didn't stay for much of the lecture. The doctor, the governor, the senior medical officer and the chaplain all came to see her over the next few days: none of them were able to change her mind. Meals were brought and refused. Jane washed her mouth out with water but neither drank nor ate. At night she dreamed of melons, peaches and nectarines.

Jane Warton wasn't bound by the same conventions as Constance Lytton. She could do anything she wanted and proved it by breaking every petty rule she could. She wouldn't wear her hat. She wore the skirt of her dress around her neck like a cloak, trying to keep warm. She lay on her bed in the day. She wouldn't do her needlework. For this she was sentenced to three days on bread and water; a meaningless punishment since she was not eating anyway. She scrawled political and religious slogans across the walls, making ink out of soap and dust. One was a quote from Thoreau: 'Under a Government which imprisons any unjustly, the true place for a just man (or woman) is also a prison', and the other was from the Bible: 'Only be ye strong and very courageous.' She tried communicating with her neighbours by tapping out the signal for 'No Surrender' on the wall, but was never sure if the answering taps she heard were imaginary.

On the fourth morning, the prison doctor came to inspect her and decided to force-feed her at once, though Jane was actually left alone for the rest of the day in a state of nervous excitement. The doctor did not come back until six in the evening, accompanied by five wardresses. He had one more go at persuading her to eat: she told him that was out of the question. That was her last chance. Now Jane felt an odd thrill: 'I had looked forward to this moment with so much anxiety lest my identity be discovered beforehand, that I felt positively glad when the time had come.'[8]

It is no exaggeration to describe force-feeding as torture. The violation of their bodies was understood by the suffragettes, though few used the word, as rape; all the more traumatising because it was state-sanctioned. Unsurprisingly, force-feeding had terrible consequences for the women's health. Nearly all became severely constipated and most continued to lose weight. Few suffragettes could stop themselves struggling, and this made their minor injuries worse: chipped teeth and bruised limbs were common,[9] to say nothing of the mental suffering caused by the anticipation of torture.

Jane knew all this, both from lurid accounts in the press and from suffragette testimony in *Votes for Women*, and must have imagined all sorts of horrors. Even so, the actual experience was beyond her worst nightmares. To do it justice, it is worth quoting her testimony at length:

> Much as I had heard about this thing, it was infinitely more horrible and more painful than I had expected. The doctor put the steel gag in somewhere on my gums and forced open my mouth till it was yawning wide. As he proceeded to force into my mouth and down the throat a large rubber tube, I felt as though I were being killed; absolute suffocation is the feeling. You feel as though it would never stop. You cannot breathe, and yet you choke. It irritates the throat, it irritates the mucous membrane as it goes down, every second seems an hour, and you think they will never finish pushing it down. After a while the sensation is relieved, then the food is poured down, and then again you choke, and your whole body resists and writhes under the treatment; you are held down, and the process goes on, and, finally, when the vomiting becomes excessive the tube is removed.[10]

Now Jane knew just how bad it was, her hours became 'a nightmare of agonised dread'.[11] The food was a mixture of milk, gruel, eggs, brandy, sugar and beef tea – Jane, of course, was a vegetarian and this added insult to injury. She was violently sick each time and then, when she was sufficiently recovered, cleaned up the mess herself. The alternative was that another female prisoner would have to do it, and Jane could not bear to see another woman suffer the humiliation. She was humiliated enough herself by the wardresses who watched and criticised her: 'Look at her! Just look at her! The way she's doing it!' Jane's general behaviour made the prison officials angry and afraid. The head wardress scolded her like a child for breaking the gas jet which served for heating, and for 'all that writing scribbled all over your cell.' The doctor went one better: 'I suppose you want to smash me with one of these?' Jane seized her chance to retaliate and asked him haughtily not to slap her again. He ignored her, and went ahead with the force-feeding in silence. Afterwards, she was uncontrollably sick on him. 'If you do that again, I shall have to feed you twice,' he said.[12]

Jane had decided to make exactly the same decisions as Constance had done in Newcastle. This was part of the test for the authorities. That meant she refused to answer medical questions but wouldn't resist medical tests. But there were no tests. Her pulse was not taken and her heart was not examined until the third time she was force-fed, when she had 'a sort of shivering fit'.[13] The doctor was alarmed and called in his junior, who gave her a perfunctory examination and pronounced her fine. The senior doctor was unconvinced and begged her to give in. Jane refused. After the feeding, she lay on the bed, utterly broken. She felt she could go on no longer. She tried recalling to mind all the women she had known or been inspired by, but it was no use. She was finished. Then, she had a spiritual hallucination in which the window frame became Christ's cross. Outside the window, she saw a woman with a baby, framed by the dying evening light. Somehow this image did what nothing else could: it gave her the strength to endure.

She pleaded with the authorities to make the feeding less painful, asking for different food, less food, a smaller tube. All were refused. Most suffragettes were fed by the doctor sitting behind the suffragette: this one chose to sit on her knees. The torment was unbearable. But the mental torment was even harder to bear than the physical suffering. 'Infinitely worse than the pain was the sense of degradation, the very fight that one made against the outrage was shattering one's nerves and one's self-control.' Jane felt there was no kindness in this gaol. 'Prisoners are made to feel in the presence of nearly every prison official that they are the scum of the earth,' she wrote, 'suspected of deceit, prejudiced and found wanting.'[14] She had to close her eyes so as not to see the people who came to torment her: she could not even bring herself to call them 'people' and instead described them as 'beings', utterly corrupted by an utterly corrupt system.[15] One of her great regrets was that she was unable to hide the fear she felt in the face of such inhumane brutality. She hoped that her evident terror gave her tormentors some satisfaction.[16]

Jane made less and less effort to keep up her pretence. It was too much trouble to style her hair differently, especially when it dragged into her sick. The glasses were painful and she abandoned them. She would have been terribly tired and weak, certainly light-headed and possibly delusional as well. Above all, she was cold, despite the heat in the cell, despite wearing her flannel nightdress in the day, and despite three blankets. It required incredible mental strength to submit to repeated force-feeding. She had little left for lying and deception. Meanwhile, her condition deteriorated.

After six feedings, Jane felt she could stand no more and longed for death. But the words 'no surrender' came to mind and she was ashamed of giving in. Jane forced herself to get up and walk up and down the cell until she felt half-alive again. The next day, for the first time, she cried after the feeding: deep, wracking sobs that convulsed her body.

The prison governor came to see her again. Jane repeated her accusations: that the doctor had hit her, that she was being fed even while being sick, that there was too much food. 'I am an abnormal looking woman with short hair and a moustache ... and it is under-standable that he should consider me fair game for his contempt,' she said. 'But this is not quite the right mood for an official, and what he could do to one woman, no matter of what type, he might possibly do to another.'[17] The governor ignored her complaints but was said that she would be allowed to write to her mother. After struggling with the practical difficulties – how could she let her mother know she was all right without giving away where she was, when her family would immediately demand that she were let out?

– the temptation was too much for her. She took a little bread and milk to gain enough strength to write lucidly, then wrote a letter to a Mrs Sleath, the Lutyens family nanny, so that it might indirectly reach Edith Lytton. The prison authorities noted that she appeared 'to be in a more manageable condition and temper'.[18]

Back in London, Emily was having dinner with a family friend, Arthur Chapman, when she received a telegram meant for Victor. It was from the *Daily News*, enquiring whether the rumours that Lady Constance Lytton was in prison in Liverpool were true. Chapman got on the telephone to the prison at once and the pieces of the puzzle were quickly put together. The prison authorities said that Jane was due to be released the next morning anyway. Emily caught the midnight train to Liverpool, where she met with the prison governor. He had suspected this was no ordinary prisoner and had been making enquiries with the Home Office. The governor told Emily that 'he had never seen such a bad case of forcible feeding … she was practically asphyxiated each time'.[19] Apparently, this was not enough to make him stop.

'She is terribly thin, her face so drawn and pinched, but a good colour and I think very pretty with her short hair. Her body just like pictures of famine people in India,' Emily reported to Betty.[20] Constance was five feet eleven inches tall – she is easily recognisable in photographs of the suffragette because she towers above the rest – and usually weighed just over nine stone. On her release from prison, she weighed only seven and a half stone.[21] Constance talked non-stop on the journey and was in half-hysterical fits of giggles most of the time. She was now a member of the only elite worth anything to her: not the social elite, but the suffragette elite – a true martyr to the cause. After a short rest, she stayed up all night to compose her experiences for *The Times*, *Votes for Women* and, most importantly, a speech to her fellow suffragettes.

On 31 January, Constance stood before a packed Queen's Hall to share her experiences. She was not a natural speaker and always relied on emotion rather than argument. She had once told Aunt T, 'I am in no way equipped to impress people, to convert them, or to stir them.'[22] Now, though, she didn't need to say a word. Her skeletal body told its own story. 'We are like an army ... we are deputed to fight for a cause, and for other people, and in any struggle or any fight, weapons must be used,' she proclaimed.[23] Constance struggled to convey the enormity of the degradation she had experienced. The pain of the force-feeding was bad enough. But the anticipation of the force-feeding, the agony of hearing others being tormented, and the 'moral blindness' of a system in which wardens, doctors and governors all treated prisoners as worse than human: all these were worse still. Many in the crowd openly wept.

Constance always insisted that she planned and executed the Jane Warton escapade entirely on her own. 'My leaders do indeed feel for you. They have not ordered or led me. I did this thing absolutely on my own responsibility,' she told her mother, who of course believed exactly the opposite.[24] Constance wished to avoid any impression of a conspiracy to deliberately entrap the authorities. It certainly wasn't unusual for suffragettes to strike out on their own without the Pankhursts knowing. Marion Dunlop's hunger strike, Emily Davison's postbox fires and Ellen Pitfield's arson campaign were all started on their own initiative and only later got the stamp of approval from headquarters.

There are, however, hints that others may have known, or at least suspected, what she was up to. The Ker family, who hosted Jane before her arrest and gave her the stewed pears, knew Constance Lytton and had hosted her before. It is difficult to imagine that Alice Ker, a doctor, didn't see through Constance's ramshackle disguise. Constance knew Ada Flatman, too, from her days in Holloway.[25] There is also a letter from Constance which was annotated by Ada in 1936 as 'for my use, being the organiser in Liverpool who planned & carried through the protest at Walton Gaol with her'.[26]

In a letter to Ada Flatman on 19 January 1910, Christabel implored her 'not to tell a soul about our friend. It had better go on to the end. She is willing we know.'[27] Christabel may not have directly given the go-ahead, but this is surely an indication that she knew what was going on. On 23 January, Emmeline Pethick-Lawrence wrote to Victor to tell him that she had been moved by Constance's action and to say that 'your sister was not led to take this action by any influence of ours'.[28] If it looked to the public that the leaders had endorsed or encouraged Constance to become Jane, it would seem as though she had been thrown to the lions.

In a campaign marked by daring feats of bravery, great moments of theatre and spectacular leaps of imagination, this act of Constance Lytton/Jane Warton still stands out. The suffragettes immediately turned her act into the stuff of legend. *Votes for Women* spoke of Constance in the most glowing terms (it sounds very much as though Emmeline Pethick-Lawrence wrote this):

> In her and in her deed the human race is ennobled. We can forget the ugly, the base, the mean of less souls in the knowledge that such beauty, grandeur and strength can exist in being made in the same likeness as ourselves. And wherever the annals of the human race are preserved, this deed of hers will be treasured up as a priceless possession.[29]

It was as if Constance/Jane had carried out a secular miracle and was being beatified. Having gone so far beyond the call of duty, she was now well on the way to becoming a suffragette saint. But still she wanted to give more. As she said at the Queen's Hall,

> Women have for so long thought it almost a virtue to despise themselves, and now they are being told that that is all wrong, that they have got something to do, that they have got to come into this

movement, and not only draw their life from it, but also to give their life to it.[30]

The suffragettes had changed her life so much that she could only thank them by giving her life away. Perhaps she was even a little disappointed that she hadn't quite managed it.

CHAPTER NINE

CONCILIATION

*'Who has the "weak heart," Lady Constance Lytton or the
Liberal Government?'*[1]

The papers called it 'Lady Constance Lytton's latest Freak'[2] and for once Constance revelled in the attention. Though she had deliberately set out to see what she could accomplish under another name, once released she took full advantage of all the benefits of being Lady Constance Lytton. The public knew about the hunger strikes and the forced feeding, of course, but for the first time they now put a name and a face to the policy. And what a name! With her profile, connections and influence, Constance could do what none of the other nameless, powerless hunger strikers could do. She could turn her personal suffering into political advantage and make the government squirm.

'She has indeed gained a victory over the Government which will make it much more difficult for them to continue forcible feeding,' wrote a gleeful Christabel to Betty.[3] On 10 February, *The Times* published a prim letter from Sir Edward Troup, Gladstone's private secretary at the Home Office. He said that 'Jane Warton' was already going to be released before her identity was discovered. As for the difference in treatment, he said that Constance Lytton was expected to resist force-feeding, which would have been bad for her heart. Jane Warton was not expected to resist and had refused medical examination which would have uncovered her weak heart. It was important to the government to make the issue one of resistance rather than of force-feeding. They stubbornly tried to keep up the pretence that force-feeding was mildly unpleasant rather than physically damaging.

Victor was appalled. He sent Constance's statement to the Home Office, saw Edward Troup, a junior Home Office minister, for a private interview and then requested a public inquiry. He wrote to Gladstone:

> This denial on the part of the Home Office implies that my sister either is not in possession of her faculties or has deliberately published a statement which she knows to be untrue. My sister is unfortunately too ill to defend herself and I have therefore undertaken the task of vindicating both her sanity and her veracity.[4]

What Victor said was true: Constance was very ill and certainly did not have the strength for a battle with the Home Office. She could barely sit down and ate her meals knelt on a cushion instead. Her jaw was sore from the gag which had held her mouth open and the crown of a tooth fell off. Her legs were swollen and her heart was erratic, sometimes trembling, sometimes racing. The formal diagnosis was 'mitral disease of the heart, with parasystolic murmur',[5] which affected the way blood was being circulated around the body. She was forbidden letters and visitors by her doctor, Marion Vaughan, and was even told to walk up the stairs backwards to avoid straining her heart. She did, however, summon the strength to write a note to Gladstone vindicating herself: 'It has been suggested that I acted as I did with a view to playing a kind of practical joke. Even if that kind of thing were in my line I could not have faced the strain and suffering entailed for such a purpose.'[6] She also wrote to her co-conspirators in Liverpool. 'The experience in prison this time was intensely grim and dreadful but now the reward seems indescribably great,' she told Alice Ker. 'To think I had who endured by far the least of all the forcibly fed should be making people wake up more than all of them.' She wrote to Ada Flatman, optimistic that Jane Warton would make a lasting difference: 'What hope that at least this feeding business will be heard of no more.'⁷ She had given everything to this heroic effort: she had to believe that it was worth it.

While Constance had been in prison, the election had produced a hung parliament, with no party winning an outright majority: the Conservatives had won more votes though the Liberals had won more seats. The Liberals now had to rely on the Irish Parliamentary Party to govern. This election had only been called so that the Liberals could strengthen their hand against the intransigent House of Lords. It was a terrible miscalculation and this result was a disaster for them; they were in no mood to compromise with the suffragettes. On 19 February, Asquith sacked Gladstone as Home Secretary and installed Winston Churchill in his place. Gladstone had been public enemy number one for the suffragettes for some time. 'The record of this man – his cruelty, his petty meanness, his wilful and deliberate misrepresentations – form a sordid chapter in this country's history, and sully a name which had been made world famous by his father by for traditions of liberty and honour,' said *Votes for Women*.⁸ But Churchill was also detested by the suffragettes and had long been singled out for particularly nasty heckling. On the other hand, he was a close friend of Victor Lytton. Would this be an advantage or not, in a case which hinged on accusations of special treatment for the privileged?

Prison bureaucracy swung into motion and, as Victor had requested, the Chief Commissioner of Prisons, Sir Evelyn Ruggles-Brise, began an internal inquiry. The Home Office files bulge with testimonies from prison staff rejecting Constance's accusations. The doctor had tested her pulse. He had not slapped her, though he had once patted her cheek to offer comfort. She had not been sick. Any food which came up was residue from the tube. Medical and bureaucratic jargon are mustered to explain how all the doctors could have missed the prisoner's obvious illness in the meantime. 'It is well known to medical observers that a murmur of this kind varies greatly in intensity at different times and in different positions of the patient and that its audibility bears little relation to the symptoms of heart-disorder, if any, which may be present.' It all sounds very convincing. They even consider going on the offensive, wondering whether the doctor might sue *The Times* for printing the accusation that he had slapped the prisoner.[9]

One piece of evidence, though, is damning. The prison doctor had drafted a letter to *The Times* to explain what, in his view, had happened. He sent it to the Home Office for approval, and the draft has been altered by a Home Office official. The doctor says there was 'some dry retching', but the Home Office corrects this to 'much'. The doctor says his assistant tested Jane's pulse: the Home Office changes this to 'senior colleague'.[10] In the event, the letter was not published, but the Home Office certainly seems nervous. Nevertheless, the Commissioner concluded that

> no case exists for a special or formal inquiry. Such allegations, if made by an ordinary prisoner on discharge, and when disposed of by such inquiry as has been made in this case, would not be deemed to call for any further action … in this case the discharged prisoner is of gentle birth, highly educated and thus enabled to make public her alleged grievances through the medium of the Press and of her influential friends.[11]

The establishment liked to pick and choose its moments to be snobbish.

This was not good enough for Victor, and he turned once more to *The Times* to put his case before the public. As Constance Lytton, his sister had been judged too ill for force-feeding. As Jane Warton, she was not. There could not be a clearer case of double standards. The fact that Jane Warton refused to answer questions about her medical history did not absolve the prison staff from their responsibility to investigate her health. Moreover, he was not asking for special treatment for Constance – quite the reverse. Rather, he wanted to make sure other 'Jane Wartons' would be treated the same as Constance Lytton. 'Your readers will form their own opinions of the justice of a Government Department which brings accusations of untruthfulness against an individual whilst refusing the only means by which the truth can be established,' he concluded, with a flourish.[12]

The Home Office still refused to hold a public inquiry and, as their justification, they brought out the letter that Jane Warton had written at the end of her sentence. 'There is nothing that you need worry about as regards me ... I am not ill ... in my case no injury results only pain and you have always said that pain is wholesome.'[13] It did not matter that this letter was designed to set Edith Lytton's mind at rest. If Jane Warton had said she was not ill and had suffered no injury, it was no use Constance Lytton claiming otherwise now. As far as they were concerned, that was that.

Or not quite. Constance and the suffragettes did not know it, but behind the scenes Churchill did intervene. Privately, he dismissed Constance's claims, 'many of which are trivial and others imaginary. The business of forcibly feeding an unruly and hysterical woman must in any case be disagreeable in its details.' He introduced a new rule which took away the discretion of prison governors and doctors: once a prisoner had been on hunger strike for twenty-four hours, force-feeding should begin immediately.[14] But he also put in place new policies which would prevent any other Jane Warton-type cases. Before any other prisoner was force-fed, a medical officer must sign a certificate showing that the prisoner had been fully examined and that no harm would result from the forced feeding. What was public knowledge, though, was Churchill's introduction of Rule 243a. It did not recognise suffragettes as political prisoners as such, but nevertheless gave WSPU members sentenced to the second and third division the privileges of those in the first division. (Robert's old friend and Judith's father, Wilfred Scawen Blunt, claimed credit for putting the idea in Churchill's head.)[15] Rule 243a put an end to the hunger strikes for several years.

This might not have been the vindication that Constance was hoping for. Nor would she ever get any credit for the new Home Office policies. But Jane Warton's suffering would, indirectly, prevent others from suffering in the same way. That was something.

Meanwhile Victor had decided that enough was enough. Inspired and moved by Constance's bravery, he was determined that her ordeal should not have been in vain. The vote simply had to be granted to women before more damage could be done. Henry Brailsford – who seems to have been rather an unsung hero of the women's suffrage movement – established a 'Conciliation Committee', which would attempt to build a consensus to deliver the vote quickly. Victor chaired the committee. Mrs Pankhurst supported the idea. With the Conciliation Committee at work and Rule 243a in place, she called a truce. Privately, Christabel was not convinced that the Conciliation Committee would succeed, but she welcomed the truce as a time to regroup.[16] The truce also, incidentally, helped keep Constance in the public eye as there were no more dramatic acts of militancy to take her place in the press. Far away on holiday in Innsbruck, Sylvia Pankhurst was asked about Jane Warton: her escapade had reached the European papers too.[17] Constance was the poster girl of the horrors of forcible feeding for the public, but particularly for the suffragettes. For them, she represented the worst excesses of a government which seemed increasingly violent and vindictive towards innocent victims.[18]

Within a few months the committee had a draft Bill – the Conciliation Bill – which they believed was moderate enough to gain enough support – from all parties – to become law. It was not a radical or far-reaching proposition, and the committee admitted as much.

> We do not claim for our Bill that it is an ideal solution; it is a working compromise. Its single merit is that, in a way which no party can consider objectionable or unfair, it breaks down the barrier which at present excludes all women from citizen rights ... it does not preclude a future advance towards Adult Suffrage; but neither does it render such an advance inevitable.[19]

It would give women property owners the vote, though a man and a woman could not represent the same house, and so would only benefit around a million women, mostly unmarried women and widows. The old objections, that these women were more likely to vote Conservative, thus resurfaced among Labour and Liberal supporters. Nevertheless, most of the suffragettes were thrilled. It was the principle of votes for women that mattered most. They could worry about extending the franchise to more women later on. 'You are playing so very important & essential part in the scheme of things. Suddenly the centre has shifted and upon you and your brother & Mr Brailsford so much rests,' wrote Emmeline Pethick-Lawrence.[20] A realistic prospect of victory was at last in sight.

Interestingly, Victor and Constance were often personally at odds in this period. 'Your speech seems splendid from your point of view,' she said, pouring cold water on it. 'It is difficult to think as you do that it will do good.' Eventually Victor grew tired of her inability to listen or compromise. 'Our minds are not tuned to the same key & our explanations therefore lead to discord instead of harmony ... You are trying all the time to misunderstand me – to misinterpret my opinions and to catch me out in some verbal inconsistency,' he wrote crossly. 'We had better work in our own ways and on our own lines. We have the same goal and we shall reach it some day. When militancy is going on I can do little and you think me lukewarm.'[21] Like the other suffragettes, Constance believed that half-hearted friends and allies were worse than enemies. They were all tired of politicians who professed support and then gave up when push came to shove. Though perhaps, too, Constance found it frustrating that she had taken all the risks and now her brother was charging in to capture the glory. Victor's biographer argues that for him, 'woman's suffrage ... was a truly knightly cause, especially when the damsel in distress was his own sister'.[22] Constance must have found this patronising and beside the point. Suffragettes wanted to speak – and vote – for themselves, not be rescued.

But the fault was not all on Victor's side. It's an indication of just how fanatical Constance had become that she was suspicious of Victor at the very moment he was staking his reputation on this controversial cause. He even lost his oldest friend, Winston Churchill, over the matter. Their relationship, already strained over the Jane Warton episode, now snapped. Victor initially overestimated Churchill's support for the Bill and then later unfairly interpreted Churchill as going cold on it, which he saw as an unforgivable betrayal. In truth, Churchill would never have supported the proposals. He despised the suffragettes, who had dogged and disrupted his career for years, and would not countenance anything that looked the least bit like the government caving in. Their friendship had survived Pamela choosing Victor over Winston; it did not survive Victor choosing the suffragettes over Winston.[23] But still Constance underestimated what he was sacrificing for her. She was single-minded in the extreme and 'did not spare her friends or family', as Betty commented drily.[24] Constance sent a piece Betty had written for *Votes for Women* titled 'Why I Believe' to a friend and said patronisingly, 'I think it an excellent presentation of the case from the point of view of the average well-to-do woman who means well.'[25] Whatever her family did to support her, unless they became militants themselves, it would never be enough. Edith always welcomed her back to Homewood. Betty and Emily disagreed with her means but absolutely supported her ends. Victor made her cause his own. But Constance always felt isolated within her family and this constant sniping threatened to overshadow all that they held in common.

On 18 June, 10,000 women marched from the Embankment to the Albert Hall in support of the Conciliation Bill. At the head of the parade were 617 women dressed in white armed with silver staves. These were women who had been to prison. Eighty-seven of them women had been on hunger strike. To her frustration, Constance was put in charge of the musicians, or, as she put it to Betty, 'My task was to work up the respectables. Oh how I hate the respectable world!'[26] All her siblings marched in the parade except Victor, who was a speaker at the main event at the Albert Hall. Watching the procession, Frances Balfour caught sight of Constance: 'A wonderful figure, so set and fixed … But Con's face is the thing that remains to me. I don't feel she is to be long amid the waves of this troublesome world.'[27] Afterwards, Constance went on holiday to Droitwich in Worcestershire with Edith for a much-needed rest. The last time she had been there was just after the John Ponsonby affair had ended so painfully. She was able to look back without regret, though, as all her focus was now directed forward, towards the Conciliation Bill and much-looked for success.

A musician of a rather different sort also reappeared in Constance's life in 1910. It was WSPU policy to contact women who distinguished themselves in public life and ask them about their stance on suffrage. Ethel Smyth had been awarded a doctorate of music by the University of Durham, and Constance, perhaps remembering their past acquaintance at the Ponsonbys', duly wrote to question her about votes for women. Ethel was indifferent and carried the letter around unanswered until a friend persuaded her that women's suffrage was 'the one really alive issue in England' and Mrs Pankhurst 'the most astounding personality'.[28] Still unconvinced, Ethel went along to a meeting, whereupon she met Mrs Pankhurst, and like thousands of women before her, was bewitched. This meeting transformed both her personal and her professional life. She gave up music for two years to become a full-time suffragette. There has been some speculation about the nature of her relationship with Mrs Pankhurst, but it is clear that it was profoundly significant to both women. Ethel and Constance renewed their own acquaintance; rather more surprisingly, Ethel was a great admirer of Edith's.

In July, Constance spoke alongside Emily Wilding Davison at yet another major demonstration in Hyde Park and, in her own spirit of conciliation, she wrote to Victor to say, 'You are paying a bitter price. I can't help hoping that, as you share the crosses, so you will share at least something of the joys.'[29] This generosity reflected the general mood of hopefulness among the suffragettes. It genuinely seemed that victory was around the corner. But they had underestimated Asquith's intransigence. He met with Millicent Fawcett – he would not see the militants – to discuss the question. She said there would be huge anger if the Conciliation Bill did not get beyond a second reading. Frances Balfour felt half the NUWSS were teetering on the bunk of militancy and told Arthur, 'We are as near revolution as we have ever been, the women determined to go forward and life and blood will be sacrificed.'[30] There had been plenty of Bills which had got so far but then were lost for lack of time. It was time the Bill needed, for it had the votes: it passed second reading by a majority of 109. But it was sent to a committee of the whole house, a delaying tactic. Victor wrote desperately saying that a week was all that was needed; Asquith would not commit to anything.[31]

Constance was now employed full-time as an 'organiser' by the WSPU and paid £2 a week. Her pay was backdated to January, in a tacit acknowledgement of her service above and beyond the call of duty in Liverpool Gaol. This meant that for the first time in her life, Constance had the means to live a life independently of her mother. She rented a small flat, at 15 Somerset Terrace, Dukes Road, just off the Euston Road and was ready to leap on a train at a moment's notice to go wherever she might be needed. Mary Neal was a near neighbour.[32] 'It will mean the week days away from home, but every Friday to Monday free. Wondrous terms; in return I give all I have to give, night and day, year in and year out,' she told Aunt T, who can't have seen these terms as wonderful at all. 'Mother on the whole pleased, and feels it to be flattering.'[33] Either Edith was gritting her teeth very hard or Constance was taking a rosy view of the situation.

Being an organiser was hard work. Most organisers were expected to co-ordinate all aspects of the campaign in their area, from posters and propaganda to large-scale demonstrations. By this time, they were experienced and hugely in demand, so much so that they were being discouraged from going to prison because their loss in the field would be too great. A few, like Constance, may have been called 'organisers' but were given the title as a reward for particularly distinguished service and in expectation that it would continue. Constance did not have any formal training in campaigning, nor did she have any particular talent for it. Her post was something more ceremonial. It was her presence the suffragettes needed, not her skills.

Being an organiser meant a packed schedule, relentless travel, snatched meals and uncomfortable nights spent on temporary beds.[34] Constance usually just spent one night in any given town before moving on; her letters did not follow as quickly and she was always trying to catch up and to make arrangements for her next visit.[35] Such a chaotic lifestyle took its toll even on the most robust of suffragettes. It was intensely draining for the sickly Constance, who developed strict rules to help manage her time on the road. 'I always carry about my own flannel sheet. I am a vegetarian, eat no meat, fish or fowls and only require the simplest of other ordinary foods. The only luxury I care much about is a fire in my room: unless I can warm up at home, I can't speak,' she informed another organiser.[36] Constance might like to imagine herself as just one of the girls, with simple needs, but her very specific requirements – especially her vegetarianism – must have seemed unusual to some of her provincial hostesses.

She took to her duties with enthusiasm and her usual wholehearted commitment. Her body, as well as her name, was now invaluable. Always thin, she did not recover the weight she had lost in prison, and was painful to look at. Some women were aged by their time in prison; Constance seemed somehow younger. 'There was a look of spirituality about her that was very moving,' Neville remembered. 'Her ethereal delicacy made a great effect on a platform, and it was important that she should show herself at meetings in order that the crowds of waverers should finally be converted by her look of suffering.'[37] So Constance found herself on something of a whirlwind tour of the country, speaking at meeting after meeting. Her correspondence at this time gives some indication of the distances she was travelling: Bath, Bristol, Lewisham, Walthamstow and Sheffield.[38] She also reappears in *The Times*, in the column announcing the day's arrangements: she was with Christabel in Liverpool in April; with Betty in West London in June and with Mrs Pankhurst in Kensington in July. She even addressed a Christian conference in September at which David Lloyd George was also a speaker.[39]

She had no illusions about her place in the movement, writing to another organiser, Mary Phillips, that she was 'content to be used socially either before or after the meeting'.[40] She was clearly in great demand, though she had become notorious enough that the Cambridge women's colleges refused to have her on the premises. An enterprising student had to hire a hall and have a married woman act as hostess. 'I don't think the Authorities can very well have any objection to that,' wrote another excited student home to her mother.[41]

The victory had to be won in all corners of the country. But she also retained her ties to Hertfordshire and often stopped in to the Letchworth branch of the WSPU to see what they were up to, though she left the day-to-day running of the organisation to others.[42] Nor did she give up her place at the centre of the movement: in October, she and Adela Pankhurst went to lobby the Chancellor of the Duchy of Lancaster into supporting the Conciliation Bill. (It was unsuccessful: he treated them on a lecture to their tactics instead).[43]

In November, after addressing the Actresses' Franchise League, she took part in *The Pageant of Great Women* in Bristol. Written by Cicely Hamilton, this play presented great heroines of the past as a way of restoring women to history and emphasising their present claims. The cast was a mixture of professional actresses and leading suffrage figures. Constance played Florence Nightingale; Annie Kenney, Christabel Pankhurst and the Pethick-Lawrences were all in the audience.[44]

But the cost to her health was increasing. In the autumn, Constance suffered a heart seizure and temporary paralysis; she spent weeks in bed, supported by a nurse, to recover.[45] Then she caught shingles and was confined to bed again, which meant she missed one of the suffragettes' most famous and bloody battles: Black Friday, 18 November 1910. Asquith had stalled and stalled over the Conciliation Bill: now he dissolved Parliament entirely and called another general election, the second that year, hoping it would give him a decisive majority. The Conciliation Bill was lost for that parliamentary session. Mrs Pankhurst was appalled and led a deputation of over three hundred women to the House of Commons. The Westminster police were well used to their tactics by now, and managed most such deputations and protests without injury. On this occasion, though, police were brought in from other parts of London who were less experienced in dealing with the suffragettes and positively seemed to enjoy exercising as much brutality as possible. For once, public sympathy was almost entirely with the suffragettes because the police had so obviously used disproportionate force. More than two hundred women were arrested but Churchill ordered them all released without charge. Though no women were killed on the day, several of the women, weaker or older, died later, and Black Friday was blamed for their injuries. One of these was Emmeline Pankhurst's sister, Mary Clarke, discovered dead in her room on Boxing Day. Mrs Pankhurst, always a patriot as well as a militant, and determined to prove that her followers were responsible citizens, re-established the truce for the coronation year, 1911. But the savagery of Black Friday meant the suffragettes started to question whether they needed to keep putting themselves in harm's way. Why keep hurling themselves at the House of Commons to no avail? Why not make their presence felt in other ways?

In the spring, Constance reappeared in the pages of *The Times* in bizarre circumstances. Lady Selborne, a prominent Conservative supporter of women's suffrage, wrote to *The Times* enclosing a letter she said was from Constance which read, 'You have often pointed out to me the undesirability of militant methods for the propagation of our reasons for demanding the vote ... I cannot help thinking that my method is far more effective than yours.' Three days later, Lady Selborne wrote again to *The Times* confessing that Constance had never actually written the letter; she had just 'borrowed her name' to show 'how hard it is for women like myself, who have no inclination to adopt militant methods, to get our views reasonably set forth'. The combination of the Lytton name and the outrageous tactics of the suffragettes were irresistible to the newspapers, whereas those struggling within the law could not get a fair hearing. But the following day, a letter appeared from Constance herself, saying that even though she had not written the letter, Lady Selborne 'wrote with my full approbation': she completely agreed with her, and no apology was necessary. Indeed, one of the reasons why militancy was so important was that otherwise, women were simply ignored.[46]

For census day, 2 April 1911, the suffragettes rediscovered their sense of fun. They decided to be naughty, rather than aggressive, and boycott the census. Many went roller skating at the Aldwych all night long, meaning they would not appear on the forms which required details of everyone in a given house on the night. Even more imaginatively, Emily Davison hid in a parliamentary broom cupboard, meaning that she could legitimately give the House of Commons as her address on that night. The historian Jill Liddington has recently completed a thorough study of suffrage tactics on census day and distinguishes between 'evaders' and 'resisters', who scrawled defiantly across their form or just refused to fill it in.[47] Constance was one of the latter, and it was completed for her by one of the census officials (which presumably accounts for the mistakes: her age is stated as 'over 60' though she was only forty-two; her place of birth is given as 'British born', though it had been Vienna). Her personal occupation is described grandly as 'daughter of sister of an Earl' and her industry marked as 'independent means'.

In May 1911, she was at last able to meet Arthur Balfour in person to discuss votes for women, accompanied by Betty and Annie Kenney. He was not especially encouraging.[48] But change at last appeared to be afoot. A second Conciliation Bill passed the second reading stage by a majority of 167 MPs, and Asquith promised a new Conciliation Bill would get the parliamentary time it needed to become law the following year. Was the end in sight at last? In June, 40,000 suffragettes and suffragists turned out to mark the coronation, to give a visible symbol of their patriotism and desire to become full citizens. There were more mass meetings at the Queen's Hall, in which Victor pledged his determination to see the Conciliation Bill through, and Arthur Ponsonby popped up to show his support, saying, 'Even a quarter of a loaf was better than no bread.'[49]

By the autumn, it was obvious Constance was becoming increasingly ill and weak. At least three times after speeches she was overcome with what she described as 'heart-seizure', which left her 'incapacitated for about a quarter of an hour'.[50] She reluctantly began to turn down invitations to speak. On one occasion, she gave the organisers a list of suggested alternative speakers – interestingly enough, about half were men – but said that both Betty and Victor were full up until after Christmas.[51]

The rank and file members loved her more than ever: for transcending class barriers, for her experiences as Jane Warton and for her determination to keep going until the fight was won, despite her obvious frailty. Constance was now a star attraction in the WSPU, adored by the suffragettes and almost as prominent as the Pankhursts themselves. She was even fictionalised as Mary O'Neil, the heroine of Constance Maud's suffrage novel *No Surrender*. Mary is Irish, but her passion, empathy and close identification with working women all belong to Constance.[52] Perhaps it was this fictional appearance in print that gave her the idea to begin writing her own book. With her name and notoriety, she hoped that it would reach a far wider audience than she would ever have access to otherwise, no matter how many speeches she made and meetings she attended. Every moment that was not given to the suffragettes or wasted on illness was now spent writing this statement of her beliefs, values and experiences.

CHAPTER TEN

BETRAYAL

'If this bill does not go through, the woman suffrage movement will not be stopped, but the spirit of conciliation of which this bill is an expression will be destroyed, and there will be war throughout the country, raging, tearing, fierce, bitter strife, though nobody wants it.'[1]

In November, Asquith inexplicably changed his mind and abandoned the idea of a Conciliation Bill. Instead, he announced the government would be introducing universal suffrage for men. There was no mention of women at all in the Bill. By way of an afterthought, Asquith eventually added that women's suffrage could be tacked on as an amendment, if MPs were so minded.

Asquith could not have done anything that was more offensive to the women's movement. As Millicent Fawcett said, 'If it has been Mr Asquith's object to enrage every Woman Suffragette to the point of frenzy, he could not have acted with greater perspicacity.'[2] The restricted franchise for men was undoubtedly outdated and problematic, but to overlook women in this way was hugely insulting. On 17 November, Constance was one of thirty women, both suffragettes and suffragists, who met with the Prime Minister to express their outrage. Constance was no longer terrified at the thought of coming face to face with him. Her experiences as Jane Warton had given her the confidence to believe that she could speak authoritatively and with credibility on behalf of other women. The other members of the deputation were Christabel and Sylvia Pankhurst, Annie Kenney and Emmeline Pethick-Lawrence: Constance was firmly among the leaders now. Betty was also at the meeting, representing the Conservative women's supporters of suffrage. But nothing they said could persuade him to change his mind. Christabel despised him. 'Mr Asquith that day was rosy-faced and smiling. He might have been Father Christmas with votes for women in his bag of presents.'[3]

The suffragettes declared war. On 21 November, there was a mass window-smashing rampage around Westminster and Victoria. Constance was accompanied by her friend Miss Lawless, armed with a hammer as well as with her usual stones. She wandered up and down Victoria Street in a state of nervous agitation. When the clock struck eight, she told Miss Lawless, 'I can wait no longer', then turned to the nearest building and began smashing away.[4] She was soon arrested but found the whole experience rather enjoyable as there were so many comrades about and the police were good-humoured, even encouraging.

She was ordered to return to Bow Street Magistrates' Court on 23 November. On the morning of the hearing she had a 'heart collapse', and found herself unable to lift her head or speak. Nevertheless, she struggled out of bed, without seeking medical attention, and made it to the magistrates' court by the afternoon, keen to use the defendants' stand as a soap box. 'This was the only effective means of protest left to us by a Government which boasts of Liberalism and representation where men are concerned', she told the court, 'but ignores the elementary principles of representation where women are concerned. Votes and riot are the only form of appeal to which this Government will respond. They refuse us votes, we fall back on riot. The wrongs they inflict on women are intolerable, and we will no longer tolerate them.' Fully warmed up, she continued, 'Although we committed the acts alleged, we were not guilty of crime, our conduct being fully justified by the circumstances of the case.'⁵ The magistrate did not agree.

Given the publicity her case had received, it is unimaginable that the authorities would have done anything that might have risked her health. But they would have been equally careful of anything that could be seen as further special treatment. So despite her obvious illness Constance was sentenced to fourteen days in Holloway. She was put in a taxi with Mary Leigh, Miss Lawless and several policemen to go to the prison, but Miss Lawless found that she had forgotten her purse and the car had to stop and get it.

'I decided,' Constance wrote in *Prisons and Prisoners*,

> that the Constable should get out with Miss Lawless, put her in charge of another policeman, then return and mount guard on us … nothing would have been easier than to open the door the other side of the pavement, and, with the noise of the street, Mrs Leigh or I could have escaped. But it was understood all round that this was not the game, and we waited quietly.⁶

The police and the suffragettes were well used to playing this game by now.

Constance was sent straight to the prison hospital and spent most of her time resting and reading. She was impressed with the changes in Holloway: suffragettes were now allowed to wear their own clothes and talk to each other: she walked arm-in-arm with Emmeline Pethick-Lawrence around the exercise yard. Small improvements, perhaps, but hard won, the results of Jane Warton's experiences and rule 243a. On 28 November, an anonymous benefactor paid her fine and she was released. The supervisor escorted her home and Constance spontaneously kissed her. She took several months off to recover from the strain of this experience, staying quietly at home.⁷

She did write to the Home Secretary to complain that her sentence had been light compared to that of Mary Leigh. Constance alleged that Mary's past convictions had been held against her, while her own had been overlooked. The Home Office brushed this aside.[8] In December, Emily Davison was arrested for setting fire to a postbox. Asked about her motives in court, she said she was protesting at the harshness of the sentence given to Mary Leigh compared with that of Constance Lytton.[9] The suffragettes would not give up their fight for equal treatment as well as equal rights.

Back in South Africa, Olive Schreiner had completed what she believed to be her life's work. The first draft of this had been destroyed in the Boer War and she had painstakingly rewritten it over a decade. This was published in 1911 as *Women and Labour* and became an incredibly important text for feminists: it had a profound impact on the young Vera Brittain, who would call it 'the Bible of the Women's Movement'. It was dedicated, in tribute to their friendship and in recognition of her service, to Constance Lytton.

In the new year, Constance went with Christabel and Emmeline Pethick-Lawrence to the wedding of a fellow suffragette, Una Dugdale, which reached the newspapers because the bride refused to use the word 'obey'.[10] Then she plunged back into a whirlwind of activity, acting as Mrs Pankhurst's deputy at speeches in Bristol, Shrewsbury and Stroud. It took an immense toll on her. 'My life is mostly a rush of continuous bodily and mental strength,' she told Alice Ker.[11] There was no time to slow down. 'From all private accounts that reach me the Cabinet are at last beginning to fear the situation they have created for themselves on this question. It is the moment therefore to "press" our advantage & more than ever to remember the helpless for whose sake we suffer,' she told Millicent Fawcett.[12] But her intelligence was too optimistic. The Cabinet might be increasingly afraid of what the suffragettes might do,

but that didn't mean they were prepared to give in. Supporters of
the Conciliation Bill had a third and final try at getting it through
the House of Commons in February and March 1912, regardless
of Asquith's suffrage bill for men. This time it was defeated, voted
down by Irish nationalists who were focusing all their energies on
a Home Rule Bill.

With the Conciliation Bill dead and buried, the suffragettes
needed a new strategy. On 16 February 1912, the Liberal MP Charles
Henry Hobhouse made a speech in which he declared that the suffragettes had done nothing on the scale of burning Nottingham
Castle or tearing up railings in Hyde Park: actions which directly
led to the Great Reform Acts in 1832 and 1867. The suffragettes took
this as the go-ahead for renewed and extreme violence. Emmeline
Pankhurst proclaimed that 'the argument of the broken pane of glass
is the most valuable argument in modern politics'.[13] The suffragettes
put this theory to the test on 1 March 1912, when there was a mass
smashing of windows in central London. Up and down Oxford
Street, Piccadilly, the Strand and elsewhere, women produced ham-
mers from their handbags and went to work on shop windows.[14]
Emmeline Pankhurst, having been taught to throw stones by Ethel
Smyth, broke the windows at 10 Downing Street. The trick was
repeated again a few days later. Constance's old friend Alice Ker
had come down especially from Liverpool for the occasion: she was
sentenced to three months. Dr Louisa Garrett Anderson, daughter
of the medical pioneer Elizabeth, and niece of Millicent Fawcett,
was also arrested for the first time.

Constance wasn't well enough for a session of smashing, nor the
inevitable prison sentence which would follow. Instead, she went
to Holloway after the event to see if she could do anything for
the women. She was amused to read the 'newspaper accounts of
the hysterical girls of 18!' and looked round at rows of women like
her, approaching middle age. Her presence, and the knowledge of

what she had done for them, gave the prisoners new strength. Ethel Smyth, waiting to be sentenced, wrote to Betty that 'the adoration of Suffragettes for "Lady Conny" is a thing to see, not tho' to wonder at'.[15] Constance began writing to Alice's daughter Margaret, to keep her up to date on what she knew of her mother's trial and situation. 'Your mother has been perfectly splendid!' she told Margaret. 'She was the only one of the lot … who was allowed bail, but she wouldn't take it as the others hadn't a chance of it … I know she is ever so happy now at her job being over & well brought off.'[16] The judge said he regretted her actions, but Alice replied that as the mother of daughters, she would do anything she could to bring about votes for women.[17] Inspired by her mother's example, Margaret Ker became a suffragette herself. Constance went down to the House of Commons, where she loitered in St Stephen's Hall to lobby MPs about the treatment of the women in Holloway. Frances Balfour saw her there 'in full costume … and looking a meek mule … She is a very yellow colour and her eyes look strained, but she was all herself.'[18]

Holloway could not accommodate the volume of prisoners. Some had to be sent out to other gaols around the country while Holloway itself had so many suffragettes that it was almost like a suffrage reunion. Striding round the exercise yard in the March chill, the suffragettes decided to cheer themselves up by singing the suffragette anthem, 'March of the Women'. From a cell above, two arms appeared, waving a toothbrush in lieu of a baton. It was Ethel Smyth, conducting her own composition in the most unlikely of circumstances.[19] But this was a light-hearted moment in an otherwise bleak time. The sentences imposed on the window breakers were severe: generally several months' hard labour. Worse still, Rule 243a did not apply where an individual had been sentenced for 'serious violence' so the privileges they had become accustomed to were taken away. The suffragettes responded by returning to their old weapon: the hunger strike. But they were sent a message to hold off while awaiting the outcome of further alarming developments.

The government did not just want the window breakers themselves in prison: they wanted the leaders there too. After the second attack on West End windows, the offices of *Votes for Women* were raided and shut down by the police. Emmeline Pankhurst and Mabel Tuke, already in prison for smashing windows, were charged alongside the Pethick-Lawrences with conspiracy to incite violence. Only Christabel was free, and after dodging the authorities for some weeks in London, she fled to Paris, where she attempted to conduct the campaign in exile. Annie Kenney took over as leader. But the government achieved its aim, in the short-term at least, as the organisation faltered without their most inspirational figureheads at the helm.

Later, Betty asked Annie why Constance wasn't asked to take on a formal leadership role at this time. With so many powerful and significant women missing, Betty believed that Constance could have filled the gap.[20] But the truth was that Constance did not have the calculating political brain needed to direct a campaign. Her talent was not for strategising, but for sacrifice. At a major event on 7 March, just after the Pethick-Lawrences had been arrested, Constance stood up and surveyed the assembled crowds. 'I believe the militant section of the movement has "collapsed",' she said. 'I congratulate you on that collapse.' The rest of the reported speech shows how far she had come as a speaker. She could now rouse a crowd with the best of them.

> They think they can seize our funds, that they can behead the movement of its leaders and the movement will come to an end. (Cries of 'Never!') It is quite true, our leaders are phenomenal. (Applause.) But they are the products of the movement which they lead: they have not created it. Nobody knows that better than themselves.

Nobody knows it better than we do in a dark hour like this. There will be a variation in our next few meetings. Our leaders will not be on the platforms, but they will be there. Whether they are in prison or whether they are dead, our leaders shall lead us. (Applause).[21]

A few weeks later, Constance was once again advertised in *Votes for Women* as a hostess for a meeting in honour of the leaders called 'all will be well'. Emmeline Pankhurst said with her usual confidence that 'the fact that this trial should be held is the very best thing that could happen to this movement … The trial, like everything else that has happened to us, is going to be a great victory for the women's cause.'[22] But privately, with Christabel so far away, she cannot have been so optimistic. This was the last time that Emmeline Pethick-Lawrence and Emmeline Pankhurst would appear together in public.

At the end of May, Mrs Pankhurst and the Pethick-Lawrences were sentenced to nine months in the second division. They threatened to go on hunger strike unless they were moved to the first division and treated as political prisoners. They were moved, but their comrades were still serving sentences for hard labour, so they went on hunger strike anyway. The government was incensed about what they saw as a complete breakdown in logic. The leaders were in the first division because they had been sentenced for incitement to violence rather than actually committing violence themselves. Their window-smashing comrades could not be expected to be put in the first division: that was not how rule 243a worked. But the suffragettes weren't interested in this distinction.

So the hunger strike was now used once more on a mass scale, for the first time in several years. It was also the first time any of the leaders were force-fed. Emmeline Pethick-Lawrence found the experience so horrendous that she fainted. Emmeline Pankhurst, listening next door, threatened to hit the doctor with a jug if he tried it on her, and was left alone. From this time on Emmeline Pankhurst was regularly on hunger strike, though she was never force-fed.

The two women were freed after a couple of days, though Fred Pethick-Lawrence was made to suffer force-feeding twice a day for ten days before his release.[23] Ethel Smyth and Louisa Garrett Anderson were both released just weeks into their lengthy sentences, which brought up all the old questions of preferential treatment. 'If it is considered just to release these two women of intellectual distinction and social position, why is not a similar course of action taken with regard to the other women still in prison?' demanded *Votes for Women*.[24] At this time, there were more than eighty women on hunger strike in Holloway. In June, Emily Wilding Davison attempted to commit suicide by throwing herself down an iron staircase. Like her old comrade Constance Lytton, she hoped to save other women pain and degradation by making herself into a martyr. On this occasion, she failed.[25]

There were a few voices still prepared to stand up for the suffragettes in public. One was their loyal friend Keir Hardie and another was Louisa Garrett Anderson, who wrote in the *British Medical Journal* that 'the reason they do not take their food is political, not pathological, and the appropriate treatment is statesmanship, not a stomach tube'.[26] Another supporter was Emily Lutyens. Though vehemently opposed to the violence of the suffragettes, she was still a strong supporter of votes for women. She wrote to *The Times* at the end of March to promote

the happy wives and mothers who, having everything that this world can give have yet been willing to face insult, imprisonment and even death if necessary because by doing so they hoped to bring a little nearer the day when their sisters would no longer toil in sweated industries or be driven on to the streets for a livelihood.[27]

But, in general, the renewed militancy horrified the public. The suffragettes were becoming more extreme and, as a result, what public support they had now began to ebb away. Even some suffragettes began to feel uneasy at the new strategy. Where once they had been an army, now they were more like a militia and individual suffragettes were no longer merely soldiers but guerrilla fighters. The fight itself, not the cause they were fighting for, seemed to become the focus of their efforts. But those who remained were prepared to go to any lengths for their beloved leaders.

Their former friends in the NUWSS were also alienated by the renewed militancy. Millicent Fawcett felt just as let down by Asquith over the failure of the Conciliation Bill as she had at his surprise support for universal male suffrage. But rather than turning to violence, the suffragists turned instead to the Labour Party. They believed that helping more Labour candidates into Parliament would put greater pressure on the Liberal Party, and set up an 'election fighting fund' to achieve this aim. The labour movement and the women's movement thus came together again: though without the suffragettes, who still refused to support any political party.

Constance drafted an angry letter to Millicent Fawcett expressing her disappointment at this new policy.

> What did working men do to ensure fair play for women … through the long drawn out struggle of over 40 years during which there was no question of violence on the part of women? When militancy began … what did the Labour party to secure … that women's deputations should be received, that women's suffragists should not be imprisoned, that if imprisoned the treatment of them should be differentiated from that of criminals? How did these defenders of the right to strike stand by the women when their hunger strike … was met by the barbaries of forcible feeding during weeks and months of imprisonment?[28]

Constance's admiration for working women obviously did not extend to working men. While, as we have seen, she regularly lobbied prominent members of the Conservative and Liberal Parties, I have not seen anything that suggests she did the same for Labour politicians. Understandably enough, she put her energy into trying to persuade those in her own social milieu whom she might reasonably be expected to influence. Later in the year, the Labour MP George Lansbury actually resigned in order to take a stand over women's suffrage. For once the suffragettes broke their own rules in order to give him their backing, but the Labour Party and the WSPU were unable to work successfully together and he lost his seat.[29]

The suffragettes became 'more violent, but also less confrontational'.[30] Where they had once deliberately sought arrest, now they did not want to waste their time in prison, nor their energy on hunger striking. Sabotage and subterfuge were the order of the day.

But Constance was not about to embark on a midnight arson attack. She was feeling worse and worse. 'I have been so utterly done with the overstrain these last weeks that I did not know what I was doing or saying – have had to come home here and collapse into bed with a fever attack,' she wrote to Margaret Ker, apologising for her silence.[31] She had flu and bronchitis, which kept her in bed for several weeks. When the hunger strikes began, she forced herself to get out of bed and put herself to work trying to get the suffragette side of the story into the press. After a couple of visits to the *Times* offices, her heart 'gave out, returning to the tricks it has often indulged in since 1912'.[32] She reluctantly concluded that the only thing she could do now was take herself off to a quiet cottage and finish her book.

Her troubles were not just physical: the old depression was creeping up on her. She was having nightmares 'about my jobs left undone, about beloved leaders in prison, fearful gloom at the separation from them and total removal of all our heads', she told Betty. She was profoundly worried about the ordinary members in prison. She felt a strong sense of obligation to do whatever she could for them, and believed she was always letting them down in some way.[33] She also was unsure whether she was going to be tried alongside the Pethick-Lawrences. 'My name was mentioned in the prosecution, & certainly if the Leaders are criminals on the grounds of "incitement", "conspiracy" etc so am I,' she told Alice Ker, still in prison. 'It seems to me our Albert Hall meeting this summer will be in Holloway.' She concluded this letter by saying, 'My thoughts are constantly with you. If you have an opportunity give my love to all my fellow-workers in Holloway & my friendly greeting to those officials who know me.'[34]

These were the last words she ever wrote with her right hand. Later that day, Constance's charwoman let herself into the Euston Road flat as usual. There, she found Constance lying on the floor, barely conscious and unable to move or speak.

CHAPTER ELEVEN

PARALYSIS

'I would rather be Con, lying broken and shattered there than any one of those men who have been false to every principle of the Liberalism they have preferred. If Con had died, she would have died gloriously.'[1]

Constance had suffered a stroke. At first it was uncertain whether she would survive. She lived at first at Emily's house in Bloomsbury Square. A nurse, Sister Kate Oram, who had previously nursed Florence Nightingale, was hired and became her constant companion. It was a long struggle back to a half-life. Two months passed before she could get out of bed. She could manage only a few steps at a time, and otherwise had a wheelchair. Nurse Oram would push the chair through Bloomsbury each day so that she might enjoy the outdoors.[2] Her right side remained paralysed and she would have to gingerly lift the right hand with the left. She could no longer write. Improbable rumours about what had happened to her spread. Olive Schreiner reported that 'a particle from the worn-out heart has got into one of the arteries in the brain … She will never be able to stand the least excite again, as there will always be the danger of particles from the worn-out heart breaking off again and getting into the circulation.'[3]

Eventually Constance was well enough to go back to Homewood. Edith's visitors' book for Homewood records, in her own handwriting, 'Constance Georgina Lytton returned home July 28th 1912.' She would not, of course, have added any comment on her feelings, but her gratitude that Constance was still alive, and recovering, would have only been heightened by the knowledge that she was home for good. Aside from a few days here or there, Constance would not leave home for over a decade.

But that did not mean that Constance lost interest in the suffragettes. Quite the contrary: even her near-fatal collapse was used in service of the cause. At the end of June, Betty wrote to *The Times* supporting the hunger-striking women in prison and informing the public of Constance's condition. Betty made it very clear that they all believed Constance's illness was an after-effect of the force-feeding. 'I feel it a public duty to mention this case of the dire result of the treatment which it is believed is still being meted out to some 70 prisoners in the Suffrage cause.'[4] Betty continued to raise their case throughout the summer, more horrified than ever at the brutality of force-feeding now that she had seen the long-term consequences. But she still kept well away from endorsing the suffragettes. 'As a non-militant I am prepared to deplore the rebellious spirit – the spirit of hate – as the motive power for the redress of any grievance,' she told the *Evening Standard*. 'But wise rulers should take care how they excite it in any section of the community.'[5]

The situation of these seventy women was debated in Parliament and the Jane Warton affair was brought up once more. Victor wrote to *The Times* to complain that Reginald McKenna, now the Home Secretary, had misled the House by telling them that Jane had refused to be force-fed. He also pointed out that McKenna had finally admitted that Jane could not keep the food down; at the time, Edward Troup had insisted that she had not been sick.[6] While *Votes for Women* mentioned these letters, is rather surprising to find that the newspaper did not cover her illness in greater depth.[7] Perhaps this was because the paper was once more packed with personal testimonies of women being force-fed. In this context, Jane Warton was old news.

Once the suffragettes knew what had happened, letters expressing what Constance had meant to them poured in. Constance had
been inspired by the suffragettes she had met – Emmeline Pethick-
Lawrence, Jessie Kenney, Laura Ainsworth – now she in her turn
became an inspiration, enabling other women to screw up their
courage and do whatever they thought necessary. 'Every life she has
ever touched has been strengthened, purified and ennobled,' wrote
Emmeline Pethick-Lawrence, while Annie Kenney said, 'How
little we feel, how small-hearted and narrow-minded compared to
her! I always think of a lamp that throws out its light that those
who are stranded can be guided to safety and security.' 'She makes
one give one's very best in words and deeds, even without speaking.
I always want to be and act my noblest because of her,' an anonymous suffragette wrote to Edith. From South Africa came a letter
signed by forty-five feminists: 'We deeply hope that we shall before
long hear that you are fully restored to labour for the cause so near
all our hearts. Across the seas we stretch hands of love & sympathy
towards you.' The last signatory was Olive Schreiner. Only Emmeline Pankhurst struck the wrong note. Preoccupied and distracted,
she wrote carelessly, 'I hope you will soon be well again and that
you will take better care of yourself in future', and used the rest
of her note to praise Christabel.[8] Meanwhile, a suffragette visiting
Constance at Emily's house asked her nephews whether they were
proud of their 'splendid Auntie'. 'No,' was the reply. 'We think she
has done very wrong.'[9]

Aside from the odd visit to her sisters, Aunt T and Emmeline
Pethick-Lawrence, Constance now lived entirely at home and
largely in bed. In such constrained circumstances, her days were now
once again dominated by family concerns, especially as the younger
generation grew up. By now, Constance had twelve nieces and five
nephews. In July 1912, Betty had a final daughter at the age of forty-
five (her eldest daughter, Eleanor, was twenty-one) and named her

Kathleen Constance.[10] Victor's children lived a short walk away and often came to visit; the others used to come for weekends and extended holidays in the summer. They all loved Constance but each responded to her, of course, according to their age and personality. Few were old enough to remember her as anything but a complete invalid. The natural tendency of the very young to see all adults as 'very old' was exacerbated by her obvious illness. She was constantly breathless and easily tired. She stayed in bed until lunchtime and then would have another nap in the afternoon. But compared with her former state, she could describe this to Alice Ker as being 'wonderfully well'.[11]

Except on her very worst days, she was still sparky and still funny, keen to involve the children in innocent conspiracies. Something of a rebel herself and already aspiring to be a composer, Elisabeth Lutyens found Constance to be a kindred spirit and an ally against her rather intimidating Grannie. 'She chuckled at things, she was anything but sanctimonious,' Elisabeth remembered. 'Aunt Con was slightly disrespectful. Nothing was sacrosanct. I felt she was on our side.' Neville's daughter Anne was a less frequent visitor, but Constance had a deep and unforgettable impact on her. 'When we were very young she used to read fairy stories to us, and though never as a child did I really believe in fairies, she made me believe … by making it quite impossible not to, she made them sound so very real,' Anne said, remembering that Constance was visibly amused by the dark morality of these fairy stories. Aunt Con was a special favourite of Anne's, and she believed to the end of her life that Con was the most impressive person she ever knew. Hermione, Victor's older daughter, remembered that her natural empathy with people was even more obvious when it came to children. She invited confidences, and the older children would turn up at her door with bunches of wild flowers and their homework, ready to share their secrets. At fifteen, Hermione left an essay with Constance to read, and it was returned full of scratches. Every time Hermione had written 'men', Constance crossed it out and wrote 'men and women'. It was also Constance, perhaps remembering Emily's disastrous honeymoon, who gave them a book to teach them the facts of life. Judith was cross about this. Anne found the book was so euphemistically written that after reading it she was still none the wiser.

The younger ones, though, could find Constance strange and a little frightening. Hermione's sister Davinia found Constance's obvious differences uncomfortable rather than interesting. Elisabeth's younger sister, Mary, found the atmosphere oppressive and dreaded the hour that she would be expected to sit with Aunt Con. 'She asked me questions, I had to sit beside her bed and I didn't know how long I'd have to stay there, I didn't like this invalidish atmosphere and I felt trapped, completely trapped,' she remembered. It always very hot in Constance's room, and there was a lingering smell of flannel sheets, mixed with the smell of her Pekingese dog. Constance would peel grapes for the dog to eat while she talked. She had shelves full of ornaments and knick-knacks which the children were allowed to inspect, play with and occasionally take home.

The children liked it better when she was well enough to come downstairs, when they could escape outside if her company got too much. Sometimes they were allowed to push her around in her chair. She was quite particular about the way the rugs should be arranged on her legs, but otherwise was content to sit back and let the children play at being horses while she sat in the carriage. At home, she sat in the sunny dining room, by far the nicest room in the house, and arranged flowers with one hand. These were 'in the Japanese style', in flat pans rather than tall vases, with individual flowers and twigs held down with stones. Occasionally she played a few notes on the piano with her left hand. She could not, of course, indulge herself in cleaning any more, but she still liked everything spick and span, detested mess and loved the smell of Brasso. Her dark hair had by now turned grey, but her deep blue eyes were still striking, and when she laughed – as often as she could manage it – her whole face lit up. She wore a long purple dress with a white lace collar, to which she pinned her suffragette medals. Her own clothes were loose and flowing, to make it easier for the nurse to get them on and off, but she had strong opinions about the children's clothes and what the 'right' shoes were.

Constance made a stark contrast with Edith, now very much a *grande dame*, who sat for hours straight up on a hard chair and demanded attention rather than affection. 'She already seemed to belong to history,' Mary recalled. 'She pronounced cucumber, cowcumber; laundry, larndry; soot, sut; and blouse and vase, bloose and vaize. She sent her hair-combings to Paris to be made up into curls which the maid pinned to the front of her head.'[12] But Elisabeth remembered that Edith was lonely too. She would sometimes sit very quietly in the dining room so that she could hear the servants' conversation. Edith was very much respected and admired in the village, and had a genuine interest in the welfare of local people, but her elevated social position also had the effect of cutting her off from company. Neville brought out the best in Edith: on visits he rubbed her back and played the flute for her. The children all saw that Edith and Constance adored each other. 'I only remember Grannie being so devoted to her and thoughtful for her comfort and making her really the care of her life,' Mary recalled. Anne said that Constance was a calming influence on Edith: if Edith threatened to get upset, Constance had a knack of saying exactly the right soothing thing.

Yet the children also sensed the unspoken complexities of this relationship, even if they didn't fully understand them. Having lived at the epicentre of a whirlwind, Constance found it hard to go back to living a life of restrictions and constraints. She remained devoted to the suffragettes and would not hear a word against them. Edith could find this difficult. Lady Selborne wrote to Betty accurately (if tactlessly): 'She is such a noble, selfless nature, that it makes one feel better to be with her, but I always do feel that life would hardly be bearable if one held one's opinions with that intensity.'[13]

It was hard to reconcile the stories of Aunt Con's wild adventures with her present illness. 'The idea of prison was the nightmare that bad nannies threatened you with,' Davinia remembered. 'The fact that one's aunt had gone to prison and that … everybody said she was nearly a saint: I couldn't work it out.' Few of the children were old enough to remember her as anything other than a complete invalid. Anne thought that she would have been happier living in modern times, with greater freedom.[14]

Outside the family, Constance's closest friend during these years was Miss Avery, the village schoolteacher. Miss Avery was a friend from the suffragette campaign: she had been the secretary of the Knebworth branch of the WSPU.[15] She now became a weekly visitor, and Constance interested herself in the running of the school. She also took an interest in several children who had been orphaned in the war and boarded out in the village; these were known as 'Lady Constance children'.[16]

After the Pethick-Lawrences had been released, they went to Canada to recover. The government seized their home as payment for the costs of their trial. When they returned from their holiday, they urged caution on the Pankhursts. They could see that popular opinion was turning vehemently against the increased militancy, and believed that a campaign to educate the public about why the shift in tactics was necessary before they continued to smash windows and start fires. But Mrs Pankhurst and Christabel were not used to being criticised within the WSPU, still less being told what to do. Their response was to eject the Pethick-Lawrences from the movement. This was heartbreaking and inexplicable to many of the suffragettes. The public version of events was that the Pethick-Lawrence finances were becoming a liability to the WSPU. The Pethick-Lawrences, to their credit, did not contradict this and kept their counsel, to ensure the break was swift and clean. They took *Votes for Women* with them and the WSPU started a new newspaper, *The Suffragette*. Christabel and Emmeline Pankhurst never spoke to the Pethick-Lawrences again. Many of the suffragettes were understandably left bewildered by this episode. Constance decided to stick with the Pankhursts until the end. But she wrote to a friend describing Emmeline Pethick-Lawrence 'as the Leader whom I am proud to follow, in whom I place whole hearted faith and love.'[17] She had brought Constance into the movement and they had served time together in Holloway; Constance would never forget her. Holloway was on her mind that spring. It was five years since she had first been imprisoned and she wrote an open letter to the friends joining together for a reunion:

> The sufferings of our fellows in prison are so much greater now and the fight has become much fiercer to some, yet it was truly a beginning, a baptism of fire, and that whatever the camp in which we may now find ourselves, we have grown in this woman's movement startlingly beyond our vision in 1909.[18]

Christabel was still abroad and Mrs Pankhurst now cut a lonely figure at the top of the organisation. Annie Kenney did her best to keep the show on the road and ran the day-to-day business while Mrs Pankhurst was in prison. She made weekly visits to Paris to take orders from Christabel and then returned to carry them out. This was an incredibly difficult time for the suffragettes. The WSPU appeared to be collapsing and the government seemed to be winning.

Though Constance had no physical strength to serve the suffragettes, she still had one asset: her name. She was determined that it

should be put to some use. In January 1913, she got out the manu-
script of her book, shelved for many months. She had reached the
moment in Holloway when she had been to communion with Emmeline Pethick-Lawrence.[19] Now she determined to finish the story,
as a way of bringing renewed publicity to the struggle and shame
on the government. This was no simple task, and the first obstacle
was purely practical. Her right hand remained paralysed, wasted and
useless. So, over many months of patient struggle, Constance taught
herself to write with her left hand. Her old handwriting had been
fluid and easy; now, the carefully formed letters stood up painfully
straight, each one formed and printed individually. She had to struggle on this way until 1917, when her friends bought her a typewriter.
There is a poignant picture of her, looking positively elderly, sat up in
bed with the typewriter on her lap. However, there are more handwritten letters than typewritten among her papers: it cannot have
been easy to press down the keys with her withered hand.

With the more cautious Pethick-Lawrences out of the picture,
and with Christabel still in Paris, unable to see the impact of her
policies at first hand, suffragette violence now reached new heights.
Though they were still careful not to risk lives – apart from their
own – they went on the rampage. Telegraph wires were cut and golf
courses were torched. The public were incensed, but the suffragettes
were unrepentant. One wrote to the *Daily Telegraph*:

> Everyone seems to agree upon the necessity of putting a stop to Suf-
> fragist outrages; but no one seems certain how to do so. There are two,
> and only two, ways in which this can be done. Both will be effectual.
>
> 1. Kill every woman in the United Kingdom. 2. Give women
> the vote.[20]

But option two now seemed further away than ever. In January
1913, the Speaker ruled that the government's proposed Bill to grant

universal suffrage for men could not be amended to include votes for women. Their last hope for this parliamentary session was gone. Militancy escalated once more. One suffragette, Lilian Lenton, re-called in her memoir that the strategy was now to make the country ungovernable, demonstrating that governments cannot rule with-out consent.[21] They were certainly succeeding in causing chaos. In February, a house that was being built for Lloyd George was blown up. Emmeline Pankhurst took responsibility, was arrested and sen-tenced to three years' hard labour.

Emmeline Pankhurst on hunger strike presented an acute prob-lem for the government. Much older than most of the other strik-ers, she was also worn out from her years on the road, and as a result was very frail and vulnerable. There was a very real risk she might die. Indeed, the authorities had only just managed to avoid killing another suffragette. Early in 1913, Lilian Lenton was force-fed while tied to a chair. She was later discovered unconscious and hurriedly released for treatment. The feeding tube had accidentally been put into her lung, not her stomach. She developed septic pneumonia and almost died.[22] Her case became almost as notorious as that of Jane Warton.

Partly as a result of such horrific accidents, and partly to avoid having to force-feed Emmeline Pankhurst, the government changed tack. It hurriedly passed what became known as the infamous 'Cat and Mouse Act'. This gave them the ability to re-lease a hunger-striking prisoner who appeared too weak and ill to continue in prison, then re-arrest them later on. Of course, once released, many 'mice' went on the run. They rested and recuperated in supporters' homes – one house in Kensington became known as 'Mouse Castle' – but then relished giving the authorities the slip and going out on the rampage again. The 'Cat and Mouse Act' did mean that the numbers of suffragettes being force-fed now dwindled to a handful: those who were thought too dangerous to let out because

their offences were particularly serious.[23] Constance felt hopelessly disconnected and wrote wistfully to Adela, 'Now that I have
more life, I do sometimes wish tremendously to be near and see
my darling suffragettes, and to hear news of them.'[24] That Christmas, she was delighted to see both Adela and Olive Schreiner.
Each was profoundly moved and joyful at the reunion. It was
sixteen years since the three of them had last been together. It
never happened again; but for all three it was among the most
significant friendships of their lives.[25] Adela's daughter was named
Olive Constance.

This last period of the suffragette campaign was marked by increasing desperation, personified by Emmeline Pankhurst.[26] She
declared herself 'a prisoner of war'.[27] She had begun thirst striking as well as hunger striking while in prison in order to get out
faster, and the impact on her health was predictably devastating.
Thirst striking, Emmeline recalled later, made the ordeal of hunger
striking seem 'a mild experience'.[28] Under the terms of the Cat and
Mouse Act, she was repeatedly released and re-arrested, and in the
first year of her sentence she served only thirty days. The suffragettes were incensed by this treatment of their beloved leader.

In June 1913, Emily Wilding Davison, who had been at Constance's side in Newcastle and for many speeches, died under the
King's horse on Derby Day. Mrs Pankhurst, on release under the
Cat and Mouse Act, was re-arrested trying to attend Emily's funeral. Constance sent a book of Whitman's poems to be placed in
her comrade's coffin. Mary Leigh carried out this request and the
book was put in Emily's lifeless hand before burial, open at her
favourite poem.[29]

With Mrs Pankhurst in and out of prison and Christabel far
away in Paris, the suffragette movement continued to spiral out
of control. They began, for example, attacking works of art, and
the government responded by closing historic buildings, galleries

and museums. This did not stop Mary Richardson, who famously walked calmly into the National Gallery the following year, armed with an axe, and attacked the Rokeby Venus 'as a protest against the Government for destroying Mrs Pankhurst, who is the most beautiful character in modern history'.[30]

Meanwhile, after running the WSPU for almost a year, Annie Kenney was finally arrested in April 1913 and became one of the highest-profile 'mice' in the movement. Like Mrs Pankhurst, she went on both hunger and thirst strike, and embarked on a cycle of release, recovery, evasion and arrest. She was carried about on a stretcher to meetings so the suffragettes could be in no doubt as to what the government was doing to her. She had a special place in Constance's heart and was never far from her thoughts. 'I am wondering what we can do for the prisoner who every time that the police see her they re-arrest her,' Constance wrote to Alice, a year into Annie's harrowing life of disguise. 'I will try all I can to bring her south, but I am almost helpless.'[31] Sylvia Pankhurst was also undergoing a harrowing experience. She was the only member of the Pankhurst family to be force-fed, and found it excruciating. It went on twice a day for more than a month, until she went on a 'rest-strike' and walked round her cell for twenty-eight hours until she was finally released; then, like Annie Kenney, she was in and out of prison and carried around on a stretcher. But suffrage remained just one of her causes; she remained a fervent socialist and supporter of the Labour Party. After speaking out in support of striking Irish workers, she was summoned to see Christabel in Paris in January 1914. Not only was she seen as insubordinate, her prominent visibility was a direct challenge to Christabel's authority. Emmeline and Christabel demanded she leave the WSPU. Adela Pankhurst – it is almost impossible not to think of her as 'poor Adela', so overshadowed was she by her dominant sisters – was also shipped off to Australia soon afterwards, forbidden to campaign for the cause. Sylvia continued her campaign for the vote independently, even going on hunger and thirst strike outside the House of Commons until Asquith agreed to meet a deputation of working women. After listening to their arguments, he said, 'If change has to come, we must face it boldly.'[32]

Constance was horrified both by the renewed use of force-feeding and by the Cat and Mouse Act. It was difficult to imagine which was worse. 'This is inhuman, like the feeding of the beast – no, of an insentient thing,' she said of the law. She used the closing pages of her testimony to warn the government would never stop the suffragettes, whatever they did, until their demands were granted. She justified the wave of arson attacks now sweeping the country by saying, 'They will burn buildings until they are treated rationally as an equal part of the human race.'[33] Victor acted as Constance's agent and placed the book with William Heinemann, who insisted on inserting a disclaimer distancing himself from the subject matter. This was extremely unusual: what publisher does agree with everything an author writes? Unfortunately, the correspondence has disappeared from the publisher's archive, so how they discussed the question and came to this compromise may never be known.

Prisons and Prisoners was the first personal testimony of a suffragette to be published in a book. Teresa Billington-Greig and Sylvia Pankhurst had written histories of the movement but not from their individual perspectives. Emmeline Pankhurst published her ghost-written autobiography *My Own Story* later in 1914, but most other suffragettes waited until long after the campaign had been completed before telling their stories: then all their pent-up memories came pouring out.[34] *Prisons and Prisoners* is written in the heat of battle by a wounded soldier who is longing to take to the field once more and does not know how the conflict will end. There was no mention of her stroke or the consequences for her health. Instead, the book concludes on a note of righteous fury that passionately makes the case for the justice of the cause and the inevitability of the victory.

Shortly after 'Jane Warton' was released, she had written up extensive notes on her experience; she drew heavily on this account when writing *Prisons and Prisoners*.[35] This earlier draft was privately printed in 1987 as *I, Constance Lytton*, and there is very little difference in the substance of these accounts. There is, however, a slight difference in tone: *I, Constance Lytton*, composed in the heat of the moment, is somewhat more tentative and hesitant. 'I think' is repeated again and again. In contrast, *Prisons and Prisoners* is more assertive, a confident story born of frequent retelling, with no room for uncertainty lest critics seize on inconsistency as evidence of inaccuracy.

Constance was understandably nervous about the reception but was thrilled at the sales and the reviews. 'It was well noticed in the press in England, America, Canada, Australia, S Africa, and I received numerous letters from strangers about it,' she noted some years later with justifiable pride and pleasure.[36] 'They had first printed 2,000 copies, then ordered 500 more and to-day I hear another 500,' she told Aunt T. 'That is good for under a week.'[37] Perhaps her greatest pleasure, though, would have come from her mother's verdict, handwritten on the inside of her own copy: 'A human document ... beautifully written ... in spite of the acute pain of the whole thing.'[38] Betty, however, received a letter which could stand for the ongoing scepticism of the Lytton family friends. 'It is an example of wonderful self-sacrifice and martyrdom which one cannot help regarding with respect – but O if all these energies and loyal devotions had been directed into wholesome and natural channels for her!'[39] Another commented that Robert would have 'adored' it.[40]

Sylvia Pankhurst designed the original cover, and Constance sent Sylvia Pankhurst half the royalties to support her paper, the *Women's Dreadnought*. This interaction, together with her ongoing support for Emmeline Pethick-Lawrence, suggests that Constance maintained relationships with her comrades even when Christabel cut them off. Sylvia recalled that Constance was so hard up she could not afford an annual subscription to the penny-a-week paper, but had to pay in instalments.[41] Constance celebrated her literary success with several long trips: first to the Pethick-Lawrences and then to Aunt T. But she was overdoing it. She was soon ill again, this time with the breathlessness that would plague her for the rest of her life.

Then in August 1914, the outbreak of war changed everything for the suffragettes, for women, and for the country.

The WSPU immediately called a truce, and offered to put their army to work serving the government. The government responded by releasing all suffragette prisoners. McKenna, the Home Secretary, said in Parliament that 'His Majesty is confident that the prisoners … will respond to the feelings of their countrymen and country-women in this time of emergency, and that they may be trusted not to stain the causes they have at heart by any further crime or disorder'. But he cannot have anticipated that Emmeline and Christabel Pankhurst would become the most patriotic of citizens.

Of all their decisions, this was among the most difficult to explain to their followers. It was one thing to suspend hostilities. It was quite another to wholeheartedly support a government that had spent the best part of a decade trying to crush them. Yet members of the WSPU now began to hand out white feathers to men they suspected of 'shirking' their 'duty'. The name of their newspaper was changed to *Britannia*, and the articles became virulently anti-German. Asked why and how they could become such staunch government allies, Christabel responded, 'The country was our country. It belonged to us and not to the Government, and we had the right and privilege, as well as the duty, to serve it.'[42] But that was only part of the story. She – and others – saw that they had a chance to prove themselves. As Millicent Fawcett said, 'Let us show ourselves to be worthy of citizenship whether our claim to it be recognised or not.'[43]

They were knocking at an open door. The government needed women – and in particular they needed the suffragettes, with their organisational nous and their gift for propaganda. Lloyd George especially recognised this. The old enmity was forgotten and he became almost friends with Emmeline Pankhurst. As Minister for Munitions, he asked her to mount one more of the suffragettes' great processions, demonstrating women's willingness to work in munitions factories. The deputation as part of this procession was the first she had ever led which was welcomed with open arms. Given that just a few years earlier she had been held responsible for blowing up his house, the transformation in their relationship was remarkable. Later in the war, following the Russian Revolution, Emmeline went to Russia to try to persuade their women to support the war effort; she would also go to the Balkans, and try – rather unsuccessfully – to start a project to help war babies. Another suffragette, Charlotte Marsh, imprisoned alongside Mary Leigh in Birmingham while protesting against Asquith, and a hunger-striker who had been force-fed hundreds of times, was Lloyd George's chauffeur in the war. One wonders what she said to him.

But not all the militants followed Christabel's lead. Sylvia Pankhurst and her new Federation of East London Suffragettes, for example, were committed to pacifism. The Federation and the Women's Freedom League were the only groups who kept up the campaign for the vote during the war: all others set it aside for the duration. The NUWSS occupied a middle ground, supporting efforts to relieve suffering rather than the war itself. But many members of the NUWSS resigned to campaign more actively for peace, and joined forces in this endeavour with former suffragettes like Emmeline Pethick-Lawrence: the war thus formed new alliances and relationships in the women's movement.

It is difficult to build up a complete picture of Constance's life during the war years. She was not, of course, writing many letters and does not appear to have restarted her diaries. Her nephews, fortunately, were too young to be called up. Victor was working for the Admiralty in London (it has recently been suggested that he may have been involved in code-breaking). Neville joined up and served as an officer on the Western Front, where he was injured, though not seriously. He was eventually awarded the Legion d'honneur by the French government. In 1917, on her mother's death, Judith became Lady Wentworth. This prompted a new outbreak of hostilities with Wilfred Scawen Blunt over the stud at Crabbet. Some horses were stolen and others were shot as father and daughter fought in the courts and in the stables over the inheritance. Judith eventually won, but it must have been a bitter victory.

Constance herself did what she could for the war effort. Her friend Dr Marion Vaughan was running a field hospital in Belgium and because of this, Belgian refugees became a major preoccupation. She and Edith had a couple sleeping in the library.[44]

But her first thought, of course, was always for her beloved suffragettes. However hard-up Constance was, she continued to give away what little she had, and reserved particular sympathy for her fellow hunger strikers. Kitty Marion, who had been with Constance in Newcastle, had a particularly horrific experience of force-feeding. In June 1913, Kitty had been imprisoned for setting fire to a grandstand at a race track; a tribute to Emily Wilding Davison after Emily's death at the Epsom Derby. She was force-fed 232 times over fourteen weeks and contemplated hanging herself. She was eventually released having lost thirty-six pounds, looking elderly and emaciated, unrecognisable to her friends. Kitty Marion's experience reminded Constance of her own. 'Jane Warton counted the hours and wondered each time how she would bear it again ... Now Kitty Marion has borne it for 4 months!' she told a friend in horror. To Kitty herself, she sent flowers from Homewood and an effusive message of devotion: 'My reverence for you is of the greatest and I feel a love for you which I cannot put on paper. I have thought of you incessantly while you were being forcibly fed. Your splendid courage is greater than anything I can conceive.'[45] What Kitty had done put her own actions in perspective, yet Kitty's experience never had the impact that Constance's had: she was an actress, not an aristocrat. When war was declared, Constance helped Kitty leave England for a new life in America. She also gave her a letter of introduction to a prison commissioner to try to help Kitty find a job. This was unsuccessful, and Kitty eventually went to work for the birth control pioneer Margaret Sanger. In 1922, Constance tried, unsuccessfully, to get Kitty a British passport so that she could accompany Margaret to China and Japan.[46]

Constance also took on responsibility for the medical care of Rachel Peace. Rachel had been arrested alongside Mary Richardson in October 1913 for arson and had gone on hunger and thirst strike. She used an alias, Jane Short, and her face appears in photos of the time as among the 'most wanted' suffragettes. Rachel was force-fed while on remand to make sure that she was fit to stand trial. Questions were asked in Parliament about how this could be allowed, given that she had not yet been found guilty of the crime. A group of suffragettes smashed windows at her trial to protest at the way she was being treated and were themselves sent to prison; another group tried to set off a bomb at Holloway. Rachel was sentenced to eighteen months' hard labour. Like Kitty, she was one of the suffragettes judged likely to reoffend and too dangerous to release and so was force-fed for several months. The experience had driven her mad.[47] Constance worked tirelessly for Rachel, who had no family of her own. She raised money to keep Rachel in a private asylum and had her to visit when she was well enough. This cannot have been easy for Constance, as Rachel was, according to Emmeline Pethick-Lawrence, 'not dangerous but quarrelsome and talkative'.[48]

The Lyttons were uncomfortable about Constance's generosity and believed that she was much too ready to believe a hard-luck story.[49] She gave away all her money and sold her belongings, helping not just the suffragettes, but other unpopular causes: Germans struggling in wartime, conscientious objectors, ex-convicts. All the legacy she had inherited from Georgina Bloomfield had long since been channelled into the suffragette cause.[50] She even got herself into £300 worth of debt by helping suffragettes who were down on their luck.[51] Edith saw Constance as utopian and impractical, and she was not far off the mark.[52]

They had to endure their fair share of hardships and discomforts during the war years. This, of course, appealed to Constance's self-denying instincts, and even Edith seems to have approached deprivation with a certain spirit of adventure. 'Mother is living in a most cruelly Spartan manner, with only one fire of wood and an oil stove. She is really crazy about it. She has a most peculiar set of servants who shout and sing and talk all day regardless of anyone's presence,' Emily reported to Edwin in horror. 'Con of course encourages them and has them in to sing to her.'[53]

With the natural passing of time and with the distraction of war, the visits from her fellow suffragettes dried up. In the summer of 1915, she told Adela that she had seen Emmeline Pethick-Lawrence twice recently, and Annie Kenney had been down, but that she had not seen Christabel for over a year.[54] This was not uncommon. Hannah Mitchell wrote in her autobiography:

I was deeply hurt by the fact that none of the Pankhursts had shown the slightest interest in my illness, not even a letter of sympathy … I did not realise that in the great battle the individual does not count and stopping to pick up the wounded delays the fighting.[55]

Emmeline Pethick-Lawrence, though, her first and best suffragette friend, remained a loyal and regular visitor.

The war changed the nature of the debate on voting rights. Existing law required men to be resident at their home for twelve months in order to be eligible to vote. This would disqualify all soldiers and sailors fighting abroad. Just before he resigned as Prime Minister in December 1916, Asquith gave this problem to the Speaker, who set up a cross-party conference on electoral reform. Though the claims of the fighting men were paramount, it was impossible to ignore the claims of women any longer. A hundred thousand had been nurses or worked in hospitals; a hundred thousand more had served in the auxiliary forces. A quarter of a million had worked on the land. But the biggest change had been in the factories, where 800,000 women had worked building munitions and in engineering.[56] Women had been clerks and typists, they had driven trains and buses. With a few exceptions – front-line fighting was still off limits, as was heavy industry – they had proven that they could do a man's job in a man's world. They had demonstrated their capability as citizens. Their efforts, their total mobilisation and their complete dedication had made it possible for the men to fight. It was unthinkable that they would not be rewarded for their sacrifice. The Speaker's conference recommended abolishing property qualifications for men and granting the vote to women over thirty, and university graduates. The Cabinet, now led by David Lloyd George, accepted. After passing the Commons, the bill went to the Lords, where votes for women had never yet been tested. But, perhaps with one eye on the Russian Revolution, the Lords chose 'the lesser of two evils',[57] and finally granted women the right to vote.

In 1918, the Representation of the People Act became law. It was not at all the triumph the suffragettes had anticipated. 'We had pictured national rejoicing, a great public celebration of our Votes for Women victory. It had come in a time of public mourning and deepening war danger,' said Christabel Pankhurst.[58] Nor was it a particularly fair settlement: in excluding young women from the vote, the government had excluded many of the women who had worked so hard for the war effort in factories and hospitals. But, in other ways, it went further than the suffragettes had dared hope for. Women could not only vote, they could also stand for election, and a few brave women did so. Constance marked it in her notebook: 'February 6th 1918: 4 years later from publication my Book Ap.[ril] 1914 By the Representation of the People Act, about 6 000 000 women of 30 years of age and over obtained the Parliamentary Vote.'[59]

CHAPTER TWELVE

THE PRICE OF VICTORY

'It is extraordinary that the spirit of the Militant Movement has been so little understood, and I wonder whether in years to come those who study history will realise the significance of it?'[1]

It is well documented that winning the vote did not change women's lives as much as the suffragettes had hoped. If anything, there was a backlash after the war, as women were expected to return home and allow soldiers to return to their jobs. But however much men – and even some women – may have wished for the old certainties and the old divisions, the world had changed for ever. Many of the suffragettes were too mentally, physically, emotionally and financially drained by their efforts to continue political activity.

Sylvia Pankhurst was perhaps the most significant exception to this rule, working tirelessly for socialism and, later, independence for Ethiopia, where she is still revered. Emmeline Pethick-Lawrence devoted the rest of her life to international peace. Fred became a respected senior member of the Labour Party in the House of Lords and, when Emmeline died, married another suffragette. Jessie Kenney qualified as the first female wireless telegraph operator. Constance and David Lloyd George gave her references for the training but, as a woman, she was unable to find a job and eventually became a school administrator. Emmeline Pankhurst spent several years recovering in Canada with the children she had adopted during the war, but struggled to manage in her old age and they were taken in by other families. Back in England, she was persuaded to become Conservative candidate for Whitechapel but died in 1928 before the election was held. Christabel had stood as a candidate in the post-war election but did not win. She became a fervent believer that the Second Coming was imminent and spent the rest of her life in America. Annie Kenney surprised everyone by getting married, having a son and living a quiet family life in Hertfordshire. Constance was delighted to hear about the wedding and sent Annie a white sapphire brooch she had worn pinned above her hunger strike medal during the suffrage campaign.[2]

As a result, few of the women who influenced the political debates in the years immediately after the vote had been won had been militants. Rather, they had been suffragists and, generally speaking, were those who had never put all their faith in the vote but had only seen it as one goal among many. (The first woman MP, Nancy Astor, however, was not associated with the women's movement at all, while the first Cabinet member, Margaret Bondfield, had strongly supported adult suffrage rather than the votes for women campaign.)

These years have sometimes been seen as a period of stagnation and fragmentation for the women's movement. Without the struggle for the vote unifying women, it is argued, the movement found it difficult to match the post-war conservative forces urging women back home. In fact, progress may have been quieter and less dramatic, but there were still many advances to be celebrated. Pioneers entered new professions in the law, in veterinary science, and in engineering. Legal changes gave women new rights over their children and their property. New organisations like the Six Point Group, led by Lady Rhondda (a former suffragette, still excluded from the House of Lords because she was a woman), worked for equality for women across a wide range of fields. It wasn't the radical transformation of society that the visionary suffragettes had hoped for, but it was a start.

Towards the end of 1919, Constance's doctor found what she believed to be a cyst. There were fears it was cancerous. Her general condition also worsened: her breathlessness became more difficult to manage.[3] Her heart condition meant the doctors were reluctant to use anaesthetics when removing the cyst and so she was simply given localised painkillers. Fortunately, she was able to stay at Homewood for the operation. She also liked the fact that the surgeon was a woman.[4] She was prepared to die, and even welcomed the prospect as a relief from her constant suffering. 'I am so tired of life,' she told Adela. 'I have long hoped to die, and since I've seen this possible road, I have felt most wonderfully happy.'[5] She did not die, and in fact everything went as well as could be expected. The cyst was not cancerous, though it was huge: the doctor said as big as a head, the nurse said as large as a football.[6] In January 1920, she had a visit from Ethel Smyth who wrote admiringly in the visitors' book: 'In memory of an impression of pluck that most certainly will Remain!'[7]

Olive Schreiner, demoralised and weak, died in 1920. Her marriage had been unhappy and she rarely lived with her husband, using her illness as an excuse to avoid him. She always remained devoted to Constance and, after twenty-five years of friendship, still called her 'one of the most beautiful souls the Gods ever made'.[8] Olive became disillusioned with the suffragettes, and sided with Sylvia and Emmeline Pethick-Lawrence when they were cast out of the WSPU. A lifelong pacifist, Olive was outraged by Emmeline and Christabel's strategy in the First World War, writing, 'They have lost nearly all their suffragette following so they have had to take up war to keep themselves before the public.'[9] Constance wrote her obituary for *Time and Tide*. 'She was the first woman I had known with a wide horizon,' Constance wrote, with deep regret.[10]

To the best of her limited abilities, Constance took up new causes once the vote was won. One of these was, unsurprisingly, women in politics. Constance was delighted that women were able to stand as candidates for election. She raised funds to help some she knew or liked, as well as donating her own money. At one time, Emily vaguely flirted with the idea of standing for Labour. Constance was also drawn to the noble ideals of the League of Nations, seeing it as a guarantor of future peace. Robert Cecil, the driving force of the League of Nations in Britain, was a cousin and colleague of Arthur Balfour's; his wife Nelly was a friend of Betty. Constance and Robert corresponded over the League and she set up a local branch to support it.[11]

She was also extremely interested in birth control and its potential to improve the lives of working-class women. So when Marie Stopes wrote asking for her support, Constance was only too pleased to help. They actually shared a publisher: A. C. Fitfield had published Constance's pamphlet 'No Votes for Women' back in 1909 as well as *Married Love* and Stopes's other early work. Fitfield had been unable to keep up with demand for these books.[12] On the back of her massive literary success, Marie was proposing to set up the first birth control clinic in Britain, and accordingly wrote to many of the great and good to ask for their assistance. Constance may have been particularly pleased to know that it would be in Holloway, only a short walk from the prison. Constance, of course, had only one asset, but freely gave permission for Marie to use it. 'You may certainly use my name as a patron for the "Mother's Clinic,"' she said, enthusiastically, and asked for a copy of *Married Love*. Emily was asked too, but turned the offer down, saying, 'It is a very difficult subject, and I have not yet made up my own mind upon it.'[13]

From then on, Constance and Marie were regular, if infrequent, correspondents. Constance was an ideal 'name' for Marie to have on her list: part of her mission was to make birth control something that 'respectable' women, not just prostitutes, might use.[14] Marie sent many invitations for Constance to go and see the clinic in action: Constance always regretfully turned her down on the grounds of ill health. There was a huge meeting at the end of May 1921 at the Queen's Hall, scene of so many suffragette set-pieces, and Constance was extremely sorry she could not attend. Later in 1921, she became a vice-president of Marie's new Society for Constructive Birth Control and Racial Progress.[15] There is no suggestion that Constance shared Marie's more dubious concerns about eugenics and racial purity. She simply believed, rightly, that the lives of working-class women would be easier if they had fewer children. 'It has been practised in our family and by their numerous friends for 3 generations,' she told Marie, with casual honesty.[16] She tried to enlist her siblings to the new cause, just as she had done with suffrage. After reading *Married Love*, Victor was interested enough to tell Marie, through Constance, that he'd also like to help her. Emily had by now decided that birth control was incompatible with her religion, though, perhaps remembering her own horrible honeymoon, gave her daughter a copy of *Married Love*.[17] Constance pondered how she might get Betty, the most 'respectable' of the sisters, to sign up to the movement.[18]

This epistolary friendship gives hints of one of the more bizarre episodes in Constance's life. It seems that her valuable name was being used by a fraudster called 'George Blackshaw' as surety at Liberty's. Then he used her name to gain an introduction to Marie Stopes, and wangled money out of her too. He was arrested and jailed. Constance was extremely apologetic to Marie, and offered to pay her back the money she had lost. But the story does not end there. She invited Blackshaw up to Homewood to see if she could make him see the error of his ways, telling Marie, 'He must be a rather clever man and it is a pity that he should spend his time in

& out of prison.' Rather surprisingly, he came and they ended up in what Constance naively saw as friendship. When Marie Stopes was involved in a libel trial the following year, Constance asked George to report back on the proceedings. It ended badly, though, with Constance once more apologising to Marie. George had been bothering Marie by pretending to know her and spreading false rumours. 'I am going to see him on Wednesday,' Constance said, 'and will do my best to recommend to him to keep away from your appeal case. It is tremendously annoying.' It is no wonder that her family thought she was always being taken in.[19] Marie had lost her trial and the unwelcome reappearance of George Blackshaw was the last thing she needed. Constance wrote to Lady Astor to see if she might intervene for Marie Stopes in the judicial proceedings; after some hesitation, Lady Astor actually did so, but was too late and the verdict had already been declared.[20]

This generation of Lyttons were not leaders but they were dedicated followers. They sought out inspiring individuals to serve, offering total faith and devotion, to sometimes very unorthodox causes. They had a strong desire to be 'modern', to be part of progressive movements and sometimes fell into fads instead. Collectively, they yearned for fulfilment and answers to spiritual questions in something other than their mother's conventional religion.

Some of the Lytton causes have stood the test of time better than others. Constance, of course, found her calling in the suffragettes and her leaders in Emmeline and Christabel Pankhurst: history is very much on her side. But Betty was involved with the Society for Psychical Research; Gerald was the president and their home was the headquarters. Not content with immersing herself wholeheartedly in Theosophy, Emily became a devoted disciple of its chosen leader, an Indian boy named Krishnamurti. Emily loved Krishnamurti; at first maternally and later wholeheartedly. She took to following him around the world, with her younger children in tow, much to Edwin's disgust. She seems only to have escaped becoming the black sheep of the family because of Constance's criminal record. But Victor's guru was an American named Homer Lane, and his belief in Lane's abilities had tragic consequences for Constance.

George Montagu, who later became the Earl of Sandwich, was a friend of Victor Lytton. Like many progressive Edwardians (and indeed, like Constance), he was deeply concerned about the harshness and ineffectiveness of English prisons, and persuaded his uncle to lend him land that could be used for an experiment to set up a more liberal institution for young offenders. Homer Lane, who was known in America for his work with young people, both in schools and prisons, was invited first to be a consultant on the project and then to run it. The Little Commonwealth was opened in 1913. It was a combination of farm and group home, designed to be democratic and to give the young people a sense of control over their lives. Victor was the chairman of the General Committee.[21]

Lane was not just a prison reformer and teacher: he saw himself as a new messiah, blessed with a unique understanding of scripture and of God's will.[22] As this suggests, he was a charlatan through and through. While his ideas on education were undoubtedly forward-thinking, the truth is that he exploited his position running the Little Commonwealth. His relationships with the vulnerable teenage girls in his care were at very best questionable but almost certainly sexual. In 1917, rumours began to circle in the local community that Lane was sleeping with some of the girls. A meeting to discuss the issue collapsed in acrimony. Lane then went on holiday; unbelievably, he took some of the other girls with him. When some of his original accusers ran away, the police were brought in. This prompted a full-scale Home Office inquiry, and though the results have never been published, the Little Commonwealth was closed.[23] Lane's biographer excuses him by saying that 'the girls were above the age of consent, and nothing that they alleged against Lane was actionable',[24] though this is hardly a vindication. Lane did himself no favours with a cod-psychology defence in which he blamed a failure of the 'transference' process: the girls were supposed to 'transfer' their allegiance to the Commonwealth but something had gone wrong and they had accidentally transferred to him instead. Victor believed whole-heartedly in his innocence, and put most of the trouble down to Lane's perverse habit of refusing to co-operate with authority.[25] He resigned from the Little Commonwealth committee in protest at Lane's treatment. Lane seems to have been a powerful and hypnotic personality: none of his influential friends saw through him, and they were so convinced of his goodness that they ignored all evidence to the contrary.

His muddled understanding of Freud and his complete lack of training did not stop Lane from setting himself up as a lecturer and consultant in psychoanalysis. Victor supported him wholeheartedly in this new venture, even going so far as to arrange lectures for him. Lane made a splash in certain circles: Betty reported that London had 'gone mad over Lane', and that Ethel Smyth had become a disciple.[26] Victor also became a patient himself, and attributed a miracle cure to Lane. Like Constance, Victor had suffered with depression: now he felt well enough to accept a senior diplomatic post in India. He saw this as nothing short of a miracle cure. He was evangelical about the benefits of Lane's therapeutic approach and began recommending other patients to Lane.

One of these was Constance who was very excited about the prospect of treatment. Psychoanalysis appealed to her interest in modern and progressive thinking. She was even more interested in the promises Lane made. He claimed that he would be able to cure her paralysis and poor health for good.

The idea of 'unconscious conflict' was, Lane believed, at the heart of the patient's problems. The troubles they suffered from – whether mental or physical – were as a result of their unconscious wishes to escape from their situation. To be cured, patients had to acknowledge and come to terms with these wishes. These are not particularly radical theories, but in Constance's case, the implications were alarming. Lane attributed her stroke to an unconscious rebellion against her suffragette activities. Her body knew that her actions were wrong and acted to prevent it. Given that this went against all her beliefs, and that she clung to her suffragette past to give her life meaning, it is incredible that Constance accepted this diagnosis. She told Betty (who might have resented her sister's ongoing belief that all her relatives disapproved of her):

> I don't understand how the self-sought ill health applies in my case – I at last had found my feet in the Votes for Women movement, was desperately happy in a world of friends. This stroke besides almost quite incapacitating me cast me back among my relations who disapproved of all my work and I was cut off practically from my friends. But no matter – Lane perhaps will find a way out.[27]

She began treatment in the summer of 1922. We cannot, of course, know exactly what went on in these sessions, but Lane's biographer has left an account of his methods and we can only hope she was spared the worst of Lane's exploitative excesses. Psychotherapy was still very much in its infancy and Lane seems to have been making much of his practice up as he went along. According to his biographer, his patients 'seem to have enjoyed an experience almost akin to that of the woman with an issue of blood who felt that she need only "touch the hem of His garment"'. Sessions were informal. Lane sat, smoked and talked and the patient was expected to listen.[28] Sometimes he would do more than talk. Lane's biographer suggests that he sometimes conducted sessions where both participants were naked and would even 'give physical demonstrations of his "love" for a pupil who could be convinced in no other way'; even his biographer concluded this was 'very stupid'.[29] It seems that Lane, who could no longer exploit vulnerable young offenders, now preyed on an equally defenceless group of psychological patients. He also charged a hefty fee for the privilege: two pounds and two shillings a week for Constance's treatment, which she, mired in debt, could ill afford.[30]

Nevertheless, Constance believed the treatment was working. She felt better than she had done for years, though this seems to be down to a shift in her own attitude and self-perception. Betty thought that she was still very breathless and her paralysed arm showed no improvement, but that she was transformed, full of high spirits and certainty that she was going to get well.[31] But Lane was not satisfied with her progress. He blamed the suffragettes for her stroke, but he blamed her inability to recover on Edith. She was too dependent on Edith, she had no incentive to recover and they were trapped in an unhealthy relationship because Edith wanted her close at home.[32] Edith herself was ignoring the whole thing. 'I suppose she looks upon it as a mild form of madness,' Betty reported to Victor, and, later:

> She hates it, doesn't really believe in it, and grudges the money it costs. Part of herself does not really want Con to get well – she does not want to lose control of her. Besides, the whole thing is unorthodox & not in her scheme of things ... nothing will cheer Mother except Con sinking back into high priestess in her illness.[33]

Regardless of Edith's feelings, it seems that Lane said what Constance needed to hear. She decided that she would leave, and move to London again to continue her 'treatment'. She justified this decision by saying that it was in Edith's interests as well as her own. 'My life here was in the grave and not vital or helpful to Mother,' she told Betty.[34] Living on her own again would make her better: a 'doctor' said so.

In December, she announced her intentions to Edith – or, as her mother described it to Betty, 'Con threw a bombshell at me … after nursing & helping her for 10 years it does seem hard … & ah the loneliness for my last days.' Constance's siblings thought, though they did not say it in so many words, that this was rather a selfish attitude to take. They tended to agree with Lane's diagnosis and Edith's response only confirmed it. Betty tried to express their position gently.

> For 10 years, Con has been on the shelf. You have been angelically & patiently & unselfishly nursing her – what for? Not for death – but for Life. If you had the choice to keep her ill & always with you – or to give her back the great gift of health & with it the freedom to work once more I am sure you love her too much to deny her that freedom, even if it means more loneliness for you.[35]

For Victor and Betty, the question was not whether Constance would be made better or worse by the move, but rather whether worrying about Edith would hamper her recovery. Victor wrote weekly letters to Edith from India urging her to let Constance go. Edith, meanwhile, continued her histrionics, telling Betty that perhaps it would be better for Constance if she died. But though Edith may have been emotional in her response, that did not mean she was wrong.[36] All the siblings, Constance included, seemed to believe that recovery, and an independent life, was just over the horizon. In Neville's words, 'She determined to take up her bed and walk; she was tired of leading an invalid life and she meant to get well or die in the attempt.'[37]

Constance felt that she had been given a new lease of life. With a sudden burst of energy, she began working on a cookbook. The idea was to gather recipes 'from Courts and Palaces – from farm houses and cottages' from countries around the world and sell it in aid of the League of Nations. She had one recipe from Queen Victoria's still room, and another (for boiled milk) from the governor of Holloway Prison; she had recipes from Egypt, India and Jamaica as well as from Britain, America and Europe. They were, of course, all vegetarian.[38] By January 1923 she felt well enough to make her long-cherished trip to Marie Stopes's clinic in Holloway and finally meet with the doctor herself.[39] Her only worry was how to pay for her ongoing treatment: with no means of earning money, she was still heavily in debt. Victor offered to make her a loan, to be paid back once she was well and working. She planned to start reviewing and writing, and even wrote some poems. She started coming down to breakfast and dinner instead of taking her meals in her room, as a way of demonstrating how well she was, though still no physical improvements were visible to Betty.[40]

Then, after more than a decade living with her mother, she left home in the spring of 1923 and returned to London. Her first thought was to go back to the Euston Road, as it was close to Lane as well as being associated with her happiest years. But this was thought unsuitable: too isolated, too cold and too uncomfortable. If she was going to be free, it would have to involve compromises: her siblings discussed a plan to put her in rooms in an occupied house where someone could keep an eye on her. Constance bridled at these restrictions. She was not a child and – at least in her head – no longer an invalid. Instead, Emily found her a flat in Tavistock Square, above the Theosophical Society's headquarters. From here, she wrote her last letter to Marie Stopes, explaining that she couldn't write a projected article on birth control because 'Mr Homer Lane told me that I must give up that kind of thing for the present'.[41] Lane was increasingly dominating her life. In her last few analytic sessions, the story of John Ponsonby came out, upsetting her deeply. She wrote to Victor that she had been reading her old letters, saying, 'I gave myself to J. P. for him to ask of me whatever he chose ... the most upsetting bit of my life.'[42] Betty told Constance that Gerald had said she was a saint; Constance answered, 'Lane says I must be a demon, and I suppose I am.'[43]

The number of stairs at Tavistock Square made it unsuitable, and after a few weeks she was forced to return to Homewood. Having made the break, though, she was determined that this homecoming would only be temporary. Adela managed to find her alternative accommodation in Paddington, in lodgings once occupied by Olive Schreiner. The landlady had been dedicated to Olive and would look after Constance for Olive's sake.[44] Towards the end of April, Constance heard the news that Jessie Kenney had at last qualified as a wireless telegraph operator, and wrote that she too was on the verge of a new life. 'My hand and arm have quite recently begun to come to life again ... it seems like a miracle after being for ten years 1/2 dead.' She told Jessie about the progress of her cookbook ('what a come down! you will perhaps think'), asked her for a recipe and said she would try to help Jessie if she could, perhaps through Maurice Baring, who had the right connections.[45]

Constance felt she was hovering on the edge of a miracle, but she was wrong. Once she had moved into Olive's old flat, she had only days to live. Though her siblings had all urged her to break free, once in London, far from recovering, she quickly began to deteriorate. Yet she did not go home. 'During the last days in London her love & thought for Mother were intense & yet never for an instant did she regret having left her,' Betty told Victor. Victor had been writing 'psychological letters' to Constance from India; Lane asked Betty to cable to him to tell him to stop; Betty thought it was too late to make a difference. Edith wrote to Victor in anguish: she believed that Victor was against Constance seeing other doctors. Victor wrote back absolving himself: 'I knew that she was certain to be ill but I never meant her to refuse to see any doctor about her symptoms.' But it was too late. Marion Vaughan, who had been her doctor after the Jane Warton episode, was brought in to assess her. One day she was able to make jokes with Marion; the next she could not speak. 'Physiologically it is easy to explain,' Betty wrote to Victor. 'The dropsy was caused by bad circulation – the kidney – liver – & lungs also failed to function & then I suppose the whole system became poisoned. I have no doubt the Heroin given during the last 3 days hurried the end but made it peaceful & painless.'[46] Lady Constance Lytton died at four o'clock in the afternoon of 22 May 1923 with her sisters beside her. Neville recorded that she said, 'I am glad to die, and at last to be free of suffering.'[47]

Hundreds of people attended her funeral and Knebworth Church was packed. There were representatives of the Actresses' Franchise League, the Catholic Women's Suffrage Society, the Women's Freedom League, and many other groups as well as the WSPU. Emmeline Pethick-Lawrence placed a palm leaf in suffragette colours on the coffin, with the message 'Dearest Comrade, you live always in the hearts of those who love you, and you live forever in the future race which inherits the new freedom you gave your life to win.' Afterwards, Neville and a family servant carried the ashes to the Knebworth Mausoleum.[48]

Many tributes were made. One told Betty, 'She was a light to our generation, lighting something which will never go out. To be heroic with a sense of humour is the most sane and lovely thing there is.'[49] Old friends like Maurice Baring and Frances Balfour, who had rarely seen her in recent years, wrote to pay their respects. *The Times* obituary, said Frances, did not do her justice, and told 'what she did, not what she was'.[50]

One of the condolence notes was sent to Victor.

May I just write to you one word that is to say how deeply, very deeply sorry I am to see the notice in today's newspaper about Lady

Conny. It is too terribly sad and although I haven't seen Lady Conny for now many years, I shall always remember past days. I won't write more, and don't answer but I feel I must just write you a word to tell you how *very* very sorry I am.[51]

It was from John Ponsonby. John Ponsonby remained in the military and commanded the fifth infantry division during the First World War, before going to India. Still single, he eventually married in 1935 when nearly seventy years old. He died in 1952.

Constance's rapid end after so many long years of drift and stagnation is startling. If her decline was so swift, how could no one have spotted that she was getting worse? Why did none of them see what appears with hindsight to have been inevitable? Perhaps she realised it herself and was hiding it from them, in order that she could die on her own terms. But it is still heartbreaking to think that her last days were lived in the shadow of Homer Lane, calling her a demon, reopening the old John Ponsonby wounds, attacking Edith and blaming Constance for her failure to get well.

If all this was not enough, he then left Betty with the sense that she and the rest of the family were actually responsible for Constance's death. 'I am not sad for Con,' Betty told Victor. 'But I am fearfully disappointed & feel a glorious experiment has failed.' She was more saddened still by the impression that 'Lane in his heart thinks her family killed her'.[52] 'Did he feel all along that it was a fight between Con & her family & that if only we had all stayed away from her she would have lived?' she asked him. 'But how could I leave her – alone in a strange house with no loved one near her & the Dr saying it was a question of hours & nothing could save her.'[53] In Constance's last days and hours, Betty, Emily and Edith had of course been constantly at her side and Lane believed this was 'a failure – not of psychoanalysis but of the attempt to apply it'. In the same letter, Betty explicitly says that 'it is much more true to say

Lane killed her', but she goes on to say, 'Better make the attempt to live & fail, than see her a prisoner.'[54] She went on picking at the events of the last days, at Lane's motives and actions, unable to understand what he had been doing. But she did not distance herself from Lane or repudiate him. On the contrary, she was desperate to see him. Lane's behaviour, though, is rather easier to understand: he seems to have been trying to blame Betty and the rest of the Lyttons so that Constance's death could not be laid at his door; then he went into hiding to let the dust settle.

Rather surprisingly, given that she had been preparing for death in 1919, Constance did not make a will. It is odd that she did not make any personal bequests to her mother, her sisters or her suffragette comrades; perhaps she believed that she had nothing worth leaving. In September, Edith's twin sister, 'Aunt Lizzie', came to stay, and Edith insisted that she take something from Constance's room to remember her by. Betty watched Aunt Lizzie standing in the middle of the room 'looking unutterably miserable', surrounded by pamphlets about suffrage and books about prison reform. 'It did seem hard for Aunt L to make her choice. It almost made me giggle & I thought how Con would have laughed.'[55] Everything passed to Edith as Constance's next of kin, but Edith did not take any steps to administrate the estate and after she died, probate was granted to Victor. Constance is described in the probate documents as 'a Spinster without Father'.[56] Edith did, however, send some mementos to Annie Kenney, including Constance's treasured medals. Annie eventually donated these to the suffrage collection housed in the Museum of London.[57]

Betty took on the responsibility for putting Constance's affairs in order. Rachel Peace – 'the poor mad thing', as Betty called her – was the most immediate question. Betty felt particularly obligated to help Rachel, because she 'was one of Con's great incentives to get well', as she told Victor. 'She wanted – if cured herself – to cure her,

& Lane was confident he could!'[58] Emmeline Pethick-Lawrence suggested that the ex-suffragettes might club together and care for her as a memorial to Constance, but this seems to have come to nothing.[59] Many suffragettes were struggling financially. An appeal a few years before to raise money for a house for Mrs Pankhurst had not been very successful. Betty and Adela each paid for a week in the private asylum; then Rachel was moved to a public asylum in Kent.[60] George Blackshaw also briefly resurfaced for one last time, as Betty told Victor: 'Con's unfortunate ex-prisoner friend who was to bring out her cookery book is again in prison.'[61] Betty had the cookbook itself typed up as a Christmas present for Edith, though unfortunately it seems to have later disappeared.

A few years later, Betty collected and edited her sister's letters, just as she had done for her father. It was the best possible tribute and though, as we have seen, the collection is incomplete, it is also invaluable. Having seen how miserable the John Ponsonby letters made her towards the end of her life, Betty and Victor decided to leave those out. Betty was reading Annie Kenney's autobiography while finishing off her collection, and compared Annie's 'buoyant cheerfulness' with Constance's apparent sadness. 'She suffered vicariously too much for effectiveness in this life,' Betty concluded.[62]

In 1925, the family of another of Homer Lane's patients complained to the police that he was taking advantage of her. It was discovered he had been relieving her of large sums of money. There was a trial. Betty testified on his behalf and Victor wrote increasingly desperate letters from India, but to no avail. Lane was deported, having failed to keep to the terms of his visa, which required him to notify the police when he changed address. He died in Paris in September, missed and mourned by Victor, who continued to try to vindicate him. Pamela was the only one of the Lyttons who seems not to have been taken in. 'My last talk to him, two years ago, just after darling Con died, completely disillusioned [me] as to him being a good man.' She acknowledged that he had been 'the strange hand that held a lamp to light Victor's way', but still 'something in me shrinks from him'.[63]

Like Robert before him, Victor returned from India a disappointed man – or rather, as he told Betty, feeling 'like a suffragette as the gates of Holloway open to let her out'.[64] Victor had gone to India full of optimism and hope about the prospects for Home Rule and became thoroughly disillusioned. When he returned home, he felt rather sidelined by the Foreign Office and his career faltered. It was not until the 1930s that he was once again given real responsibility, and this time his work had global repercussions. He was asked by the League of Nations to investigate the war in Manchuria between Japan and China. His report accurately concluded that Japan was to blame. Japan withdrew from the League, which helped hasten its demise.

Edith Lytton lived until 1936, a widow for forty-five years, in a world that was unrecognisable from that of her childhood. It was a delightful surprise to find buried in an archive a touching correspondence with Jessie and Annie Kenney, apparently begun after Constance had died. Much as Constance loved her mother, she always saw Edith as an immovable obstacle to her suffragette career. But these letters reveal Edith's open mind and caring heart. Edith wrote as an intimate friend, and as equals, to Annie and Jessie; Dowager Countess to former mill girls. She gave Annie advice about getting her book to Queen Mary. 'My dear daughter Con friend [sic] and my own also I hope,' she says once; even more remarkably, she once signs herself 'Red Grannie Lytton'.[65] Edith's obituary in *The Times* called her 'a great lady of the old school', praised her 'courage, dignity, unswerving rectitude and loving kindness' and said she was 'a rare instance of increasing breadth of outlook as she grew older'.[66] That, of course, was not necessarily out of choice. But she loved her children, and accepted them and their causes, however much they baffled her. She was ninety-five when she died.

Emily remained unconventional and unapologetic. She followed Theosophy until Krishnamurti left the movement; then she followed him. She was often in India at the same time as Victor, though she disagreed with him on many Indian issues. Her autobiographies are astounding in their candour; her letters are staggering in number. Both are invaluable sources for historians in a variety of fields. Emily died in 1964, on the cusp of an age of freedom she would have been far more suited to. Betty remained interested in the occult, the afterlife and the spirit world. Just before the Second World War broke out, she 'contacted' Constance at a séance, through a medium. In the Balfour papers at the Scottish Archives, among the reams of official government business, there is a transcription of this event. 'I see ... a woman who passed to this life some time ago. She looks as if in some way in life she was a lonely person. She shows me Prison clothes. But she does not say what crime she committed ... She says "Prison gave me my freedom."'The 'spirit' of Constance told Betty not to be afraid, and that she was not coming to the spirit world yet.[67] Betty died in 1942.

Neville and Judith were divorced in 1923. He remarried, lived in France and had another daughter. This second life seems to have been much more stable and content than his relationship with Judith. He was a member of the Société Nationale des Beaux Arts and exhibited regularly. They had to escape France during the Second World War, but returned to England afterwards, where he died in 1951. Victor's sons, Anthony and John, both predeceased him, Anthony in a plane crash and John in the Second World War. Neville inherited Victor's earldom when he died in 1947, which then passed to Neville's son. Knebworth, though, was inherited by Victor's eldest daughter, Hermione Cobbold. Hermione's son, David, with his wife Chrissie, were responsible for introducing the rock concerts that have made Knebworth famous in recent years, while also keeping it solvent. Their son Henry is the present occupant. Like generations of Lyttons before him, he is both extremely literary and very interested in family history. A screenwriter by profession, he is working on a biography of Emily, Robert Lytton's sister. His wife, Martha, oversees the running of the extensive estate: it is a model for other similar estates in Britain. The interior of the house honours all their extraordinary forebears. Constance's achievements are celebrated alongside those of her father and grandfather.

After Edith died, Davinia lived at Homewood until Victor died and Hermione inherited it with the rest of the estate, whereupon it was let to a series of diplomatic families. In the early 1970s it was brought by the Pollock-Hill family, who still live there. In recent years, they have restored most of the inside of the house to Lutyens's original plans, aside from the addition of much-needed bathrooms. Constance would recognise her Homewood in the house which stands today, with her bedroom just next door to Edith's.

Constance's nieces took full advantage of the freedom that had been won by their aunt and her contemporaries. They went on to live interesting lives with distinguished careers, making their mark in fields which would not have been open to them a generation before. Eve Balfour was one of the first women to study agriculture at university, was a pioneer of organic farming and co-founded the Soil Association. Ruth Balfour studied medicine at Newnham College, Cambridge, and became a doctor. Elisabeth Lutyens became a composer of significant note, championed by William Walton. Mary Lutyens became a scholar. In an eclectic career, she collected and edited the philosophy of Krishamurti, was the first to put forward the theory of John Millais's notorious wedding night, and took on the mantle of family biographer. She was also a novelist and agony aunt. None of the women went into politics, though Davinia married a prominent MP. Constance would surely have been pleased at the opportunities these women had and the choices they were able to make.

In 1928, Parliament voted to give women the vote on the same terms as men. Fred Pethick-Lawrence, a Labour MP since 1923, said he had never cast a vote for anything that had given him greater pleasure. During the debate, he referred to Constance in the same breath as Mary Wollstonecraft and John Stuart Mill and suggested that 'with a heroism that has rarely been equalled, [she] placed herself in the humblest position in order that she might suffer and share the lot of many of her humble sisters'.[68] Nancy Astor, the first woman MP, also paid tribute to Constance, 'very frail and delicate, who fought so long and so hard'. The elderly Millicent Fawcett was in Parliament to witness the debate and the fulfilment of all her hopes. Mrs Pankhurst had died just a few weeks earlier.

After Constance was cremated, her white urn was placed in the small family mausoleum in the grounds of Knebworth. Victor and his daughters are in St Mary's Church, a few moments away. Her father was already there: her mother was also placed there after her death and the two lay side by side, opposite the door. To the right is Robert's sister Emily Lytton, the aunt she never knew, and to the left is the unbearably small coffin of her brother, Henry. At some point in the 1950s, the mausoleum was broken into and Emily's coffin stripped of its lead. To stop this happening again, the mausoleum was bricked up. Towards the end of her life, Lady Hermione Cobbold, Victor's daughter, decided to invest in restoring the mausoleum. The bricks were torn down and the door broken in. At that point, it was discovered that during the previous break-in, Constance's urn had been knocked over and some of her ashes spilled. She was restored as best as she could be, and now rests next to her brother, adjacent to her father, under a domed roof open to the sky. Outside, next to the formal tribute to her parents, there is a large inscription commemorating her life and her achievements. A group of women have begun to lay flowers here each International Women's Day. Her epitaph concludes with an extract from a poem by Maurice Baring.

Constance Georgina Lytton
Born February 12 1869
Died May 21 1923

Endowed with
A celestial sense of humour
Boundless sympathy
And rare musical talent
She devoted the later years
Of her life to the political
Enfranchisement of women
And sacrificed her health
And talents in helping to
Bring victory
To this cause

You were a summer's day all warmth and tune
Your soul a harbour dark beneath the moon
And flashing with soft lights of sympathy

The tree that had been planted in the Bath garden to honour Constance's achievements lasted into the 1950s. In 1951, Mary Blathwayt sent Annie Kenney a cutting from the tree, along with samples of her own tree, Christabel's and Elsie Howey's. It was as well she did, because the following year a huge overnight gale uprooted and destroyed Constance's tree. Mary told Annie, 'Lady Constance Lytton's tree was a splendid one, and would have been all right, if it had not come up by the roots.'[69]

AFTERWORD

'My job in going to prison was a very small thing tho' like our other women, I gave my all. Jane Warton did good, was of use, for a very little time.'[1]

'Women died to get you the vote!' is often remarked sternly in response to political apathy around election times. It is now over a hundred years since Emily Wilding Davison died under the King's horse on Derby Day. Her spectacular death is burned into the public consciousness for ever. But those who die quietly, away from the spotlight, are easily forgotten. The story of the suffragettes, as the suffragette historian Sandra Stanley Holton writes,

> revolves around the wilful acts of heroic individuals bent on making themselves forces of change ... history is made when change is wrested from the established order by its overthrow. Such change has to be willed by, and requires sacrifice from, those individuals heroic enough to resist tyranny and in this way render themselves forces of history.[2]

Lady Constance Lytton is one of those forgotten martyrs and heroic individuals.

We should not overlook her flaws. She was undoubtedly sincere in her wish for solidarity, but she could be embarrassingly patronising and naive. Marie Mulvey-Roberts, an expert both on Constance Lytton and on her grandmother Rosina, points out that her fellow prisoners are described almost as if they were children: prisons are her 'hobby' and cleaning is a 'craft', in a way which is almost self-indulgent.[3] Moreover, the Jane Warton episode demonstrates the difficult line the suffragettes were treading in their public relations. Many, like Constance, believed that the process of campaigning for the vote, as well as the vote itself, could promote broader social change, like prison reform. But with hunger striking, as with many of their more militant and violent actions, there was a real risk of the focus shifting away from the cause they were fighting for and onto the fight itself.

But as her confidence grew and her commitment deepened, it is remarkable just how far she set aside her class and upbringing to align herself with the ordinary women and their struggle. After joining the suffragettes, Constance was only Lady Constance Lytton if there was something the suffragettes might gain from her title. The rest of the time, she was desperate to prove that she was just one of the gang. Constance ignored the rules and stood shoulder to shoulder with the oppressed and miserable. Having grown up in a society so defined by class and gender, her willingness to defy expectations and stick to her principles is truly admirable.

Of course, she could never truly know what it was like to be a working-class woman: to experience the grind of delivering a child every year and watch some of them die; to live in cramped conditions with never enough to eat; to tolerate the everyday dangers of the factory or the mill; to accept early widowhood and early death as inevitable and even preferable to old-age drudgery and the shadow of the workhouse. There is no comparison between a week in disguise and a life in poverty. But Constance did what she could to bridge the divide. The other suffragettes knew this and loved her for it. 'Our reverence for her is as deep as our love,' Emmeline Pethick-Lawrence told Betty after Constance's stroke.[4] 'Jane Warton' may be all but forgotten today except among a select group of historians and feminists, but her escapades were one of the most dramatic set-pieces of the entire suffrage campaign, and made Constance a beloved heroine. As the scholar Barbara Green puts it, 'She refused the right to speak for other women and instead earned the right to speak.'[5]

Yet because both her family and the suffragettes idolised her, albeit in different ways, it is difficult to uncover and know the 'real' Constance. She has been hidden behind her own myth. I have sometimes felt, like Adela Smith, that 'it is as difficult to write of Con as it is to grasp running water'.[6] She is such a mass of contradictions: painfully shy but publicly outspoken; usually gentle but sometimes violent; frequently frightened but often brave.

It is in her letters, not her autobiography, that we see more of what Constance was 'really' like. That is not surprising, since they were written for private perusal not public consumption. *Prisons and Prisoners* gives only a glimpse of the sense of humour, the kindness and the deep humanity that defined her. It represents her public persona, not her private self. The truth is, she was neither the Francis of Assisi of her siblings' imagination, nor the shrieking harridan portrayed in the press, nor even the model suffragette, obedient to the leaders and fanatical about the cause, that she constructs in *Prisons and Prisoners*. She was all these things but she was also much more.

Constance gave her life to the cause twice over. Once when she gave up everything to devote herself entirely to the WSPU and twice when her efforts paralysed and ultimately killed her. It was an extraordinary sacrifice from an otherwise ordinary life. But Constance herself was always extremely modest about her contribution. Her story, however dramatic, is only one of many astonishing tales from the suffragette movement. In that sense, Constance was just what she wanted to be: a typical suffragette.

Some years after her suffragette adventure, Constance wrote this note to herself:

> In this women's war they gave themselves to destroy property but never to acquire it; and their bodies to the hunger strike in prison, but never to take the life of another, or to do any injury to life. Some died, some were driven mad, many suffered in this fight; but all who took part in it were privileged to see and know many things to which their eyes were shut before, and they experienced the joy of doing their part in removing the shackles from women and children.[7]

Constance gave everything she had to this 'women's war'. She certainly suffered for it, but she found joy in it too. That was her greatest privilege of all.

NOTES

EPIGRAPHS

1   Christabel Pankhurst, quoted in Midge Mackenzie, *Shoulder to Shoulder: A Documentary* (Penguin, 1975), p. 57; Mrs Combe Tennant, quoted in Betty Balfour (ed.), *Letters of Constance Lytton* (Heinemann, 1925), p. 266; Constance Lytton, *Prisons and Prisoners* (Virago, 1988), p. 283.

PROLOGUE

1   For accounts of Constance Lytton's first suffragette demonstration, see Constance Lytton, *Prisons and Prisoners*, pp. 36–52, and also Antonia Raeburn, *The Militant Suffragettes* (Michael Joseph, 1973), p. 90.

2   For accounts of Jane Warton's force-feeding, see Constance Lytton, speech at the Queen's Hall on 31 January 1910, quoted in Cheryl R. Jorgensen-Earp, *Speeches and Trials of the Militant Suffragettes, The Women's Social and Political Union 1903–1918* (Associated University Presses, 1999) and Constance Lytton, *Prisons and Prisoners*, pp. 268–93.

3   Constance Lytton, *Prisons and Prisoners*, p. 269.

4   Emmeline Pankhurst, *My Own Story* (Virago, 1979), p. 187.

CHAPTER I: DIPLOMAT'S DAUGHTER

1   C. M. Woodhouse, unpublished biography of Victor Lytton, p. 1. Christopher 'Monty' Woodhouse was Victor's son-in-law.

2   For Bulwer-Lytton's career insofar as it influenced his son Robert, see, for example, Aurelia Brooks Harlan, *Owen Meredith: A Critical Biography of Robert, First Earl of Lytton* (Columbia University Press, 1946), Mary Lutyens, *The Lyttons in India: An Account of Lord Lytton's Viceroyalty 1876–1880* (John Murray, 1979) pp. 3–10, and E. Neill Raymond, *Victorian Viceroy: The Life of Robert, the First Earl of Lytton* (Regency Press, 1980) pp. 1–100; see also his entry in the *Oxford Dictionary of National Biography*, and T. H. S. Escott, *Edward Bulwer: First Baron Lytton of Knebworth: A Social, Personal and Political Monograph* (Routledge, 1910).

3   For Anna Wheeler's career, see the *Oxford Dictionary of National Biography* and Barbara Taylor, *Eve and the New Jerusalem: Socialism and Feminism in the Nineteenth Century* (Virago, 1983), especially pp. 22–3 and pp. 59–65.

4   See, for example, Susie Steinback, *Women in England 1760–1914: A Social History* (Weidenfeld & Nicholson, 2004), p. 235.

5   See Joanna Goldsworthy and Marie Mulvey-Roberts, 'Revolutionary Mothers, Revolting Daughters: Mary Wollstonecraft and Mary Shelley, Anna Wheeler and Rosina Bulwer-Lytton', in Carolyn D. Williams, Angela Escott and Louise Duckling (eds.), *Woman to Woman: Female Negotiations During the Long Eighteenth Century* (University of Delaware Press, 2010), p. 69. The article explains why Wollstonecraft is remembered and Wheeler forgotten.

6   Lord Cobbold, 'Rosina Bulwer Lytton: Irish Beauty, Satirist, Tormented Victorian Wife, 1802–1882' in Allan Conran Christensen, (ed.), *The Subverting Vision of Bulwer Lytton* (University of Delaware Press, 2004), p. 153.

7   The story of Bulwer-Lytton and his mistresses really needs a book of its own. These details were pieced together around fifteen years ago by Beth Thomson, a descendent of Edward D'Ewes Tomson, who was brought up by Marion Lowndes. Unfortunately, Beth now lives in Australia and I have not been able to trace her again to ask for permission to quote her research.

8   Lord Cobbold, 'Rosina Bulwer Lytton', in Allan Conran Christensen, (ed.), *The Subverting Vision of Bulwer Lytton*, p. 153.

9   E. Neill Raymond, *Victorian Viceroy: The Life of Robert, the First Earl of Lytton* (Regency Press, 1980), p. 42. Rosina's pronouncement appears in T. H. S. Escott, *Edward Bulwer: First Baron Lytton of Knebworth: A Social, Personal and Political Monograph* (Routledge, 1910), p. 297, and it is much too delicious to leave out.

10 Marie Mulvey-Roberts, 'Militancy, Masochism or Martydom? The Public and Private Prisons of Constance Lytton', in June Purvis and Sandra Stanley Holton, *Votes for Women* (Routledge, London, 2000), p. 168.

11 Andrew Lycett, *Wilkie Collins: A Life of Sensation* (Windmill, 2014), pp. 194–5.

12 T. H. S. Escott, *Edward Bulwer*, pp. 331–2, quoted in Marie Mulvey-Roberts, 'Writing for Revenge: The Battle of the Books of Edward and Rosina Bulwer Lytton', in Allan Conran Christensen (ed.), *The Subverting Vision of Bulwer Lytton*, p. 164.

13 Edward Bulwer-Lytton to Robert Lytton, 1 June 1854, quoted in Mary Lutyens, *The Lyttons in India: An Account of Lord Lytton's Viceroyalty 1876–1880* (John Murray, 1979), p. 4.

14 Mary Lutyens, *The Lyttons in India*, p. 4.

15 Aurelia Brooks Harlan, *Owen Meredith: A Critical Biography of Robert, First Earl of Lytton* (Colombia, 1945), p. 45.

16 Barbara Palmer, née Villiers, Countess of Castlemaine, http://www.oxforddnb.com/view/article/28285.

17 Mary Lutyens, *The Lyttons in India*, p. 7.

18 Mary Lutyens, *The Lyttons in India*, p. 9 and p. 8.

19 Constance Lytton to Adela Villiers, undated but approximately 1893, in Betty Balfour (ed.), *Letters of Constance Lytton*, p. 23.

20 Edith Lytton, *Lady Lytton's Court Diary, India 1876–1880* (privately printed, Chiswick Press, 1899), p. 93.

21 See Elizabeth Longford, *A Pilgrimage of Passion: The Life of Wilfred Scawen Blunt* (Weidenfeld & Nicholson, 1979), pp. 45–9 for their initial relationship. Just as Browning had encouraged Lytton's talent so now Lytton supported Blunt, still finding his feet as a poet.

22 Elisabeth Lutyens described Constance as 'a seven-month baby' but I have not found any other references to this. Brian Harrison Interviews, LSE Library Collections, 8/SUF/B/049.

23 See Knebworth Archive, DIEK/036/172.

24 Mary Lutyens, *The Lyttons in India*, p. 1.

25 David Gilmour, *The Ruling Caste: Imperial Lives in the Victorian Raj* (John Murray, 2005), p. 309.

26 Mary Lutyens, *The Lyttons in India*, p. 10 and p. 26.

27 E. Neill Raymond, *Victorian Viceroy*, p. 131.

28 See, for example: David Gilmour, *The Ruling Caste: Imperial Lives in the Victorian Raj*, Chapter One, and on this period in Robert's life, see E. Neill Raymond, *Victorian Viceroy*, as well as Mary Lutyens, *The Lyttons in India* and Edith Lytton, *Lady Lytton's Court Diary, India 1876–1880*.

29 Mary Lutyens, *The Lyttons in India*, p. 14.

30 David Gilmour, *The Ruling Caste: Imperial Lives in the Victorian Raj* (John Murray, 2005), p. 229.

31 Mary Lutyens, *The Lyttons in India*, p. 37.

32 David Gilmour, *The Ruling Caste*, p. 227.

33 Mary Lutyens, *The Lyttons in India*, p. 48.

34 Edith Lytton, *Lady Lytton's Court Diary, India 1876–1880*, p. 27.

35 Mary Lutyens, *The Lyttons in India*, p. 41 and Edith Lytton, *Lady Lytton's Court Diary, India 1876–1880*, p. 25.

36 Mary Lutyens, *The Lyttons in India*, p. 48.

37 Mary Lutyens, *The Lyttons in India*, p. 52 and p. 149.

38 Victor Lytton, *Set in Remembrance* (unpublished memoir), p. 1.

39 Mary Lutyens, *The Lyttons in India*, p. 35.

40 Aurelia Brooks Harlan, *Owen Meredith*, p. 220.

41 David Gilmour, *The Ruling Caste*, pp. 115–16.

42 On this period see, for example, Mary Lutyens, *The Lyttons in India*, pp. 103–69.

43 Mary Lutyens, *The Lyttons in India*, p. 94.

44 Other women named by Mary Lutyens, *The Lyttons in India*, p. 155; godson rumour noted by Jane Ridley, *Edwin Lutyens: His Life, His Wife, His Work* (Pimlico, 2003), p. 85. On the previous page, she states that his valet tried to steal his nightshirts, hoping Robert's good luck with women would rub off on him. Mrs Plowden and Scawen Blunt described in Elizabeth Longford, *Pilgrimage of Passion*, p. 162.

45 Robert Lytton to Edith Lytton, 22 March 1880, quoted in E. Neill Raymond, *Victorian Viceroy*, pp. 221–2.

46 Edith Lytton, *Lady Lytton's Court Diary, India 1876–1880*, p. 62.

47 Edith Lytton to Elizabeth Villers, 31 May 1880, quoted in E. Neill Raymond, *Victorian Viceroy*, p. 226.

48 Letters from Edith Lytton: Edith Lytton to Elizabeth Villiers, undated by Lutyens, in Mary Lutyens, *The Lyttons in India*, p. 175; Edith Lytton to Mrs Forster, 21 February 1877, *Lady Lytton's Court Diary, India 1876–1880*, p. 99. 'Illuminating on very small things' from Edith Lytton, *Lady Lytton's Court Diary, India 1876–1880*, p. 118.

49 Edith Lytton, *Lady Lytton's Court Diary, India 1876–1880*, p. 38 and p. 151.

50 Edith Lytton, *Lady Lytton's Court Diary, India 1876–1880*, p. 37 and p. 154.

51 Edith Lytton, *Lady Lytton's Court Diary, India 1876–1880*, p. 203, p. 157 and p. 162.

52 Emily Lutyens, *A Blessed Girl: Memoirs of a Victorian Girlhood Chronicled in an Exchange of Letters, 1887–1896* (Heinemann, 1954), pp. 8–12.

53 Edith Lytton, *Lady Lytton's Court Diary, India 1876–1880*, p. 189. Edith Lytton to Mrs Forster, 10 October 1876, quoted in Edith Lytton, *Lady Lytton's Court Diary*, p. 51.

54 Edith Lytton, *Lady Lytton's Court Diary, India 1876–1880*, p. 240.

55 Robert Lytton to Edith Lytton, 15 September 1877, quoted in E. Neill Raymond, *Victorian Viceroy*, p. 168 and Edith Lytton to Mrs Forster, 10 October 1876, *Lady Lytton's Court Diary, India 1876–1880*, p. 49.

56 Edith Lytton to Elizabeth Villers, 31 May 1880, quoted in E. Neill Raymond, *Victorian Viceroy*, p. 226.

57 Edith Lytton, *Lady Lytton's Court Diary, India 1876–1880*, p. 45; Edith Lytton to Elizabeth Villiers, 13 February 1879, quoted in Edith Lytton, *Lady Lytton's Court Diary, India 1876–1880*, p. 190 and Edith Lytton, *Lady Lytton's Court Diary*, p. 99.

CHAPTER 2: A MISFIT AMONG ECCENTRICS

1 Neville Lytton, *The English Country Gentleman* (Camelot, 1925), p. 256.

2 For example, 'Parsimony in famine policy, combined with an expensive and pointless war against Afghanistan, were the main features of an irresponsible Viceroyalty,' says David Gilmour, *The Ruling Caste*, p. 115.

3 See *Knebworth House: Hertfordshire Home of the Lytton Family since 1490* (Heritage House Group, 2005).

4 Victor Lytton *Set in Remembrance*, pp. 6–10.

5 Hermione Cobbold, *Memory Lane: Tales of Long Ago, 1905–1930* (unpublished memoir), p. 23.

6 Victor Lytton, *Set in Remembrance*, p. 5.

7 Betty Balfour (ed.), *Letters of Constance Lytton*, p. 88.

8 Emily Lutyens, *A Blessed Girl*, p. 18 and Victor Lytton, *Set in Remembrance*, p. 11.

9 Constance Lytton, *Prisons and Prisoners*, p. 2.

10 Sylvia Pankhurst, *The Suffragette Movement: An Intimate Account of Persons and Ideals* (Longmans, 1931), p. 332.

11 Emily Lutyens to the Reverend Whitwell Elwyn, 17 November 1892, in Emily Lutyens, *A Blessed Girl*, p. 177.

12 Emily Lutyens to the Reverend Whitwell Elwyn, 9 September 1891 and 23 July 1892, in Emily Lutyens, *A Blessed Girl*, p. 58 and p. 146.

13 Emily Lutyens, *A Blessed Girl*, p. 18.

14 Emily in particular was extremely indiscreet. Aged thirteen, she began an intimate friendship with a 71-year-old clergyman, the Reverend Whitwell Elwyn, exchanging correspondence which describes her feelings and fears with great honesty. This series of letters was published as *A Blessed Girl* in 1953 and is a tremendously interesting record of Lutyen family life at this time, albeit seen through the eyes of an often disgruntled teenager.

15 Perhaps she didn't have time to keep them during her suffrage years or perhaps they were lost as she lived a life on the road.

16 According to her niece, Mary Lutyens. Cited in Clayre Percy and Jane Ridley, *The Letters of Edwin Lutyens to his wife, Lady Emily* (Collins, 1985), p. 35.

17 Neville Lytton, *The English Country Gentleman*, p. 249.

18 Constance Lytton to Betty Balfour, 21 August 1892, in Betty Balfour (ed.), *Letters of Constance Lytton*, p. 29.

19 Emily Lutyens to the Reverend Whitwell Elwyn, 16 December 1890, in Emily Lutyens, *A Blessed Girl*, p. 37.

20 Neville Lytton, *The English Country Gentleman*, p. 249.

21 Neville Lytton, *The English Country Gentleman*, p. 251.

22 Emily Lutyens, *A Blessed Girl*, p. 122.

23 Neville Lytton, *The English Country Gentleman*, p. 257.

24 Emily Lutyens, *A Blessed Girl*, p. 8.

25 Constance Lytton to Adela Villiers, January 1897, in Betty Balfour (ed.), *Letters of Constance Lytton*, p. 71.

26 Neville Lytton, *The English Country Gentleman*, p. 250.

27 Constance Lytton to Teresa Earle, 16 August 1897, in Betty Balfour (ed.), *Letters of Constance Lytton*, p. 77.

28 Quoted in Mary Lutyens, *The Lyttons in India*, p. 185.

29 Constance Lytton to Teresa Earle, August 1888, in Betty Balfour (ed.), *Letters of Constance Lytton*, p. 11.

30 Victor Lytton, *Set in Remembrance*, p. 17.

31 Frances Balfour to Emily Faithfull, 26 July 1887, Women's Library 7EFA/096.

32 Constance Lytton to Gerald Balfour, 31 July 1887, Balfour Papers, National Archives of Scotland GD433/2/280/8–9.

33 Constance Lytton to Betty Balfour, 9 January 1901, Balfour Papers, National Archives of Scotland, GD433/2/324/1/6–8.

34 Victor Lytton, *Set in Remembrance*, p. 15.

35 Constance Lytton to Teresa Earle, August 1888, in Betty Balfour (ed.), *Letters of Constance Lytton*, p. 16.

36 Victor Lytton, *Set in Remembrance*, p. 18.

37 Robert Lytton to Teresa Earle, 23 January 1888, quoted in E. Neill Raymond, *Victorian Viceroy*, p. 277. For this period in Robert's life see E. Neill Raymond, *Victorian Viceroy*, pp. 234–77.

38 Constance Lytton to Teresa Earle, August 1888, in Betty Balfour (ed.), *Letters of Constance Lytton*, p. 14; the price she paid for Gerald's life is on p. 16.

39 Emily Lutyens, *A Blessed Girl*, p. 19.

40 Neville Lytton, *The English Country Gentleman*, p. 253.

41 Constance Lytton to Teresa Earle, August 1888, in Betty Balfour (ed.), *Letters of Constance Lytton*, p. 13.

42 Betty Balfour (ed.), *Letters of Constance Lytton*, pp. 40–41.

43 Victor Lytton, *Set in Remembrance*, p. 19.

44 Neville Lytton, *The English Country Gentleman*, p. 256.

45 Betty Balfour to Frances Balfour, 25–26 November 1891, Balfour Papers, National Archives of Scotland, GD433/2/205.

46 Balfour Papers, National Archives of Scotland, GD433/2/305/36.

47 Emily Lutyens to the Reverend Whitwell Elwyn, 14 July and 17 July 1893, in Emily Lutyens,

A Blessed Girl, p. 210 and Emily Lutyens to the Reverend Whitwell Elwyn, 3 March 1893, in Emily Lutyens, *A Blessed Girl*, p. 189.

48 Betty Balfour to Gerald Balfour, 17 November 1891, Balfour Papers, National Archives of Scotland, GD433/2/282.

49 Emily Lutyens to the Reverend Whitwell Elwyn, 4 July 1893, in Emily Lutyens, *A Blessed Girl*, p. 206 and Neville Lytton, *The English Country Gentleman*, p. 249.

50 Constance Lytton to Emily Lytton, 23 September 1891, in Betty Balfour (ed.), *Letters of Constance Lytton*, p. 6.

CHAPTER 3: THE PONSONBYS

1 Constance Lytton to Adela Villiers, July 1893, Knebworth Archive, 01274.

2 Constance Lytton to Adela Villiers, 4 December 1892, in Betty Balfour (ed.), *Letters of Constance Lytton*, p. 37.

3 See Ruth First and Ann Scott, *Olive Schreiner* (André Deutsch, 1980).

4 Rachel Holmes, *Eleanor Marx: A Life* (Bloomsbury, 2014), p. 218.

5 Constance Lytton to Olive Schreiner, 2 November 1892, Balfour Papers, National Archives of Scotland, GD433/2/307.

6 Rachel Holmes, *Eleanor Marx*, p. 219.

7 Constance Lytton to Adela Villiers, undated 1893, Betty Balfour (ed.), *Letters of Constance Lytton*, p. 43.

8 For the full history of this interesting couple, see William M. Kuhn, *Henry and Mary Ponsonby: Life at the Court of Queen Victoria* (Duckbacks, 2003).

9 Martha Vicinus, *Intimate Friends: Women Who Loved Women 1778–1928* (University of Chicago Press, 2004), p. 133. On the same page, Vicinus suggests that 'after her husband's death, Lady Ponsonby moved almost exclusively in a world of women who loved women'.

10 Quoted in Martha Vicinus, *Intimate Friends*, p. 134.

11 William M. Kuhn, *Henry and Mary Ponsonby*, p. 117 and p. 185.

12 She was a Magdalen not a Margaret, and seems most often to have been called Maggie, but Constance usually called her Maggy and so have I. Princess Louise had several tangential connections to Constance: she was a patron of Edwin Lutyens in the first part of his career and was Frances Balfour's sister-in-law and friend. Unlike the Queen, she was a supporter of suffrage. See Lucinda Hawksley, *The Mystery of Princess Louise: Queen Victoria's Rebellious Daughter* (Chatto & Windus, 2014), p. 271.

13 Constance Lytton to Teresa Earle, 7 November 1893, in Betty Balfour (ed.), *Letters of Constance Lytton*, p. 48.

14 Betty Balfour to Constance Lytton, July 1893, Knebworth Archive, 01274, p. 1.

15 Constance Lytton to Teresa Earle, 7 November 1893, in Betty Balfour (ed.), *Letters of Constance Lytton*, p. 47.

16 Leo Maxse was married to Kitty, said to be the model for Mrs Dalloway.

17 Emily Lytton to Rev. Whitwell Elwyn, 3 October 1893, in Emily Lutyens, *A Blessed Girl*, p. 238.

18 Constance Lytton, *National Review*, January 1894, p. 713.

19 However, I did not see another review attributed to Constance Lytton in the *National Review*, nor did I see an unsigned review which might be attributed to Constance. It is not clear to me, therefore, where all this work was going, or if it was simply practice.

20 Constance Lytton to Aunt T, 25 August 1900, Knebworth Archive, 01274, p. 28.

21 Emily Lytton to Rev. Whitwell Elwyn, 15 December 1893 in Emily Lutyens, *A Blessed Girl*, p. 263.

22 For example, Journals of Constance Lytton, 30 December 1893.

23 Constance Lytton to Teresa Earle, Knebworth Archive, 01274, p. 3.

24 Constance Lytton to Betty Balfour, August 1894, Knebworth Archive, 01274, p. 4.

25 See Journals of Constance Lytton for 1895, Knebworth Archive, box 110.

26 John's remarks were copied out for Betty's benefit. Constance Lytton to Betty Balfour, August 1894, Knebworth Archive, 01274, p. 4. Constance Lytton to Betty Balfour, September 1894, Knebworth Archive, 01274, p. 5.

27 Constance Lytton to Aunt T, 25 August 1900, Knebworth Archive, 01274, p. 28.

28 Constance Lytton to Aunt T, March 1895, in Betty Balfour (ed.), *Letters of Constance Lytton*, p. 50.

29 Betty Balfour (ed.), *Letters of Constance Lytton*, p. 50.

30 Ethel Smyth, *As Time Went On* (Longmans, 1930), p. 91.

31 Constance Lytton to Betty Balfour, 16 May 1895, Knebworth Archive, 01274, p. 7.

32 Constance Lytton to Betty Balfour, 27 May 1895, Knebworth Archive, 01274, p. 8.

33 Betty Balfour (ed.), *Letters of Constance Lytton*, p. 124.

34 Letter from the Queen, Edith Lytton, ed. by Mary Lutyens, *Lady Lytton's Court Diary, 1895–1899* (Rupert Hart-Davis, 1961), preface; Gerald's role in Edith's decision on p. 13.

35 Journals of Constance Lytton, 26 October, 22 November and 28 December 1895.

36 Constance Lytton to Adela Villiers, April 1896, Knebworth Archive, 01274, p. 8.

37 Constance Lytton to Adela Villiers, 12 July 1896, in Betty Balfour (ed.), *Letters of Constance Lytton*, p. 65.

38 Constance Lytton to Adela Villiers, 26 August 1896, Knebworth Archive, 01274, p. 10.

39 Constance Lytton to Adela Villiers, 23 November 1896, Knebworth Archive, 01274, p. 11.

40 Betty Balfour (ed.), *Letters of Constance Lytton*, p. 39.

41 Constance Lytton to Adela Villiers, January 1897, in Betty Balfour (ed.), *Letters of Constance Lytton*, p. 71.

42 Journal of Constance Lytton, 12 February 1897, Knebworth Archive, box 110.

43 The busy day on 28 May is from Mrs C. W. Earle, *Pot Pourri from a Surrey Garden* (Thomas Nelson and Sons, 1919), p. 120; weeding on p. 104, instructions for the blacksmith on p. 154 and thoughts on celeriac p. 29.

44 Mrs C. W. Earle, *Pot Pourri from a Surrey Garden*, p. 328 and p. 331.

45 Mrs C. W. Earle, *Pot Pourri from a Surrey Garden*, preface.

46 Patricia Miles and Jill Williams, *An Uncommon Criminal: The Life of Lady Constance Lytton: Militant Suffragette 1869–1923* (Knebworth House Education and Preservation Trust, 1999), p. 9.

47 Constance Lytton to Aunt T, 25 August 1900, Knebworth Archive, 01274.

48 Betty Balfour (ed.), *Letters of Constance Lytton*, p. 72.

49 Journals of Constance Lytton, 5 August 1897, Knebworth Archive, box 110.

50 Betty Balfour (ed.), *Letters of Constance Lytton*, p. 78.

51 Journals of Constance Lytton, 2 August and 17 September 1897, Knebworth Archive, box 110.

52 Constance Lytton to Adela Villiers, 5 November 1897, Knebworth Archive, 01274, p. 12.

53 John Ponsonby to Constance Lytton, 22 December 1897, Knebworth Archive, 01274, p. 13.

54 Constance Lytton to Adela Villiers, December 1897, Knebworth Archive, 01274, pp. 13–14.

55 Constance Lytton to Mrs Mansel, 23 March 1898, Knebworth Archive, 01274, p. 14.

56 Constance Lytton to Mrs Mansel, 23 March 1898, Knebworth Archive, 01274, p. 15.

57 Constance Lytton to Adela Villiers, 30 June 1898, Knebworth Archive, 01274, p. 17.

58 Constance Lytton to Adela Villiers, 23 March 1899, Knebworth Archive, 01274, p. 19.

59 Constance Lytton to Teresa Earle, 7–11 November 1899, Balfour Papers, National Archives of Scotland, GD433/2/321/55–7.

60 Constance Lytton to Teresa Earle, 17 November 1899, Knebworth Archive, 01274, p. 20.

61 See Journals of Constance Lytton, 1899, for example 24 April, 11 September, 16 September, Knebworth Archive, box 110.

62 Journals of Constance Lytton, 15 December 1899, Knebworth Archive, box 110.

63 Constance Lytton to Adela Villiers, 23 July 1900, Knebworth Archive, 01274, p. 22.

64 Constance Lytton to Adela Villiers, 28 August 1900, Knebworth Archive, 01274, p. 26.

65 Constance Lytton to Aunt T, 7–11 November 1899, Balfour Papers, National Archives of Scotland, GD433/2/321/55–7.

66 Neville Lytton, *The English Country Gentleman*, p. 259.

67 Constance Lytton to Aunt T, 25 August 1900, Knebworth Archive, 01274, p. 28.

68 Journals of Constance Lytton, 14 January 1901, Knebworth Archive, box 110 and Constance Lytton to Adela Villiers, 26 January 1901, Knebworth Archive, 01274, p. 30.

69 Constance Lytton to Teresa Earle, undated, in Betty Balfour (ed.), *Letters of Constance Lytton*, p. 108.

70 Constance Lytton to Edward Marsh, 7 March 1901, Knebworth Archive, 41943.

71 Journals of Constance Lytton, 24–25 March 1901.

72 Constance Lytton to Adela Villiers, 11 June 1901, Knebworth Archive, 01274, p. 31.

73 Journals of Constance Lytton, 13 June, 24 June, 29 June and 30 June 1901, Knebworth Archive, box 110.

74 Constance Lytton to Adela Villiers, 13 July 1901, Knebworth Archive, 01274, p. 32.

75 *The Times*, 26 July 1901, in Journals of Constance Lytton 1901, Knebworth Archive, box 110.

76 Constance Lytton to Adela Villiers, 2 August 1901, Knebworth Archive, 01274, p. 33.

77 Constance Lytton to Adela Villiers, 2 August 1901, Knebworth Archive, 01274, p. 33.

78 Constance Lytton to Aunt T, 26 August 1901, Knebworth Archive, 01274, p. 36.

79 Journals of Constance Lytton, 12 August 1901.

80 Journals of Constance Lytton, August 1901. I have not been able to trace the author.

81 Constance Lytton to Adela Smith, 7 February 1902, and Constance Lytton to Teresa Earle, 31 January 1903, Knebworth Archive, 01274, p. 38 and 40.

82 Constance Lytton to Betty Balfour, 16 April 1905, Knebworth Archive, 01274, p. 40.

83 Journals of Constance Lytton, 6 June 1906 and 25 December 1906, Knebworth Archive, box 110.

84 Journals of Constance Lytton, 18 October 1903, Knebworth Archive, box 110.

85 Journals of Constance Lytton, 23 December 1904, Knebworth Archive, box 110.

86 Constance Lytton to Adela Smith, 6 September 1907, Knebworth Archive, 01274, p. 43.

87 Constance Lytton to Adela Villiers, 27 May 1895, Knebworth Archive, 01274, p. 8.

88 Victor Lytton to Betty Balfour, 24 December 1924, quoted in Michelle Myall, "'Only be ye strong and very courageous': the militant suffragism of Lady Constance Lytton', *Women's History Review*, Vol. 7, No. 1 (1998).

89 Emily Lutyens to Edwin Lutyens, 11 April 1897, quoted in Clayre Percy and Jane Ridley, *The Letters of Edwin Lutyens to his wife Lady Emily*, p. 41.

90 Neville Lytton, *The English Country Gentleman*, p. 259.

91 See Emily Lutyens, *A Blessed Girl*, p. 215 and Elizabeth Longford, *Pilgrimage of Passion*, pp. 303–20.

92 Emily Lytton to Rev. Whitwell Elwyn, 24 August 1893, quoted in Emily Lutyens, *A Blessed Girl*, p. 215.

93 Elizabeth Longford, *Pilgrimage of Passion*, p. 319. This was not the only triangle connecting Emily and Judith: Emily had at one time been pursing Gerald Duckworth, who proposed to Judith. Jane Ridley, *Edwin Lutyens*, p. 95 and Elizabeth Longford, *Pilgrimage of Passion*, p. 339.

94 Edith Lytton, ed. by Mary Lutyens, *Lady Lytton's Court Diary, 1895–1899*, p. 90.

95 Mary Links interview with Brian Harrison, 8/SUF/B/085, LSE Library collections.

96 A selection of which are published in Clayre Pierce and Jane Ridley, *The Letters of Edwin Lutyens to his wife, Lady Emily* (Collins, 1985).

97 Elizabeth Longford, *Pilgrimage of Passion*, p. 339.

98 Constance Lytton to Aunt T, 20 July 1899, Balfour Papers, National Archives of Scotland, GD433/2/320/1/49–51.

99 Elizabeth Longford, *Pilgrimage of Passion*, p. 339.

100 Jane Ridley, *Edwin Lutyens: His Life, His Wife, His Work*, p. 142. The subsequent page describes the reality.

101 Constance Lytton, *Prisons and Prisoners*, p. 1.

102 Constance Lytton to Betty Balfour, 10 January 1908, Balfour Papers, National Archives of Scotland, GD433/2/271/2.

103 Olive Schreiner to Edward Carpenter, 6 February 1908, National English Literary Museum, Grahamstown, Olive Schreiner Letters Project transcription SMD 30/32/gii, line 15.

104 Lisa Appignanesi, *Mad, Bad and Sad: A History of Women and the Mind Doctors from 1800 to the Present* (Virago, 2009), p. 171.

105 Lisa Appignanesi, *Mad, Bad and Sad*, p. 115.

106 Constance Lytton to Betty Balfour, 24 April 1907, Balfour Papers, National Archives of Scotland, GD433/2/335/51–2.

107 Lena Leneman, 'The Awakened Instinct: Vegetarianism and the Women's Suffrage Movement in Britain', *Women's History Review*, Vol. 6, No. 2 (1997), p. 275.
108 Kathryn Gleadle, *British Women in the Nineteenth Century* (Palgrave, 2001), p. 183.
109 Constance Lytton to Betty Balfour, 26 July 1899, in Betty Balfour (ed.), *Letters of Constance Lytton*, p. 130.
110 Constance Lytton to Teresa Earle, 25 August 1900, Knebworth Archive, 01274, p. 28.
111 Constance Lytton to Adela Smith, 12 June 1908, Knebworth Archive, 01274, p. 44.

CHAPTER 4: THE CAUSE

1 Constance Lytton, *Prisons and Prisoners*, p. 12.
2 There is endless historical debate about the degree to which 'separate spheres' was just an idea, or whether it really reflected the way people lived their lives. The most obvious example is paid work: for most working-class women, work outside the home was a necessity, and even middle- and upper-class women had important, if unpaid, philanthropic and charitable service in their community. But by the end of the century, even trade unions were arguing that men should be paid wages that would allow their wives (and children) to stay at home. Other examples abound, like the degree of political influence women could exert, even though they could not formally vote.
3 Susie Steinbach, *Women in England 1760–1914: A Social History* (Weidenfeld & Nicholson, 2004), p. 257.
4 Kathryn Gleadle, *British Women in the Nineteenth Century*, p. 163.
5 Susie Steinbach, *Women in England 1760–1914*, p. 248.
6 Joyce Marlow, *The Virago Book of Suffragettes*, p. 25.
7 Jill Liddington and Jill Norris, *One Hand Tied Behind Us* (Virago, 1978) is the classic text on this issue.
8 Susie Steinbach, *Women in England 1760–1914*, p. 269.
9 Kathryn Gleadle, *British Women in the Nineteenth Century*, p. 168.
10 Sophia A. Van Wingerden, *The Women's Suffrage Movement in Britain, 1866–1928* (Macmillan, 1999), p. 40.
11 Susie Steinbach, *Women in England 1760–1914*, p. 277.
12 Sophia A. van Wingarden, *The Women's Suffrage Movement in Britain*, p. 47.
13 Sophia A. Van Wingerden, *The Women's Suffrage Movement in Britain*, p. 38.
14 Kathryn Gleadle, *British Women in the Nineteenth Century*, p. 158.
15 Sophia A. Van Wingerden, *The Women's Suffrage Movement in Britain*, pp. 36–7.
16 The most complete version of the Pankhurst story is Martin Pugh, *The Pankhursts: The History of One Radical Family* (Allen Lane, 2001).
17 Katherine Connolly, *Sylvia Pankhurst: Suffragette, Socialist and Scourge of Empire* (Pluto Press, 2013), p. 5.
18 Sophia A. van Wingerden: *The Women's Suffrage Movement in Britain*, p. 77.
19 Emmeline Pankhurst, *My Own Story*, p. 42.
20 Antonia Raeburn, *Militant Suffragettes*, p. 19.
21 Emmeline Pethick-Lawrence, *My Part in a Changing World* (Gollancz, 1938), preface.
22 Sylvia Pankhurst, *The Suffragette Movement*, p. 221.
23 Christabel Pankhurst, *Unshackled: The Story of How we Won the Vote* (Hutchinson & Co., 1987), p. 84.
24 Sophia A. Van Wingerden, *The Women's Suffrage Movement in Britain*, p. 74.
25 Martin Pugh, *The Pankhursts*, p. 177.
26 Michelle Myall, *Flame and Burnt Offering*, p. 113.
27 Emmeline Pankhurst, *My Own Story*, p. 50.
28 Emmeline Pethick-Lawrence, *My Part in a Changing World*, p. 240.
29 See, for example, Lisa Tickner, *The Spectacle of Women: imagery of the suffrage campaign, 1907–1914*, (Chatto & Windus, 1988) and Barbara Green, *Spectacular Confessions: Autobiography, Performative Activism, and the Sites of Suffrage* (Macmillan, 1997).
30 Sophia A. van Wingerden, *The Women's Suffrage Movement in Britain, 1866–1928*, p. 79.
31 Krista Cowman, *Women of the Right Spirit: Paid Organisers of the Women's Social and Political Union 1904–1918* (Manchester University Press, 2007), p. 79.

32 Sophia A. van Wingerden, *The Women's Suffrage Movement in Britain, 1866–1928*, p. 79.

33 Sheila Rowbotham, *A Century of Women: The History of Women in Britain and the United States* (Viking, 1997), p. 10.

34 Christabel Pankhurst, *Unshackled*, p. 73.

35 Susie Steinbach, *Women in England 1760–1914*, p. 285.

36 Jil Liddington: *Selina Cooper: The Life and Times of a Respectable Rebel* (Virago, 1984), p. 193 and p. 199.

37 Quoted in Frank Meeres, *Suffragettes: How Britain's Women Fought and Died for the Right to Vote* (Amberley, 2014), p. 34.

38 They left the Independent Labour Party, one of the constituent bodies that made up the Labour Party.

39 Quoted in Katherine Connelly, *Sylvia Pankhurst*, p. 28.

40 Jill Liddington and Jill Norris, *One Hand Tied Behind Us*, p. 205.

41 Jill Liddington, *Rebel Girls: Their Fight for the Vote* (Virago, 2006), p. 224.

42 June Purvis, 'Christabel Pankhurst and the Women's Social and Political Union', in Maroula Joannou and June Purvis, *The Women's Suffrage Movement: New Feminist Perspectives* (Manchester University Press, 1998), p. 157.

43 Katherine Connelly, *Sylvia Pankhurst*, p. 34.

44 Quoted in Katherine Connelly, *Sylvia Pankhurst*, p. 34.

45 Reported in *Votes for Women*, 9 July 1908, quoted in Katherine Connelly, *Sylvia Pankhurst*, p. 25.

46 Betty says this is £1,000 in the Letters (p. 133) but the will itself says £2,000, as well as a blue bracelet and heart given to her by the late Duchess of Gloucester. The will was proved on 29 June 1905; the total value of the estate was nearly £59 000.

47 Constance Lytton to Teresa Earle, 28 July 1907, Betty Balfour (ed.), *Letters of Constance Lytton*, p. 134.

48 *The Times*, 4 July 1908 p. 15.

49 www.maryneal.org has a wealth of information about this very interesting woman.

50 Constance Lytton to Adela Smith, 10 September 1908, in Betty Balfour (ed.), *Letters of Constance Lytton*, p. 136.

51 Constance Lytton to Edward Carpenter, 17 January 1909, Sheffield Archives, MSS 386–164.

52 Constance Lytton to Adela Smith, 10 September 1908, in Betty Balfour (ed.), *Letters of Constance Lytton*, p. 136

53 Constance Lytton, *Prisons and Prisoners*, p. 10.

54 Constance Lytton, *Prisons and Prisoners*, p. 10 and Constance Lytton to Betty Balfour, 24 August 1908, quoted in Joyce Marlow, *Votes for Women: The Virago Book of Suffragettes*, p. 71.

55 Constance Lytton to Adela Smith, 10 September 1908, in Betty Balfour (ed.), *Letters of Constance Lytton*, p. 136.

56 Constance Lytton, *Prisons and Prisoners*, p. 10.

57 Ada Wright quoted in Barbara Green, *Spectacular Confessions*, p. 58.

58 Constance Lytton to Adela Smith, 10 September 1908, in Betty Balfour (ed.), *Letters of Constance Lytton*, p. 136.

59 Constance Lytton, *Prisons and Prisoners*, p. 9.

60 Constance Lytton, *Prisons and Prisoners*, p. 12.

61 Constance Lytton, *Prisons and Prisoners*, pp. 13–14.

62 See Maroula Joannou, '"She who would be politically free herself must strike the blow": Suffragette Autobiography and Suffragette Militancy' in Julia Swindells, *The Uses of Autobiography* (Taylor and Francis, 1995).

63 Emily Lytton to Rev. Whitwell Elwyn, 6 October 1893, in Emily Lutyens, *A Blessed Girl*, p. 240.

64 Constance Lytton to Aunt T, 23 January 1907, in Betty Balfour (ed.), *Letters of Constance Lytton*, p. 131 and Constance Lytton to Dorothea Ponsonby, 30 May 1907, in Betty Balfour (ed.), *Letters of Constance Lytton*, p. 132.

65 Emily Lutyens, *Candles in the Sun* (Williams Clowes and Sons, 1957), p. 14.

66 Jane Ridley, *Edwin Lutyens*, p. 169.

67 Quoted in Jane Ridley, *Edwin Lutyens*, p. 183.

68 Constance Lytton to Aunt T, 20 September 1908, Balfour Papers, National Archives of Scotland, GD/433/2/337/103.
69 Emmeline Pethick-Lawrence to Constance Lytton, 28 October 1908, in the Autograph Collection, Vol. XX, Women's Library.
70 Emmeline Pethick-Lawrence, 'The Autumn Campaign' in *Votes for Women*, 8 September 1908, p. 441.
71 Constance Lytton to Teresa Earle, 22 November 1908, Balfour Papers, National Archives of Scotland, GD433/2/337/109–110.
72 Constance Lytton to Teresa Earle, 20 September 1908, Balfour Papers, National Archives of Scotland, GD/433/2/337/103.
73 Betty Balfour to Constance Lytton, undated but autumn 1908, Balfour Papers, National Archives of Scotland, GD433/2/337/104.

CHAPTER 5: THE PANKHURSTS
1 Sylvia Pankhurst, *The Suffragette Movement*, p. 226.
2 Christabel Pankhurst, *Unshackled*, p. 104.
3 Antonia Raeburn, *The Militant Suffragettes*, p. 64.
4 *Daily Chronicle*, 14 October 1908.
5 *Daily Mail* and *Daily Express*, both 14 October 1908.
6 Emmeline Pethick-Lawrence, *My Part in a Changing World*, p. 198.
7 Constance Lytton, *Prisons and Prisoners*, p. 26.
8 Constance Lytton to Edith Lytton in Betty Balfour (ed.), *Letters of Constance Lytton*, p. 144.
9 Constance Lytton to Edith Lytton, 10 October 1908, in Betty Balfour (ed.), *Letters of Constance Lytton*, p. 146.
10 Emmeline Pethick-Lawrence, *My Part in a Changing World*, p. 198.
11 Christabel Pankhurst, *Unshackled*, p. 105.
12 Constance Lytton to Edith Lytton, 14 October 1908, in Betty Balfour (ed.), *Letters of Constance Lytton*, p. 147.
13 Constance Lytton, *Prisons and Prisoners*, p. 27.
14 Anonymous suffragette, quoted in Antonia Raeburn, *The Militant Suffragettes*, p. 63.
15 Women were not allowed to practise law until the Sex Disqualification (Removal) Act was passed in 1919.
16 Jane Marcus, *Suffrage and the Pankhursts* (Routledge, 1987) prints documentary evidence of this trial; this summary covers pp. 70–106.
17 Frank Meeres, *Suffragettes*, p. 67.
18 *Saturday Review*, 24 October 1909.
19 Constance Lytton, *Prisons and Prisoners*, p. 27.
20 *The Times*, 27 October 1908.
21 Constance Lytton to Lady Lytton, 14 October 1908, in Betty Balfour (ed.), *Letters of Constance Lytton*, p. 149.
22 *Daily Chronicle*, 26 October 1908.
23 Cheryl R. Jorgensen-Earp, *Speeches and Trials of the Militant Suffragettes*, p. 81.
24 *Daily Telegraph*, 26 October 1908.
25 For example, *Daily Telegraph*: 'Ability which may be misused, and courage, possibly, shown in a wrong cause', 26 October 1908; *Daily News*: 'It is deplorable that so much courage and intelligence should be wasted in advocating a course which already has behind it a sufficient majority in Parliament', 29 October 1908.
26 Frank Meeres, *Suffragettes*, p. 66.
27 Constance Lytton to Teresa Earle, undated 1908, in Betty Balfour (ed.), *Letters of Constance Lytton*, p. 152.
28 A 1921 note in Constance's scrapbook, which follows the obituary she wrote of Olive Schreiner.
29 Constance Lytton, *Prisons and Prisoners*, p. 30.
30 Emily Lutyens to Edwin Lutyens, 15 October 1908 and Edwin Lutyens to Emily Lutyens, 16 October 1908, quoted in Clayre Percy and Jane Ridley (eds), *The Letters of Edwin Lutyens to his wife Lady Emily*, p. 163.

31 *The Times*, Obituary of Edith Lytton, 19 September 1936.

32 Lady Lytton to Constance Lytton, 28 November 1908, in Betty Balfour (ed.), *Letters of Constance Lytton*, p. 156.

33 Constance Lytton to Edith Lytton, quoted in *Prisons and Prisoners*, p. 32.

34 Constance Lytton to Edward Carpenter, 17 January 1910, quoted in Michelle Myall, '"Only be ye strong and very courageous": the militant suffragism of Lady Constance Lytton', *Women's History Review*, Vol. 7, No. 1, 1998, p. 70.

35 Neville Lytton, *The English Country Gentleman*, p. 268.

36 Neville Lytton, *The English Country Gentleman*, p. 268.

37 Constance Lytton to Adela Smith, 28 August 1900, 01274, p. 26.

38 Ray Strachey quoted in June Purvis, '"A Pair of ... Infernal Queens": A Reassessment of the Dominant Representations of Emmeline and Christabel Pankhurst, First Wave Feminists in Edwardian Britain', *Women's History Review*, Vol. 5, No. 2 (1996), p. 262.

39 Constance Lytton to Aunt T, 19 August 1888 in Betty Balfour (ed.), *Letters of Constance Lytton*, p. 10.

40 *Votes for Women*, 24 October, 1909, quoted in Jill Liddington, *Vanishing for the Vote: suffrage, citizenship and the battle for the census* (Manchester University Press, 2014), p. 71.

41 Constance Lytton to Teresa Earle, August 1888, in Betty Balfour (ed.), *Letters of Constance Lytton*, p. 11.

42 Constance Lytton, speech at the Queen's Hall on 31 January 1910, quoted in Cheryl R. Jorgensen-Earp, *Speeches and Trials of the Militant Suffragettes*, p. 107.

43 Michelle Myall, *Flame and Burnt Offering*, p. 94.

44 Ray Strachey, *The Cause: A Short History of the Women's Movement in Great Britain* (G. Bell & Sons, 1928), p. 305.

45 Constance Lytton to Teresa Earle, 12 April 1909, in Betty Balfour (ed.), *Letters of Constance Lytton*, p. 163.

46 Alice Kedge quoted in Joyce Marlow, *Votes for Women: The Virago Book of Suffragettes*, p. 80.

47 Margaret Haig, *This Was My World*, p. 120, quoted in Krista Cowman, *Women of the Right Spirit*, p. 26.

48 *Votes for Women*, 25 June 1908, quoted in Katherine Connelly, *Sylvia Pankhurst*, p. 35.

49 Martin Pugh, *The Pankhursts*, p. 164.

50 Krista Cowman, *Women of the Right Spirit*, p. 18.

51 Neville Lytton, *The English Country Gentleman*, p. 268.

52 Constance Lytton to Teresa Earle, 30 November 1908, GD433/2/337/114–116 Balfour Papers, National Archives of Scotland,

53 Constance Lytton to Herbert Gladstone, 21 December 1908, British Library Add MSS 46066/200.

54 Constance Lytton to Teresa Earle, 24 December 1908, in Betty Balfour (ed.), *Letters of Constance Lytton*, p. 155.

55 Constance Lytton to Annie Kenney, 14 December 1908, KP/AK/2/LyttonC/3.

56 Jessie Kenney's unpublished autobiography, KP/JK/4/2/2/3.

57 Constance Lytton, 'No Votes for Women: A Reply to Some Recent Publications' (Fitfield, 1909), p. 23.

58 Constance Lytton, 'No Votes for Women', p. 30.

59 Constance Lytton, 'No Votes for Women', p. 26.

60 Constance Lytton, 'No Votes for Women', p. 31.

61 Constance Lytton to Betty Balfour, 9 January 1909, Balfour Papers, National Archives of Scotland, GD/433/2/338/7.

CHAPTER 6: HOLLOWAY

1 Emmeline Pankhurst, *My Own Story*, p. 101.

2 Christabel Pankhurst, *The Times*, 16 February 1909.

3 Constance Lytton to Betty Balfour, 4 February 1909, Balfour Papers, National Archives of Scotland, GD433/2/338/14–15.

4 Constance Lytton to Betty Balfour, undated, Balfour Papers, National Archives of Scotland, GD433/2/338/13.
5 Betty Balfour (ed.), *Letters of Constance Lytton*, p. 157.
6 Olive Schreiner to Edward Carpenter, 19 February 1909, Sheffield Libraries, Archives & Information, Edward Carpenter 359/94, Olive Schreiner Letters Project transcription ll. 14–16 and accompanying note.
7 Constance Lytton to Edith Lytton, 24 February 1909 in the Suffragette Fellowship Collection, Museum of London, 5082/1119. This is a postscript to the letter published in *Prisons and Prisoners*, p. 31.
8 Constance Lytton, *Prisons and Prisoners*, p. 43.
9 Constance Lytton, *Prisons and Prisoners*, pp. 50–51.
10 Emily Lutyens to Edwin Lutyens, 9 February 1909, in Clayre Percy and Jane Ridley, *The Letters of Edwin Lutyens to his wife Lady Emily*, p. 167.
11 Notes on the trial from Christabel Pankhurst, *Unshackled*, p. 123; Constance's statement reported in *The Times*, 26 February 1909.
12 Constance Lytton, *Prisons and Prisoners*, p. 58.
13 Beatrice Webb to Betty Balfour, 28 February 1909, Balfour Papers, National Archives of Scotland, GD433/2/338/21.
14 Neville Lytton to Lady Lytton, 25 February 1909, in the Suffragette Fellowship Collection, Museum of London 50.82/1119.
15 *The Times*, 25 February 1909 and Betty Balfour in *The Times*, 26 February 1909.
16 Marie Mulvey-Roberts: 'Militancy, Masochism or Martydom? The public and private prisons of Constance Lytton', in June Purvis and Sandra Stanley Holton (eds), *Votes for Women*, p. 168.
17 Constance Lytton, *Prisons and Prisoners*, p. 113 and p. 108.
18 Constance Lytton, *Prisons and Prisoners*, p. 123.
19 Constance Lytton, *Prisons and Prisoners*, p. 154–6.
20 Constance Lytton, *Prisons and Prisoners*, p. 166.
21 For a full discussion of the significance of this act, see Marie Mulvey-Roberts, 'Militancy, Masochism or Martydom? The public and private prisons of Constance Lytton', in June Purvis and Sandra Stanley Holton (eds), *Votes for Women* (Routledge, 2000).
22 Constance Lytton, *Prisons and Prisoners*, pp. 133–4.
23 Neville Lytton, *The English Country Gentleman*, p. 270.
24 Constance Lytton, *Prisons and Prisoners*, p. 135.
25 Constance Lytton, *Prisons and Prisoners*, p. 103, p. 96 and p. 61.
26 Constance Lytton, *Prisons and Prisoners*, p. 188.
27 *The Times*, 25 March 1909.
28 Mary Neal to Betty Balfour, 25 March 1909, Balfour Papers, National Archives of Scotland, GD433/2/338/24.
29 Constance coined this description of a prison sentence which was adopted by other suffragettes. Sylvia Pankhurst, *The Suffragette Movement*, p. 359.
30 Constance Lytton to Teresa Earle, 25 March 1909, in Betty Balfour (ed.), *Letters of Constance Lytton*, p. 160.
31 Betty Balfour (ed.), *Letters of Constance Lytton*, p. 159.
32 Judith Blunt to Betty Balfour, 28 March 1909, Knebworth Archive, 125, quoted in Marie Mulvey-Roberts, 'Militancy, Masochism or Martydom? The public and private prisons of Constance Lytton', in June Purvis and Sandra Stanley Holton (eds), *Votes for Women*, p. 176.
33 'Them' is Constance and Edith. Frances Balfour to Betty Balfour, 29 March 1909, Balfour Papers, National Archives of Scotland, GD433/2/338/25–6.
34 Noel Lytton to Jessie Kenney, 16 January 1964, KP/JK/3/Lytton/n2a.
35 Emmeline Pethick-Lawrence *My Part in a Changing World*, pp. 223–4.
36 http://hansard.millbanksystems.com/commons/1909/apr/07/lady-constance-lytton-holloway-prison
37 See, for example, Constance Lytton to Betty Balfour, 1 May 1910, Balfour Papers, National Archives of Scotland, GD433/2/340/49–50.

38 Constance Lytton to Herbert Gladstone, undated, British Library Add MSS 46066/312.
39 Constance Lytton to Herbert Gladstone, 4 April 1909, British Library Add MS 46067/2.

CHAPTER 7: MILITANT

1 Emmeline Pethick-Lawrence: *My Part in a Changing World*, p. 240.
2 Christabel Pankhurst, 6 April 1909, Balfour Papers, National Archives of Scotland, GD433/2/338/32–33.
3 Elizabeth Crawford, *The Women's Suffrage Movement in Britain and Ireland: A Regional Survey* (Routledge, 2006), p. 107.
4 Martin Pugh, *The Pankhursts*, p. 210.
5 A photograph of the occasion can be seen at www.bathintime.co.uk/image/251611/suffragette-emmeline-pethick-lawrence-planting-with-annie-kenney-&-lady-constance-lytton-23-april-1909, accessed 26 January 2015.
6 'Tackle Hertfordshire' and 'do something' are from Constance Lytton to Annie Kenney, 23 April 1909, KP/AK/2/LyttonC/5; admiration for Annie Constance Lytton to Annie Kenney, 4 May 1909, KP/AK/2/LyttonC/6; 'terror-making claws' in Constance Lytton to Annie Kenney, 27 May 1909, KP/AK/2/LyttonC/7.
7 *Votes for Women*, 7 May 1909, Vol. 2, p. 625.
8 *Votes for Women*, 21 May 1909, Vol. 2, p. 690.
9 *Daily Mail*, 13 May 1909, p. 3.
10 Constance Lytton to Betty Balfour, 12 May 1909, National Archives of Scotland, GD433/2/338 Balfour Papers.
11 Constance Lytton to Teresa Earle, 17 June 1909, in Betty Balfour (ed.), *Letters of Constance Lytton*, p. 164.
12 Constance Lytton to Herbert Gladstone, 5 August 1909, in British Library Add MS 46067/118.
13 See the Arthur Balfour papers Add 49793 in the British Library.
14 Dorothy Gladstone to Betty Balfour, Knebworth Archive, 41972.
15 Constance Lytton to Teresa Earle, 23 April 1909, in Betty Balfour (ed.), *Letters of Constance Lytton*, p. 163.
16 Edwin Lutyens to Emily Lutyens, 16 August 1909, quoted in Clayre Percy and Jane Ridley, *The Letters of Edwin Lutyens to his wife Lady Emily*, p. 178.
17 Edwin Lutyens to Emily Lutyens, 9 August 1909, quoted in Clayre Percy and Jane Ridley, *The Letters of Edwin Lutyens to his wife Lady Emily*, p. 173.
18 Betty's comments from Betty Balfour (ed.), *Letters of Constance Lytton*, p. 155; letter from Emily Lutyens to Teresa Earle in Betty Balfour (ed.), *Letters of Constance Lytton*, p. 159.
19 Victor Lytton, 15 June 1909, speech at St James Theatre, quoted in Marie Mulvey-Roberts and Tamas Mizuta, *The Militants: Suffragette Activism* (Routledge, 1994), p. 1.
20 Quoted in C. M. Woodhouse, unpublished biography of Victor Lytton, p. 80.
21 Davinia Woodhouse 8/SUF/B/051.
22 Constance Lytton, *The Times*, 14 July 1909.
23 Michelle Myall, *Flame and Burnt Offering*, p. 135.
24 This was Marion's second attempt at this action: the first time she had just been escorted off the premises.
25 Sylvia Pankhurst, *The Suffragette Movement*, p. 307 and Frank Meeres, *Suffragettes*, p. 79.
26 Christabel Pankhurst to C. P. Scott, 22 July 1909, quoted in Martin Pugh, *The Pankhursts*, p. 193.
27 Lisa Appignanesi, *Mad, Bad and Sad*, p. 434; see also p. 428.
28 Emmeline Pankhurst, *My Own Story*, p. 153.
29 Sylvia Pankhurst, *The Suffragette Movement*, p. 312.
30 Private Secretary to Herbert Gladstone, 13 August 1909, quoted in Joyce Marlow, *Votes for Women: The Virago Book of Suffragettes*, p. 94.
31 For an account of Mary's story, see Michelle Myall, 'No Surrender: The militancy of Mary Leigh, a working-class suffragette', in Maroula Joannou and June Purvis, *The Women's Suffrage Movement: New Feminist Perspectives* (Manchester University Press, 1998), p. 174; the figures are from Sylvia Pankhurst, *The Suffragette Movement*, p. 319. For Mary Leigh's statement to her solicitor, see Midge Mackenzie, *Shoulder to Shoulder* (Alfred A Knopf, 1975), p. 126.

32 Sylvia Pankhurst, *The Suffragette Movement*, p. 441.
33 Gladstone in the National Archives HO144/1038/180782/71, quoted in J. F. Geddes, 'Culpable Complicity: the medical profession and the forcible feeding of suffragettes', in *Women's History Review*, Vol. 17, No. 1 (2008), p. 82.
34 On 4 October 1909; for a copy of the letter see Joyce Marlow, *Votes for Women: The Virago Book of Suffragettes*, p. 97.
35 J. F. Geddes, 'Culpable Complicity: the medical profession and the forcible feeding of suffragettes', in *Women's History Review*, Vol. 17, No. 1 (2008), p. 83.
36 *The Times*, 29 September 1909.
37 Frances Balfour to Betty Balfour, 2 October 1909, Balfour Papers, National Archives of Scotland, GD/433/2/339/19.
38 Eleanor Cecil to Constance Lytton, 4 October 1909, Balfour Papers, National Archives of Scotland, GD/433/2/339/21.
39 Sandra Stanley Holton, *Suffrage Days: Stories from the Women's Suffrage Movement* (Routledge, 1996), p. 146.
40 Emmeline Pethick-Lawrence, *My Part in a Changing World*, p. 242.
41 Sylvia Pankhurst, *The Suffragette Movement*, p. 312.
42 Michelle Myall, *Flame and Burnt Offering*, p. 138; see also Constance Lytton to Annie Kenney, 22 September 1909, KP/AK/2/LyttonC/9.
43 Constance Lytton, *Prisons and Prisoners*, pp. 202–3.
44 Elizabeth Crawford, *The Women's Suffrage Movement: A Reference Guide*, p. 5.
45 Antonia Raeburn, *The Militant Suffragettes*, p. 119. As usual, Raeburn gives a very good account of the events that followed.
46 Elizabeth Crawford, *The Women's Suffrage Movement: A Reference Guide*, p. 5.
47 Constance Lytton, *Prisons and Prisoners*, p. 210.
48 Constance Lytton to Arthur Balfour, 8 October 1909, in the Arthur Balfour Papers ADD/49793/148.
49 Constance Lytton, *Prisons and Prisoners*, p. 205.
50 Henry Brailsford, *The Times*, 19 October 1909.
51 Christabel Pankhurst, *Unshackled*, p. 141.
52 Constance Lytton, *Prisons and Prisoners*, p. 211.
53 *Votes for Women*, 15 October 1909, Vol. 3, p. 35.
54 Constance Lytton, *Prisons and Prisoners*, p. 217.
55 *The Times*, 11 October 1909.
56 Both letters were published in *The Times* on 14 October 1909.
57 11 October 1909, Suffragette Fellowship Collection 50.82/1119.
58 Constance Lytton to Betty Balfour, 11 October 1909, Balfour Papers, National Archives of Scotland, GD/433/2/339/24–5 and Constance Lytton to Edith Lytton, October 1909, GD/433/2/339/33–5.
59 Constance Lytton to Betty Balfour, 11 October 1909, Balfour Papers, National Archives of Scotland, GD/433/2/339/24–5.
60 Humane staff, Constance Lytton, *Prisons and Prisoners*, pp. 228–9; slept on a plank, Constance Lytton to Edith Lytton, October 1909, Balfour Papers, National Archives of Scotland, GD/433/2/339/33–5; wrote to Gladstone, Constance Lytton, *Prisons and Prisoners*, p. 227.
61 Constance Lytton, *Prisons and Prisoners*, p. 230.
62 Constance Lytton and Jane Brailsford, *The Times*, 15 October 1909.
63 Quoted in Joyce Marlow, *Votes for Women: The Virago Book of Suffragettes*, p. 100.
64 *Evening Dispatch*, 23 October 1909.
65 Joyce Marlow, *Votes for Women, The Virago Book of Suffragettes*, p. 103.
66 Henry Brailsford, *The Times*, 19 October 1909 and George Bernard Shaw, *The Times*, 23 November 1909.
67 Hansard, 27 October 1909, Vol. 12, cc. 1001–3, http://hansard.millbanksystems.com/commons/1909/oct/27/suffragist-prisoners-forced-feeding, accessed 1 June 2013.
68 Constance Lytton to Teresa Earle, 19 October 1909 and Edith Lytton to Adela Smith, 20 October 1909, in Betty Balfour (ed.), *Letters of Constance Lytton*, p. 180 and p. 182.

69 Margot Asquith to Frances Balfour, October 1909, Balfour Papers, National Archives of Scotland, GD433/2/338/36–8.

70 Olive Schreiner to Constance Lytton, undated but assumed to be at this time, Balfour Papers, National Archives of Scotland, GD433/2/338/39.

71 Anonymous to Constance Lytton, 24 October 1909, Balfour Papers, National Archives of Scotland, GD433/2/339/42, http://www.scottisharchivesforschools.org/suffragettes/ladyConstanceLytton.asp, accessed 10 February 2015.

72 Constance Lytton to Teresa Earle, 6 November 1909, in Betty Balfour (ed.), *Letters of Constance Lytton*, p. 182.

73 Betty Balfour to Arthur Balfour, 20 November 1909; Betty's speech reported in *The Times*, 20 November 1909.

74 Constance Lytton to Edward Marsh, 5 December 1909, Knebworth Archive, 41945.

75 Kitty Marion, unpublished autobiography, p. 197, 7/KMA, LSE Library Collections.

CHAPTER 8: BECOMING JANE

1 Constance Lytton, speech to the Queen's Hall, 30 January 1910, reported in *Votes for Women*, 3 February 1910, Vol. 4, p. 288.

2 Constance Lytton, *Prisons and Prisoners*, p. 236.

3 Quoted in Joyce Marlow, *Votes for Women: The Virago Book of Suffragettes*, p. 113.

4 Constance Lytton, *Prisons and Prisoners*, p. 235.

5 To read how this unfolded in Constance's own words, see Constance Lytton, *Prisons and Prisoners*, Chapters 12 and 13.

6 Constance Lytton to Lady Lytton, 14 January 1910, Suffragette Fellowship Collection 50.82/1119.

7 Ada Flatman to Jane Warton, 14 January 1910, Suffragette Fellowship Collection 50.82/1119.

8 Constance Lytton, *Prisons and Prisoners*, p. 268.

9 Barbara Green, *Spectacular Confessions*, p. 3.

10 Constance Lytton, speech at the Queen's Hall on 31 January 1910, quoted in Cheryl R. Jorgensen-Earp, *Speeches and Trials of the Militant Suffragettes*, p. 107.

11 Constance Lytton, *Prisons and Prisoners*, p. 271.

12 Constance Lytton, *Prisons and Prisoners*, pp. 272–4.

13 Constance Lytton, *Prisons and Prisoners*, p. 274.

14 Constance Lytton, *Prisons and Prisoners*, p. 281.

15 Constance Lytton, speech at the Queen's Hall on 31 January 1910, quoted in Cheryl R. Jorgensen-Earp, *Speeches and Trials of the Militant Suffragettes*, p. 110.

16 Constance Lytton, *The Times*, 26 January 1910, Knebworth Archive, 41960.

17 *I, Constance Lytton* (privately printed, 1987).

18 Home Office Records 187986/3 National Archives.

19 Constance Lytton, *Prisons and Prisoners*, p. 298.

20 Emily Lutyens to Betty Balfour, 24 January 1910, in Betty Balfour (ed.), *Letters of Constance Lytton*, p. 189.

21 From Constance's own notes on her health in the Suffragette Fellowship Collection 50.82/1119.

22 Constance Lytton to Teresa Earle, 5 November 1908, in Betty Balfour (ed.), *Letters of Constance Lytton*, p. 152.

23 Constance Lytton, speech at the Queen's Hall on 31 January 1910, quoted in Cheryl R. Jorgensen-Earp, *Speeches and Trials of the Militant Suffragettes*, p. 108.

24 Constance Lytton to Lady Lytton, January 1910, in Betty Balfour (ed.), *Letters of Constance Lytton*, p. 194.

25 There is a photograph of them together in 1909 in the Suffragette Fellowship Collection 56.59/9. They were also correspondents, as Ada was an organiser and often requested that Constance should speak at her meetings.

26 In the Suffragette Fellowship Collection, Ada Flatman note, 13 October 1936.

27 Christabel Pankhurst to Ada Flatman, 19 January 1910, in the Ada Flatman Papers, Suffragette Fellowship Collection, Museum of London.

28 Emmeline Pethick-Lawrence to Victor Lytton, 23 January 1910, Knebworth Archive, 41930.

29 *Votes for Women*, 28 January 1910, Vol. 3 ,p. 274.
30 *Votes for Women*, 3 February 1910, Vol. 4, p. 288.

CHAPTER 9: CONCILIATION

1   WSPU election literature, National Archives HO 144/1054/187986/6.
2   Emily Lutyens to Betty Balfour, 24 January 1910, in Betty Balfour (ed.), *Letters of Constance Lytton*, p. 187.
3   Christabel Pankhurst to Betty Balfour, 24 January 1910, in Betty Balfour (ed.), *Letters of Constance Lytton*, p. 192.
4   Victor Lytton to Herbert Gladstone, 15 February 1910, HO 144/1054/187986/15.
5   Constance Lytton, *Prisons and Prisoners*, pp. 300–302.
6   Constance Lytton to Herbert Gladstone, 25 January 1910, HO 144/1054/187986/12.
7   Constance Lytton to Alice Ker, 26 January 1910, 9/21/09, LSE Library collections and Constance Lytton to Ada Flatman, 8 February 1910, 9/21/10, LSE Library collections.
8   *Votes for Women*, 28 January 1910, Vol. 3, p. 274.
9   National Archives HO 144/1054/187986/3 and National Archives HO 144/1054/187986/4.
10 National Archives HO 144/1054/187986/7.
11 National Archives HO 144/1054/187986/11.
12 Victor Lytton, *The Times*, 10 March 1910.
13 A copy of this letter is in the National Archives at 187986/7.
14 Winston Churchill, 1 March 1910, Home Office Records 187986/17.
15 Elizabeth Longford, *Pilgrimage of Passion*, p. 386.
16 Christabel Pankhurst, *Unshackled*, p. 153.
17 Sylvia Pankhurst, *The Suffragette Movement*, p. 336.
18 Christabel Pankhurst, *Unshackled*, p. 154.
19 Conciliation Committee Bill.
20 Emmeline Pethick-Lawrence to Constance Lytton, 29 May 1910, in the Suffragette Fellowship Collection 50.82/1119.
21 Constance Lytton to Victor Lytton, 7 May 1910, Knebworth Archive, item 41954, and Victor Lytton to Constance Lytton, 14 June 1910, Knebworth Archive, item 41936.
22 C. M. Woodhouse, unpublished biography of Victor Lytton, p. 76.
23 C. M. Woodhouse, unpublished biography of Victor Lytton, p. 88.
24 Betty Balfour, *Letters of Constance Lytton*, p. 214.
25 Constance Lytton to Mrs Terraro, 3 July 1911, 9/21/18, LSE Library collections.
26 Constance Lytton to Betty Balfour, 19 June 1910, in Betty Balfour (ed.), *Letters of Constance Lytton*, p. 207.
27 Frances Balfour to Betty Balfour, 18 June 1910, Balfour Papers, National Archives of Scotland, GD/433/2/340/70–1.
28 Ethel Smyth, *Female Pipings in Eden* (Peter Davis Limited, 1933), p. 191.
29 Constance Lytton to Victor Lytton, 16 July 1910, Knebworth Archive, 41938.
30 Frances Balfour to Betty Balfour, 18 June 1910, Balfour Papers, National Archives of Scotland, GD/433/2/340/70–1.
31 Christabel Pankhurst, *Unshackled*, pp. 157–9.
32 Elizabeth Crawford, *The Women's Suffrage Movement: A Reference Guide 1866–1928*, p. 361.
33 Constance Lytton to Teresa Earle, June 1910, Betty Balfour (ed.), *Letters of Constance Lytton*, p. 209.
34 Krista Cowman's *Women of the Right Spirit* describes the life of WSPU organisers. Specific facts in this and the preceding paragraph are from p. 5, p. 124 and p. 56.
35 Constance Lytton to Rose Lamartine Yates, undated, 7EWD/B/3/2/FL554, LSE Library collections.
36 Constance Lytton to Ada Flatman, 5 November 1909, 9/21/03, LSE Library collections.
37 Neville Lytton, *The English Country Gentleman*, p. 273.
38 Michelle Myall, *Flame and Burnt Offering*, p. 205.
39 *The Times*, 15 April 1910, p. 13; 13 June 1910, p. 13; 13 July 1910, p.15.
40 Constance Lytton to Mary Phillips, 3 July 1910, quoted in Martin Pugh, *The Pankhursts*, p.188.

41 Elsie Bowerman to Mrs Chibnell, 23 October 1910, ELB/B/2/17/395/12, LSE Library collections.

42 Papers of Molly Mortimer, 7MLY/A, LSE Library collections.

43 *The Times*, 10 October 1910, p. 10.

44 Katharine Cockin, 'Cicely Hamilton's Warriors: Dramatic Reinventions of Militancy in the British Women's Suffrage Movement', *Women's History Review*, Vol. 14, Nos 3 and 4 (2005), p. 532, and Lucienne Boyce, *The Bristol Suffragettes* (Silverwood Books, 2013), p. 40.

45 Constance Lytton, *Prisons and Prisoners*, p. 310.

46 Lady Selborne to *The Times*, 11 March 1911, p. 10; 13 March 1911, p. 10; and 15 March 1911.

47 Jill Liddington, *Vanishing for the Vote: suffrage, citizenship and the battle for the census* (Manchester University Press, 2014), Constance's form can be accessed through websites like ancestry.co.uk.

48 Betty Balfour (ed.), *Letters of Constance Lytton*, p. 219.

49 Christabel Pankhurst, *Unshackled*, p. 185.

50 Constance Lytton, *Prisons and Prisoners*, p. 325.

51 Constance Lytton to Rose Lamartine Yates, 11 September 1911, 9/21/20, LSE Library collections.

52 *No Surrender* was reprinted in its centenary year by Persephone Books.

CHAPTER 10: BETRAYAL

1 Quoted in Emmeline Pankhurst, *My Own Story*, Vol III, Chapter IV.

2 Quoted in Christabel Pankhurst, *Unshackled*, p. 188.

3 Christabel Pankhurst, *Unshackled*, p. 188.

4 Constance Lytton, *Prisons and Prisoners*, p. 322.

5 Constance Lytton, *Prisons and Prisoners*, p. 327.

6 Constance Lytton, *Prisons and Prisoners*, pp. 328–9.

7 Constance Lytton, *Prisons and Prisoners*, p. 334.

8 *The Times*, 13 December, 1911, p. 13.

9 *Daily Mail*, 22 December 1911, p. 7.

10 *The Times* 15 January 1912, p. 11.

11 Constance Lytton to Alice Ker, 20 February 1912, quoted in Michelle Myall, *Flame and Burnt Offering*, p. 221.

12 Constance Lytton to Millicent Fawcett, 6 February 1912, 9/21/22, LSE Library Collections.

13 Quoted in Joyce Marlow, *Votes for Women: The Virago Book of Suffragettes*, p. 157.

14 Christabel Pankhurst, *Unshackled*, p. 200.

15 Ethel Smyth to Betty Balfour, 6 March 1912, in Betty Balfour (ed.), *Letters of Constance Lytton*, p. 229.

16 Constance Lytton to Margaret Ker, 4 March 1912, 9/21/28, LSE Library collections.

17 *Votes for Women*, 5 April 1912, p. 432.

18 Frances Balfour to Betty Balfour, 4 March 1912, Balfour Papers, National Archives of Scotland, GD/433/2/344/23–3.

19 *Votes for Women*, 15 March 1912, p. 378.

20 Betty Balfour to Annie Kenney, KP/AK/2/BalfourB/2.

21 *Votes for Women*, 15 March 1912, p. 374.

22 *Votes for Women*, 20 April 1912, p. 469.

23 Emmeline Pankhurst, *My Own Story*, p. 255.

24 *Votes for Women*, 12 April 1912.

25 Figures quoted in Emmeline Pankhurst, *My Own Story*, p. 251; Emily Davison's experience described in Joyce Marlow, *Votes for Women: The Virago Book of Suffragettes*, p. 168.

26 Louisa Garrett Anderson in *British Medical Journal*, quoted in J. F. Geddes, 'Culpable Complicity: The medical profession and the forcible feeding of suffragettes', in *Women's History Review*, Vol. 17, No. 1 (2008), p. 86.

27 Emily Lutyens, *The Times*, 29 March 1912, quoted in *Votes for Women*, 5 April 1912, p. 429.

28 This is marked as draft; it is not clear whether she sent a version or not. Constance Lytton to Millicent Fawcett, 6 February 1912, 9/21/23, LSE Library collections.

29 Joyce Marlow, *Votes for Women: The Virago Book of Suffragettes*, p. 179.

30   Sophia A. van Wingerden, *The Women's Suffrage Movement in Britain*, p. 131.
31   Constance Lytton to Margaret Ker, 17 March 1912, 9/21/30, LSE Library collections.
32   Constance Lytton to Alice Ker, 24 May 1912, 9/21/31, LSE Library collections.
33   Constance Lytton to Betty Balfour, 23 March 1912, in Betty Balfour (ed.), *Letters of Constance Lytton*, p. 230.
34   Constance Lytton to Alice Ker, 4 May 1912, 9/21/32, LSE Library collections.

CHAPTER 11: PARALYSIS

1   Olive Schreiner to Mrs Francis Smith, 27 August 1912, Balfour Papers, National Archives of Scotland, GD/433/2/342.
2   Betty Balfour, (ed.), *Letters of Constance Lytton*, p. 236. Nurse Oram's connection with Florence Nightingale is mentioned by Hermione Cobbold, *Memory Lane*, p. 19.
3   Olive Schreiner to Minnie or Mimmie Murray née Parkes, 6 July 1912, National English Literary Museum, Grahamstown, Olive Schreiner Letters Project transcription 2001.24/33 l. 41 and ll. 47–9. Olive repeated the unlikely story of the particles to several of her correspondents.
4   Betty Balfour in *The Times*, 27 June 1912.
5   Betty Balfour, *Evening Standard*, 25 July 1912, quoted in *Votes for Women*, 2 August 1912, p. 718.
6   Victor Lytton, *The Times*, 1 July 1912.
7   *Votes for Women*, 5 July 1912, p. 649.
8   Emmeline Pethick-Lawrence to Betty Balfour, 14 May 1912, and Annie Kenney to Betty Balfour, May 1912 in Betty Balfour (ed.), *Letters of Constance Lytton*, p. 233; Anonymous to Lady Lytton, undated, in Betty Balfour (ed.), *Letters of Constance Lytton*, p. 226; Multiple signatories to Constance Lytton, 8 June 1913, in the Suffragette Fellowship Collection 50.82/1119; Emmeline Pankhurst to Constance Lytton, 12 April 1912, 9/20/12 LSE Library Collections.
9   Sylvia Pankhurst, *The Suffragette Movement*, p. 333.
10   There would be one more niece, Madeline, born in 1921, to Neville and his second wife.
11   Constance Lytton to Alice Ker, 19 March 1914, 9/21/34.
12   Mary Lutyens, *To Be Young* (Corgi, 1989), p. 60.
13   Lady Selborne to Betty Balfour, in Betty Balfour (ed.), *Letters of Constance Lytton*, p. 233.
14   Recollections of Constance by her nieces are on CD in the LSE library as part of the 'Brian Harrison Interviews' – a series he conducted in the 1970s with surviving campaigners for the vote and their relatives to inform his books. The material also covers their memories of Victor and Emily. The interview with Elisabeth Lutyens is at 8/SUF/B/049; with Davinia (Lytton) Woodhouse at 8/SUF/B/051; with Mary (Lutyens) Links at 8/SUF/B/085; and with Hermione (Lytton) Cobbold at 8/SUF/B107.
15   Elizabeth Crawford, *The Women's Suffrage Movement in Britain and Ireland, A Regional Survey*, p. 108.
16   Betty Balfour (ed.), *Letters of Constance Lytton*, p. 258, and Brian Harrison interview with Lady Hermione Cobbold, 8SUF/B/107.
17   Constance Lytton to Daisy Solomon, 20 February 1913, 9/21/32 LSE Library collections.
18   Constance Lytton to Friends, 24 February 1913, 9/21/36 LSE Library collections.
19   Note in the MSS, Knebworth Archive.
20   Bertha Brewster, *Daily Telegraph*, 26 February 1913, quoted in Joyce Marlow: *Votes for Women: The Virago Book of Suffragettes*, p. 182.
21   Quoted in Joyce Marlow, *Votes for Women: The Virago Book of Suffragettes*, p. 205.
22   Jill Liddington, *Rebel Girls: Their Fight for the Vote*, p. 269.
23   J. F. Geddes, 'Culpable Complicity: The medical profession and the forcible feeding of suffragettes', in *Women's History Review*, Vol. 17, No. 1 (2008), p. 89.
24   Constance Lytton to Adela Smith, 20 May 1913, in Betty Balfour (ed.), *Letters of Constance Lytton*, p. 241.
25   Betty Balfour (ed.), *Letters of Constance Lytton*, p. 242. This is a bit surprising as Olive Schreiner remained in England during the First World War and did not return to South Africa until 1920; presumably their respective illnesses kept them apart.
26   Jill Liddington, *Rebel Girls*, p. 275.
27   Christabel Pankhurst, *Unshackled*, p. 243.

28 Emmeline Pankhurst, *My Own Story*, p. 316.

29 http://womanandhersphere.com/2012/08/06/suffrage-stories-what-else-is-in-emily-wilding-davisons-grave, accessed 14 January 2015.

30 *The Times*, 11 March 1914, quoted in the Oxford Dictionary of National Biography.

31 Constance Lytton to Alice Ker, 19 March 1914, 9/21/34 LSE Library collections. Annie is not named, perhaps in case the letter was intercepted, but I cannot believe she means anyone else.

32 Katherine Connelly: *Sylvia Pankhurst*, pp. 54–8 and Asquith quoted on p. 66.

33 Constance Lytton, *Prisons and Prisoners*, p. 336–7.

34 For a full discussion of the significance of suffragette autobiography see Maroula Joannou, '"She who would be politically free herself must strike the blow": Suffragette Autobiography and Suffragette Militancy', in Julia Swindells, *The Uses of Autobiography* (Taylor & Francis, 1995), p. 32 onwards.

35 See Constance Lytton, *I, Constance Lytton* (privately printed, 1987), introduction.

36 In an unpublished notebook, primarily about her nurse, quoted in Betty Balfour (ed.), *Letters of Constance Lytton*, p. 240. Unfortunately, Betty did not publish any of these letters, nor are any in Constance's file at Knebworth.

37 Constance Lytton to Teresa Earle, 20 March 1914, in Betty Balfour (ed.), *Letters of Constance Lytton*, p. 241.

38 Lady Lytton's note in her copy of *Prisons and Prisoners*, a gift from Constance. This is in the Knebworth Archive.

39 Philip Burne-Jones to Betty Balfour, 10–14 March 1914, Balfour Papers, National Archives of Scotland, GD433/2/347/31–3. Burne-Jones was angry at the attacks on works of art.

40 Annie Matheson to Betty Balfour, 7 March 1914, Balfour Papers, National Archives of Scotland, GD433/2/347/34.

41 Sylvia Pankhurst, *The Suffragette Movement*, p. 333.

42 Christabel Pankhurst, *Unshackled*, p. 288.

43 Quoted in Kate Adie, *Fighting on the Home Front: The Legacy of Women in World War One* (Hodder & Stoughton, 2014), p. 295.

44 Betty Balfour (ed.), *Letters of Constance Lytton*, p. 245.

45 Constance Lytton to Miss Robins, 19 April 1914, 9/21/35 and Constance Lytton to Kitty Marion, in Kitty Marion's unpublished autobiography, p. 264, 7/KMA LSE Library collections.

46 Kitty Marion's unpublished autobiography, p. 319, Women's Library 7/KMA.

47 It was actually Rachel Peace's case that clarified the distinction between 'considered dangerous' = force-fed and 'considered safe' = let out under the Cat and Mouse Act. See Hansard for 16 February 1914, Vol. 58, cc. 573–4. See also J. F. Geddes, 'Culpable Complicity: The medical profession and the forcible feeding of suffragettes' in *Women's History Review*, Vol. 17, No. 1 (2008), p. 87.

48 Emmeline Pethick-Lawrence to Mrs Solomon, 13 June 1923, Women's Library 9/20/07.

49 Neville Lytton, *The English Country Gentleman*, p. 270.

50 Betty Balfour (ed.), *Letters of Constance Lytton*, p. 256.

51 Michelle Myall, *Flame and Burnt Offering*, p. 271.

52 Neville Lytton, *The English Country Gentleman* p. 279.

53 Emily Lutyens to Edwin Lutyens, 26 November 1919, quoted in Clayre Percy and Jane Ridley, *The Letters of Edwin Lutyens to his wife Lady Emily*, p. 373.

54 Constance Lytton to Adela Smith, 29 July 1915, in Betty Balfour (ed.), *Letters of Constance Lytton*, p. 248.

55 Hannah Mitchell, quoted in Joyce Marlow, *Votes for Women: The Virago Book of Suffragettes*, p. 55.

56 Figures are from Frank Meeres, *Suffragettes*, pp. 7–8.

57 Jill Liddington, *Selina Cooper*, p. 284.

58 Christabel Pankhurst, *Unshackled*, p. 294.

59 Unpublished notebook, Knebworth Archive.

CHAPTER 12: THE PRICE OF VICTORY

1 Emmeline Pethick-Lawrence to Mrs Solomon, 23 October 1929, Women's Library 9/20/081.

2   Constance Lytton to Annie Kenney, 5 February 1921, KP/AK/2/LyttonC/17.

3   Betty Balfour (ed.), *Letters of Constance Lytton*, p. 254.

4   Constance Lytton to Jessie Kenney, 17 October 1919, KP/JK/3.

5   Constance Lytton to Adela Smith, 3 September 1919, in Betty Balfour (ed.), *Letters of Constance Lytton*, p. 255.

6   Constance Lytton to Olive Schreiner, 5 November 1919, written on the back of Olive Schreiner to Betty Molteno, November 1919, BC16/Box7/Fold2/Aug–Dec1919/22, UCT Manuscripts & Archives, Olive Schreiner Letters Project transcription.

7   Ethel was an admirer of Edith as well as Constance. In one of her many volumes of autobiography, she commented on the letters collection by saying: 'From these pages emerges a beautiful picture of a parent, confronted in her old age by a new spiritual force fantastically alien to her own epoch and breeding; facing this ordeal as only a loving mother and great lady could … a wave of sympathy and admiration in the direction of the heroine's mother.' Ethel Smyth, *A Final Burning of Boats* (Longmans, 1928), p. 164. It is surprising that more suffragettes do not appear in the Homewood visitors' book.

8   Olive Schreiner to Joan Hodgson née Wickham, 29 August 1919, Harry Ransom Research Center, University of Texas at Austin, Olive Schreiner Letters Project transcription, HRC/OliveSchreinerLetters/OS-JOANHodgson/8, line 31.

9   Olive Schreiner to Havelock Ellis, undated, quoted in Ruth First and Ann Scott, *Olive Schreiner*, p. 303.

10 Constance Lytton in *Time and Tide*, 31 December 1920, p. 712.

11 See Betty Balfour's foreword to Constance's projected cookery book, Knebworth Archive, 40438.

12 June Rose, *Marie Stopes and the Sexual Revolution* (Tempus, 2007), p. 156.

13 Constance Lytton to Marie Stopes, 25 February 1921, British Library, Add MSS 58688/45 and Emily Lutyens to Marie Stopes, 21 March 1921, British Library, Add MSS 58688/78.

14 June Rose, *Marie Stopes and the Sexual Revolution*, p. 194.

15 Constance Lytton to Marie Stopes, 23 April 1921, British Library, Add MSS 58688/136 and Constance Lytton to Marie Stopes, 4 July 1921, British Library, Add MSS 58689/152.

16 Constance Lytton to Marie Stopes, 14 February 1921, British Library, Add MSS 58693/64.

17 Constance Lytton to Marie Stopes, 15 October 1921, 58690/62 and Christmas 1921, Add MSS 58691/1.

18 Constance Lytton to Marie Stopes, 26 July 1921, British Library, Add MSS 58689/187; 15 October 1921, 58690/62 and 27 September 1921, 58690/28.

19 Constance Lytton to Marie Stopes, 10 October 1922, Add MSS 56891/82 and Constance Lytton to Marie Stopes, 5 March 1923, Add 58693/109.

20 Constance Lytton to Marie Stopes, 5 March 1923, Add 58693/109.

21 W. David Wills, *Homer Lane: A Biography* (George Allen & Unwin, 1964), p. 153.

22 W. David Wills, *Homer Lane*, p. 23.

23 See W. David Wills, *Homer Lane*, pp. 161–72.

24 W. David Wills, *Homer Lane*, p. 186.

25 Victor Lytton in E. T. Bazeley, *Homer Lane and the Little Commonwealth* (George Allen & Unwin, 1928), p. 20.

26 Betty Balfour to Victor Lytton, 6 April 1922, Knebworth Archive, 40503.

27 Constance Lytton to Betty Balfour, 27 May 1922, Knebworth Archive, 40485.

28 W. David Wills, *Homer Lane*, p. 203.

29 W. David Wills, *Homer Lane*, p. 207.

30 Betty Balfour to Victor Lytton, 12 July 1922, Knebworth Archive, 49514.

31 Betty Balfour to Victor Lytton, 26 July 1922, Knebworth Archive, 49514.

32 Marie Mulvey-Roberts: 'Militancy, Masochism or Martyrdom? The Public and Private Prisons of Constance Lytton', June Purvis and Sandra Stanley Holton, *Votes for Women* (Routledge, 2000), p. 173.

33 Betty Balfour to Victor Lytton, 26 July 1922, Knebworth Archive, 40516.

34 Constance Lytton to Betty Balfour, 6 January 1923, Balfour Papers, National Archives of Scotland, GD433/2/369/6.

35 Edith Lytton to Betty Balfour, 5 December 1922, Knebworth Archive, 40432a and Betty Balfour to Edith Lytton, 6 December 1922, Knebworth Archive, 40432 (copy sent to Victor Lytton).

36 Betty Balfour to Victor Lytton, 30 September 1922.

37 Neville Lytton, *The English Country Gentleman*, p. 279.

38 Betty Balfour's draft foreword to the cookbook, Knebworth Archive, 40438 and Constance Lytton to Jessie Kenney, Knebworth Archive, 24 April 1923, JP/JK/3.

39 Constance Lytton to Marie Stopes, 13 January 1923, Add MSS 58693 10.

40 Victor Lytton to Edith Lytton, 15 February 1923, Knebworth Archive, 40173 and Betty Balfour to Victor Lytton, Knebworth Archive, 21 December 1922, 40534.

41 Constance Lytton to Marie Stopes, undated but sent from Tavistock Square, Add MS 58694.

42 Constance Lytton to Victor Lytton, 4 April 1923, quoted in Michelle Myall, *Flame and Burnt Offering*, p. 71.

43 Betty Balfour to Victor Lytton, 14 August 1923, Knebworth Archive, 40437.

44 Ruth First and Ann Scott, *Olive Schreiner*, p. 302. They give two possible locations for this address, but because Constance's death certificate gives her place of death as Paddington, I believe that it was Olive's home at 9 Porchester Place.

45 Constance Lytton to Jessie Kenney, 24 April 1923, KP/JK/3. This is, I think, Constance's last extant letter.

46 Betty Balfour to Victor Lytton, 14 August 1923, Knebworth Archive, 40437; Victor Lytton to Edith Lytton, 23 May 1923, Knebworth Archive, 40186 and Betty Balfour to Victor Lytton, 23 July 1923, Knebworth Archive, 40434.

47 Neville Lytton, *The English Country Gentleman*, p. 281. He wasn't actually there.

48 *The Times*, 28 May 1923, p. 15.

49 Quoted in Betty Balfour (ed.), *Letters of Constance Lytton*, p. 265.

50 Frances Balfour to Betty Balfour, May 1923, Balfour Papers, National Archives of Scotland, GD433/2/369/68–72.

51 John Ponsonby to Victor Lytton, 25 May 1923, Knebworth Archive, 51120/A.

52 Betty Balfour to Victor Lytton, 23 July 1923, Knebworth Archive, 40434.

53 Betty Balfour to Victor Lytton, 14 August 1923, Knebworth Archive, 40437.

54 Betty Balfour to Victor Lytton, 23 July 1923, Knebworth Archive, 40434.

55 Betty Balfour to Victor Lytton, 18 September 1923, Knebworth Archive, 40442.

56 Probate record, 12 November 1936.

57 University of East Anglia Archive, KP/AK/5.

58 Betty Balfour to Victor Lytton, 3 July 1923, Knebworth Archive, 40434.

59 Emmeline Pethick-Lawrence to Mrs Solomon, 13 June 1923, 9/20/07, LSE Library Collections.

60 There is frustratingly scant information to be found about Rachel. She does not have an entry in Elizabeth Crawford's magisterial account of the movement. Some Google search results describe her as one of the most prominent suffragettes. This is not true. There are, however, several surveillance photographs of her in existence, which show how dangerous she was considered to be.

61 Betty Balfour to Victor Lytton, 18 July 1923, Knebworth Archive, 40436.

62 Betty Balfour to Annie Kenney, KP/AL/2/BalfourB/2.

63 Pamela Lytton to Betty Balfour, 20 May 1925, Knebworth Archive, 40422.

64 Victor Lytton to Betty Balfour, 24 March 1924, Knebworth Archive, 40404.

65 Edith Lytton to Annie Kenney, 4 April 1925 KP/AK/2/LyttonE/1 and 24 April 1925 KP/AK/2/LyttonE/2, advice on Queen Mary, 22 September 1924, KP/AK/2/LyttonE/11. The Kenney sisters' own mother had died in 1905, just before Annie met Christabel.

66 *The Times*, 19 September 1936, consulted in the Knebworth Archive.

67 Record of seance with Gerald Balfour and Betty Balfour, 9 June 1939, GD433/2/386, Balfour Papers, National Archives of Scotland

68 Fred Pethick-Lawrence, in the second reading of the Representation of the People Bill, HC Deb 29 March 1928, Vol. 215, cc. 1359–481, accessed 1 June 2013. http://hansard.millbanksystems.

com/commons/1928/mar/29/representation-of-the-people-equal#S5CV0215P0_19280329_
HOC_318.

69 Mary Blathwayt to Annie Kenney, 25 February 1951, KP/AK/2/Blathwayt/4 and Mary Blathwayt to Annie Kenney, 19 November 1952, KP/AK/2/Blathwayt/5. The arboretum itself was
destroyed in the 1960s and the only original tree left standing belongs to Rose Lamartine
Yates. In 2012, staff from Bath Spa University arranged for new trees to be planted.

AFTERWORD

1   Constance Lytton to Miss Robins, 19 April 1914, 9/21/35 LSE Library Collections.

2   Sandra Stanley Holton, 'The Making of Suffrage History', in June Purvis and Sandra Stanley
Holton, *Votes for Women*, p. 21.

3   Barbara Green, *Spectacular Confessions*, p. 63.

4   Emmeline Pethick-Lawrence to Betty Balfour, 14 May 1912, in Betty Balfour (ed.), *Letters of
Constance Lytton*, p. 233.

5   Barbara Green, *Spectacular Confessions*, p. 68.

6   Quoted in Betty Balfour (ed.), *Letters of Constance Lytton*, p. 268.

7   In her unpublished notebook, quoted in Betty Balfour (ed.), *Letters of Constance Lytton*, p. 240.

SOURCES

In the 1970s, as second wave feminism gained a foothold, and women looked back at their pioneering foremothers, a landmark BBC series on the suffragette movement, *Shoulder to Shoulder*, dedicated an entire episode to Constance. The nieces felt that the programme had accurately portrayed her gentle character and sympathetic nature, though they didn't approve of the actor's red hair at all. For dedicated fans of the suffragettes, and those who want to see this story dramatised, *Shoulder to Shoulder* can be found on YouTube.

Unpublished Work

Cobbold, Hermione, *Memory Lane: Tales of Long Ago, 1905–1930*

Lytton, Victor, *Set in Remembrance*

Marion, Kitty, Autobiography, Women's Library, LSE Library Collections

Myall, Michelle, '"Flame and Burnt Offering": A Life of Constance Lytton, 1869–1923', PhD thesis, University of Portsmouth, 1999

Woodhouse, C. M., unpublished and untitled biography of Victor Lytton

Archive Collections

The Balfour Papers, National Archives of Scotland

The Kenney Papers, University of East Anglia

The Lytton Papers, Knebworth House

Letters of the Militant Suffragettes, Women's Library, LSE Library Collections

Letters of Constance Lytton, Women's Library, LSE Library Collections

The Suffragette Fellowship Collection, Museum of London

Home Office Records of the Jane Warton episode: HO 144/1054/187986, National Archives, Kew

Newspapers

Votes for Women
Daily Chronicle
Daily Express
Daily Mail
Daily News
Daily Telegraph
Evening Dispatch
National Review
The Realm
The Times

Online Sources

www.ancestry.co.uk
www.maryneal.org
www.oliveschreiner.org (Olive Schreiner letters online)
www.oxforddnb.com (Oxford Dictionary of National Biography)

Publications

Adie, Kate, *Fighting on the Home Front: The Legacy of Women in World War One* (London: Hodder & Stoughton, 2014)

Appignanesi, Lisa, *Mad, Bad and Sad: A History of Women and the Mind Doctors from 1800 to the Present* (London: Virago, 2008)

Balfour, Betty (ed.), *Letters of Constance Lytton* (London: William Heinemann, 1925)

Bazeley, E. T., *Homer Lane and the Little Commonwealth* (London: George Allen & Unwin, 1928)

Boyce, Lucienne, *The Bristol Suffragettes* (Bristol: Silverwood Books, 2013)

Brooks Harlan, Aurelia, *Owen Meredith: A Critical Biography of Robert, First Earl of Lytton* (New York: Colombia University Press, 1946)

Cobbold, Lord David, 'Rosina Bulwer Lytton: Irish Beauty, Satirist, Tormented Victorian Wife, 1802–1882', in Allan Conrad Christensen (ed.), *The Subverting Vision of Bulwer Lytton* (Newark: University of Delaware Press, 2004)

Cockin, Katherine, 'Cicely Hamilton's Warriors: Dramatic Reinventions of Militancy in the British Women's Suffrage Movement', *Women's History Review*, Vol. 14, Nos 3 and 4 (2005)

Connelly, Katherine, *Sylvia Pankhurst: Suffragette, Socialist and Scourge of Empire* (London: Pluto Press, 2013)

Cowman, Krista, *Women of the Right Spirit: Paid Organisers of the Women's Social and Political Union 1904–1918* (Manchester: Manchester University Press, 2007)

Crawford, Elizabeth, *The Women's Suffrage Movement: A Reference Guide* (London: UCL Press, 1999)

— —, *The Women's Suffrage Movement in Britain and Ireland: A Regional Survey* (London: Routledge, 2006)

Earle, Mrs C. W., *Pot Pourri from a Surrey Garden* (London: Thomas Nelson and Sons, 1919)

Escott, T. H. S., *Edward Bulwer: First Baron Lytton of Knebworth: A Social, Personal and Political Monograph* (London: Routledge, 1910)

First, Ruth and Scott, Ann, *Olive Schreiner* (London: André Deutsch, 1980)

Geddes, J. F., 'Culpable Complicity: the medical profession and the forcible feeding of suffragettes', *Women's History Review*, Vol. 17, No. 1 (2008), pp. 79–94

Gleadle, Kathryn, *British Women in the Nineteenth Century* (Basingstoke: Palgrave, 2001)

Gilmour, David, *The Ruling Caste: Imperial Lives in the Victorian Raj* (London: John Murray, 2005)

Goldsworthy, Joanna and Mulvey-Roberts, Marie, 'Revolutionary Mothers, Revolting Daughters: Mary Wollstonecraft and Mary Shelley, Anna Wheeler and Rosina Bulwer-Lytton', in Carolyn D. Williams, Angela Escott and Louise Duckling (eds), *Woman to Woman: Female Negotiations During the Long Eighteenth Century* (Delaware: University of Delaware Press, 2010)

Green, Barbara, *Spectacular Confessions: Autobiography, Performative Activism, and the Sites of Suffrage* (London: Macmillan, 1997)

Hawksley, Lucinda, *The Mystery of Princess Louise: Queen Victoria's Rebellious Daughter* (London: Chatto and Windus, 2014)

Heritage House Group, *Knebworth House: Hertfordshire Home of the Lytton Family since 1490* (Heritage House Group, 2005)

Holmes, Rachel, *Eleanor Marx: A Life* (London: Bloomsbury, 2014)

Joannou, Maroula, '"She who would be politically free herself must strike the blow": Suffragette Autobiography and Suffragette Militancy', in Julia Swindells, *The Uses of Autobiography* (London: Taylor and Francis, 1995)

Jorgensen-Earp, Cheryl R., *Speeches and Trials of the Militant Suffragettes, The Women's Social and Political Union 1903–1918* (London: Associated University Presses, 1999)

Kuhn, William M., *Henry and Mary Ponsonby: Life at the Court of Queen Victoria* (Croydon: Duckbacks, 2003)

Leneman, Leah, 'The Awakened Instinct: Vegetarianism and the Women's Suffrage Movement in Britain', *Women's History Review*, Vol. 6, No. 2 (1997), pp. 271–87

Liddington, Jill and Norris, Jill, *One Hand Tied Behind Us: Rise of the Women's Suffrage Movement* (London: Virago, 1979)

Liddington, Jill, *Selina Cooper: The Life and Times of a Respectable Rebel* (London: Virago, 1984)

— —, *Rebel Girls: Their Fight for the Vote* (London: Virago, 2006)

— —, *Vanishing for the Vote: suffrage, citizenship and the battle for the census* (Manchester University Press, 2014)

Longford, Elizabeth, *A Pilgrimage of Passion: The Life of Wilfred Scawen Blunt* (London: Weidenfeld & Nicholson, 1979)

Lutyens, Emily, *A Blessed Girl: Memoirs of A Victorian Girlhood Chronicled in an Exchange of Letters, 1887–1896* (London: Heinemann, 1954)

— —, *Candles in the Sun* (London: Rupert Hart-Davis, 1957)

Lutyens, Mary, *The Lyttons in India: An Account of Lord Lytton's Viceroyalty 1876–1880* (London: John Murray, 1979)

— —, *To Be Young* (Corgi, 1989)

Lycett, Andrew, *Wilkie Collins: A Life of Sensation* (London: Windmill, 2014)

Lytton, Constance, *'No Votes for Women': A Reply to Some Recent Publications By Lady Constance Lytton* (London: A. C. Fitfield, 1909)

— —, *I, Constance Lytton* (London: privately printed, 1987)

— —, *Prisons and Prisoners* (London: Virago, 1988)

Lytton, Edith, *Lady Lytton's Court Diary, India 1876–1880* (London: Chiswick Press, 1899)

— —, ed. by Mary Lutyens, *Lady Lytton's Court Diary, 1895–1899* (London: Rupert Hart-Davis, 1961)

Lytton, Neville, *The English Country Gentleman* (London: Hurst and Blackett, 1925)

Mackenzie, Midge, *Shoulder to Shoulder: A Documentary* (London: Allen Lane, 1975)

Marcus, Jane, *Suffrage and the Pankhursts* (London: Routledge, 1987)

Marlow, Joyce, *The Virago Book of Suffragettes* (London: Virago, 2000)

Maud, Constance and Fillet, Lydia, *No Surrender* (London: Persephone, 2011)

Meeres, Frank, *Suffragettes: How Britain's Women Fought and Died for the Right to Vote* (Stroud: Amberley, 2014)

Miles, Patricia and Williams, Jill, *An Uncommon Criminal: The Life of Lady Constance Lytton: Militant Suffragette 1869–1923* (Knebworth: Knebworth House Education and Preservation Trust, 1999)

Mulvey-Roberts, Marie and Mizuta, Tamas: *The Militants: Suffragette Activism* (London: Routledge, 1994)

Mulvey-Roberts, Marie, 'Militancy, Masochism or Martydom? The Public and Private Prisons of Constance Lytton', in June Purvis and Sandra Stanley Holton, *Votes for Women* (London: Routledge, 2000)

— —, 'Writing for Revenge: The Battle of the Books of Edward and Rosina Bulwer Lytton' in Allan Conran Christensen (ed.), *The Subverting Vision of Bulwer Lytton* (Newark: University of Delaware Press, 2004)

Myall, Michelle, 'No Surrender: The militancy of Mary Leigh, a working-class suffragette', in Joannou, Maroula and Purvis, June, *The Women's Suffrage Movement: New Feminist Perspectives* (Manchester: Manchester University Press, 1998)

— —, '"Only be ye strong and very courageous": The militant suffragism of Lady Constance Lytton', *Women's History Review*, Vol. 7, No. 1 (1998)

Neill Raymond, E., *Victorian Viceroy: The Life of Robert, the First Earl of Lytton* (London: Regency Press, 1980)

Pankhurst, Christabel, *Unshackled: The Story of How we Won the Vote* (London: Hutchinson & Co., 1987)

Pankhurst, Emmeline, *My Own Story* (London: Virago, 1979)

Pankhurst, Sylvia, *The Suffragette Movement: An Intimate Account of Persons and Ideals* (London: Longmans & Co. 1931)

Percy, Clayre and Ridley, Jane, *The Letters of Edwin Lutyens to his wife, Lady Emily* (London: Collins, 1985)

Pethick-Lawrence, Emmeline, *My Part in a Changing World* (London: Gollancz, 1938)

Pugh, Martin, *The Pankhursts* (London: Allen Lane, 2001)

Purvis, June, '"A Pair of … Infernal Queens": A Reassessment of the Dominant Representations of Emmeline and Christabel Pankhurst, First Wave Feminists in Edwardian Britain', *Women's History Review*, Vol. 5, No. 2 (1996), pp. 259–80

— —, 'Christabel Pankhurst and the Women's Social and Political Union', in Joannou, Maroula and Purvis, June, *The Women's Suffrage Movement: New Feminist Perspectives* (Manchester: Manchester University Press, 1998)

Raeburn, Antonia, *The Militant Suffragettes* (London: Michael Joseph, 1973)

Ridley, Jane, *Edwin Lutyens: His Life, His Wife, His Work* (London: Pimlico, 2003)

Rowbotham, Sheila, *A Century of Women: The History of Women in Britain and the United States* (London: Viking, 1997)

Smyth, Ethel, *A Final Burning of Boats* (London: Longmans & Co., 1928)

— —, *As Time Went On* (London: Longmans & Co., 1930)

— —, *Female Pipings in Eden* (London: Peter Davis Limited, 1933)

Stanley Holton, Sandra, *Suffrage Days: Stories from the Women's Suffrage Movement* (London: Routledge, 1996)

— —, 'The Making of Suffrage History', in June Purvis and Sandra Stanley Holton, *Votes for Women* (London: Routledge, 2000)

Steinbach, Susie, *Women in England 1760–1914: A Social History* (London: Weidenfeld & Nicholson, 2004)

Strachey, Ray, *The Cause: A Short History of the Women's Movement in Great Britain* (London: G. Bell & Sons, 1928)

Taylor, Barbara, *Eve and the New Jerusalem: Socialism and Feminism in the Nineteenth Century* (London: Virago, 1983)

Tickner, Lisa, *The Spectacle of Women: imagery of the suffrage campaign, 1907–1914* (London: Chatto & Windus, 1988)

Vicinus, Martha, *Intimate Friends: Women Who Loved Women 1778–1928* (Chicago: University of Chicago Press, 2004)

Wills, W. David, *Homer Lane: A Biography* (London: George Allen & Unwin, 1964)

van Wingerden, Sophia A., *The Women's Suffrage Movement in Britain, 1866–1928* (Basingstoke: Macmillan, 1999)

INDEX

EBOOK, £8.99

chel Beer was both a rebel and a pioneer. In the late nineteenth
ury, at a time when women were still denied the vote, she became
e first woman ever to edit a national British newspaper – in fact
, the *Sunday Times* and *The Observer*. It was to be over eighty years
before another woman took the helm of a Fleet Street paper.

vever, whilst other female journalists were restricted to frocks, frills and frippery, Rachel
aged to raise her formidable voice on national and foreign political issues – including the
torious Dreyfus Affair – as well as on social and women's issues, often controversially.

ing on a wealth of original material, *The First Lady of Fleet Street* paints a vivid picture of a
arkable woman and of the times in which she lived. It also provides an important history
of two venerable Jewish families, their origins and their rise to eminence.

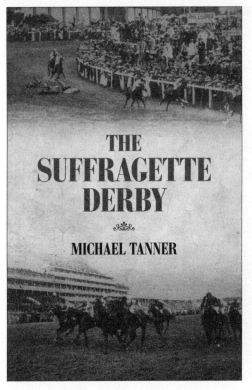

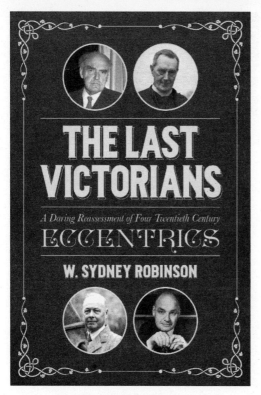

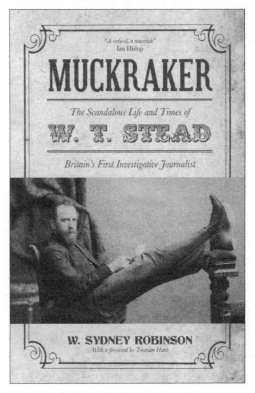